Franklin in His Own Time

T0346052

WRITERS IN THEIR OWN TIME

Joel Myerson, *series editor*

FRANKLIN

in His Own Time

A BIOGRAPHICAL

CHRONICLE OF HIS LIFE,

DRAWN FROM RECOLLECTIONS,

INTERVIEWS, AND

MEMOIRS BY FAMILY,

FRIENDS, AND

ASSOCIATES

EDITED BY

Kevin J. Hayes and Isabelle Bour

University of Iowa Press
Iowa City

University of Iowa Press, Iowa City 52242
Copyright © 2011 by the University of Iowa Press
www.uiowapress.org
Printed in the United States of America

The University of Iowa Press is a member of Green Press Initiative
and is committed to preserving natural resources.

Printed on acid-free paper

Library of Congress Cataloging-in-Publication Data
Franklin in his own time: a biographical chronicle of his life, drawn from recollections, interviews,
and memoirs by family, friends, and associates / edited by Kevin J. Hayes and Isabelle Bour.
p. cm.—(Writers in their own time)
Includes bibliographical references and index.
ISBN-13: 978-1-58729-982-7, ISBN-10: 1-58729-982-8 (pbk.)
ISBN-13: 978-1-58729-983-4, ISBN-10: 1-58729-983-6 (e-book)
1. Franklin, Benjamin, 1706–1790. 2. Franklin, Benjamin, 1706–1790—Friends and
associates. 3. Statesmen—United States—Biography. 4. Scientists—United States—
Biography. 5. Inventors—United States—Biography. 6. Printers—United States—
Biography. I. Hayes, Kevin J. II. Bour, Isabelle.
E302.6.F8F844 2011
973.3092—dc22 2010049281
[B]

Contents

Introduction

IN HIS TIME Benjamin Franklin was the most famous American in the world. Those personally unacquainted with him knew Franklin as the inventor of the Pennsylvania fireplace; the author of *The Way to Wealth*, a pithy book of financial advice; a pioneer in the study of electricity; the inventor of the lightning rod; and a leader of the American Revolution. Those who were acquainted with him personally had a somewhat different view. Aware of all the famous things he had done, they also knew him as a faithful friend, a brilliant conversationalist, a great wit, an entertaining storyteller, and an intellectual filled with curiosity.

Franklin's vast store of knowledge complemented his conversational skill. Whatever topic someone else brought up, he seemed to have an appropriate anecdote to suit. Relating one particular conversation with him, Thomas Jefferson explained that Franklin "gave his sentiments, as usual, by way of Apologue."[1] Sometimes Franklin's apologues came from what he read, but often they emanated from his personal experience. These apologues and anecdotes were so memorable that those who heard them remembered and often retold them to others. Furthermore, many of Franklin's friends and associates wrote down what he said in their personal reminiscences.

When they first appeared in print, the anecdotes typically formed part of a personal narrative. But the individual anecdotes themselves were so poignant that editors of newspapers, magazines, and jestbooks frequently excerpted them. Franklin's anecdotes proved to be ideal texts for filling the spare white spaces of a newspaper column. He became such a memorable figure in the anecdotal literature that many old chestnuts that had circulated widely before his time were attributed to him and recirculated.[2]

Though the present volume reprints many of Franklin's renowned stories, it is not designed as another collection of anecdotes. Rather, it seeks to restore those oft-told anecdotes to their contexts, to situate Franklin within his time by reprinting the original documents in which those anecdotes occur, documents written by friends and associates, people who knew him during different stages of his life. These documents help clarify several aspects of Franklin's life, aspects he himself sometimes obscured.

Franklin retold many anecdotes in his autobiography. There is no evidence that he fictionalized his life story, but the autobiography does tell a highly selective version of Franklin's personal experience.[3] He had accomplished so much over the course of his life that he could pick and choose particular episodes to emphasize, episodes that suited his general purpose behind the book: to make himself an example for others to emulate. Franklin's autobiography codifies what would become known as the American Dream.[4] It is the story of a young man who works hard, perseveres, and gets ahead in the world. But it is not the whole story of his life, not by any means.

Benjamin Franklin's father, Josiah, for example, gets short shrift in the autobiography. A tallow-chandler and soap-boiler by trade, he emerges from his youngest son's autobiography as a man with so little grasp of Benjamin's genius that he tries to turn the boy into a tallow-chandler and soap-boiler, as well. By all accounts, Benjamin Franklin loved and respected his father, but he realized that it would not do to give him too much credit in his autobiography, the ur-story of the self-made man. Actually Josiah Franklin had a much greater intellect and a much greater influence on his youngest son than that son let on in his autobiography, as Pehr Kalm's record of his personal encounter with Benjamin Franklin reveals.

Kalm's *Travels into North America*,[†] which contains the first extended record of Franklin in conversation, is important for many reasons, including what it says about Josiah Franklin. A well-educated Swedish botanist, Kalm came to America in 1748 with the support of his institution, Åbo Academy. His main purpose was to gather information about North American flora and fauna. He and Franklin met *before* Franklin established an international scientific reputation for his electrical experiments. Yet Kalm's portrayal shows that Franklin was doing all he could to encourage the development of science in North America. Learning the purpose of Kalm's visit, Franklin recalled many pertinent anecdotes concerning the natural history of North America.

One story Franklin told Kalm concerns a practical experiment about the herring fishery his father had made. As his son told the story, Josiah Franklin exhibits curiosity, keen powers of observation, deductive abilities, a willingness to experiment, and a great sense of satisfaction when his experiment succeeds: all characteristics Benjamin would come to exemplify. A tallow chandler he may have been, but Josiah Franklin was no ordinary tallow-chandler. Besides relating information about natural history that he learned from his father and others, Benjamin Franklin also told Kalm a humorous anecdote pertaining to asbestos and related an experiment of his own concerning how ants communicate. Kalm was quite impressed with Franklin, and the two corresponded once Kalm left Philadelphia to continue his travels through North America.

Franklin himself loved to travel, and his growing responsibilities as deputy postmaster general of North America took him to many places during the mid 1750s. On January 22, 1754, he found himself in Annapolis, Maryland. Since January 22 happened to fall on a Tuesday that year, Franklin took the opportunity to attend a meeting of the Tuesday Club, which met at the home of Dr. Alexander Hamilton that evening. As secretary, Hamilton kept the club's minutes, which he transformed into *The History of the Ancient and Honorable Tuesday Club*, one of the masterworks of early American literature. Hamilton's record of Franklin's Annapolis visit is brief, yet delightful.

For *The History of the Tuesday Club*, Hamilton assigned club members and visitors typenames. He named himself Loquacious Scribble. Maryland printer Jonas Green he called Jonathan Grog, and their distinguished visitor that evening he labeled Mr. Electro Vitrifice, a name acknowledging Franklin's profound contributions to the study of electricity. Over the past three years, in fact, Franklin had published *Experiments and Observations of Electricity* (1751), performed his famous kite experiment proving that lightning is electrical in nature, invented the lightning rod, published *Supplemental Experiments and Observations on Electricity* (1753), and received the Copley Medal from the Royal Society of London for his work in electricity.

In *The History of the Tuesday Club*, Loquacious Scribble poses a question regarding a long-standing member of the club who was leaving Annapolis. Should the club alter his membership status, allowing him to become an honorary member instead of a long-standing member? Jonathan Grog responds: "Why, Mr. Secretary, you would not have us dock the Gentleman, I suppose the member, however he may stand now at this Juncture, is as

Furankurin to kaminari no zu (*Benjamin Franklin and Lightning*). Woodcut print, ca. 1870. Library of Congress, Prints and Photographs Division (reproduction number LC-DIG-jpd-02514).

long as ever." Another club member laughs at Jonathan Grog's remark and interjects, "The longstanding members methinks are waggish." Mr. Electro Vitrifice takes advantage of this setup to deliver a salacious punch line: "Longstanding members, I think Gentlemen, with Submission, are not so properly waggish, because if they stand they cannot wag." [5]

Since *The History of the Tuesday Club* is a partly fictionalized retelling of the club's story, its contents sometimes cannot be taken as documentary evidence, but in this instance they can. The words Mr. Electro Vitrifice speaks in *The History* are the same as those Franklin speaks in Hamilton's unvarnished *Minutes of the Tuesday Club*.[6] The bawdy humor and sexual innuendo provide another dimension of Franklin's wit that the published anecdotes often efface.

In 1755, Franklin set up postal communications for Major-General Edward Braddock, commander of the British forces in North America. That April he traveled to Frederick, Maryland, to confer with Braddock and agreed to supply his forces with wagons for their march against the French at Fort Duquesne. Braddock's march provides the historical backdrop for the diary of Daniel Fisher,[†] a Virginia merchant and tavern keeper who came to Philadelphia in search of opportunity. The person Fisher had come to see, however, left Philadelphia before he got a chance to see him. Consequently, Fisher was stuck in Philadelphia, where he did not know a soul. He did know about one person, however, the man who had made a reputation for himself with his electrical experiments. Fisher boldly decided to approach Franklin for help.

Fisher's behavior was not unheard of. Franklin's growing fame prompted many down-and-out characters to seek his help, much to his wife Deborah's chagrin. Fisher recorded Deborah Franklin's frustrations with all the wretches who approached her husband. Benjamin Franklin took a liking to Fisher and did what he could to help. Fisher's diary shows Franklin's kind heart and his willingness to help those in need. It also provides much information about what Philadelphia was like in 1755. Whereas Kalm and Hamilton were excellent writers who consciously shaped their encounters with Franklin as part of a greater literary work, Fisher artlessly recorded his on-the-spot impressions of what he encountered. His frankness and his immediacy are what makes his diary an important contribution to the story of Franklin's life.

Join or Die. Woodcut print by Benjamin Franklin from the *Pennsylvania Gazette,* 9 May 1754, considered America's first political cartoon. Library of Congress, Prints and Photographs Division (reproduction number LC-USZ62-9701).

Fisher left Philadelphia before the growing tensions between Franklin and the Penn family—the Proprietors of Pennsylvania—came to a head. The latest members of the family to take control of Pennsylvania lacked the altruism of their ancestor William Penn. They saw the colony of Pennsylvania as their own private cashbox and made administrative decisions based on how much they could profit by them. In August 1755 Franklin joined forces with the Quaker party, which generally opposed the Penns, to demand that the Proprietors' landholdings be taxed to raise money for the defense of the frontier. Two years later the Pennsylvania Assembly elected Franklin to travel to England to serve as its agent in an effort to negotiate the ongoing conflict with the Proprietors.

Franklin left for London in 1757. Terrified of the ocean crossing, his wife, Deborah, stayed behind and looked after her husband's personal and financial interests in his absence. Franklin returned to Philadelphia in 1762, but two years later the Pennsylvania Assembly elected Franklin to serve as its London agent again. Franklin left Philadelphia in 1764. Once more Debo-

B. Franklin of Philadelphia — L.L.D., F.R.S. Mezzotint engraved by James McArdell after a painting by Benjamin Wilson, 1761. Library of Congress, Prints and Photographs Division (reproduction number LC-USZ62-45191).

rah refused to cross the Atlantic. This time her husband was gone for over a decade. Deborah passed away in 1774, the year before Benjamin returned to Philadelphia. His second term as the Assembly's agent in London coincided with Parliament's passage of the Stamp Act in 1765.

Stephen Sayre, a New Yorker who had come to London to enter the mercantile trade, befriended Franklin and spoke with him about the Stamp Act. In a note to a political pamphlet, Sayre recorded something Franklin had said that succinctly conveyed his attitude toward the act:

Dr. Franklin, a gentleman of great abilities, and commands a great share of inoffensive wit, and true humour, was desired by a particular person to point out the particularly grievous parts, and clauses in this act; and after reading the same over very carefully, returned it to his lordship, with the alteration of only one word, as the only alteration which could possibly be admitted, or to any purpose be advised; and this was, that instead of one thousand seven hundred and sixty-five, it should take place in two thousand seven hundred and sixty-five.[7]

The Stamp Act forms the subject of the fullest Franklin interview that survives. After the law passed in early 1765, and again after it went into effect later that year, protests, sometimes violent protests, erupted throughout colonial America. Parliament had greatly underestimated colonial opposition to the Stamp Act. By the second week of February 1766, the House of Commons met as a Committee of the Whole to consider what to do. They called several witnesses, the principal one being Benjamin Franklin. On February 13, he came before the House to testify. The clerk assistant kept a detailed transcription of the legislators' questions and Franklin's responses. By law the publication of such proceedings was illegal, but they were often leaked to the press. Such was the case with Franklin's interview, which was published in 1766 as *The Examination of Doctor Benjamin Franklin*.[†]

The Examination presents a very different view of Franklin from the humor-filled reminiscences. Franklin understood that humor was inappropriate on this occasion. He comes off in this document as informed, serious, and dedicated to the cause of colonial American rights. His answers were effective: Parliament soon repealed the Stamp Act. The London printer William Strahan informed Philadelphia printer David Hall:

> To this very Examination, more than to anything else, you are indebted to the speedy and total Repeal of this odious Law. The Marquis of Rockingham told a Friend of mine a few Days after, That he never knew Truth make so great a Progress in so very short a Time. From that very Day, the Repeal was generally and absolutely determined, all that passed afterwards being only mere Form, which even in Business the most urgent must always be regarded. — Happy Man ! — In Truth, I almost envy him the inward Pleasure, as well as the outward Fame, he must derive from having it in his Power to do his Country such eminent and seasonable Service. So striking and so indubitably authentic a Proof of his Patriotism must, I imagine, for ever silence his Enemies with you; and must afford you and his other Friends the greatest Pleasure.[8]

B. Franklin of Philadelphia — L.L.D., F.R.S. Mezzotint engraved by Edward Fisher after a painting by Mason Chamberlain, ca. 1763–1785. Library of Congress, Prints and Photographs Division (reproduction number LC-DIG-ppmsca-10083).

In short, *The Examination* established Franklin's reputation as a political genius.

Though colonial politics gave Franklin a reason for remaining in Great Britain for so long, he enjoyed the rich social and intellectual opportunities the metropolis offered and befriended London's leading scientists. The contemporary scientific literature yields further evidence regarding what Franklin said in conversation. Consider a contribution to the *Philosophical Transactions of the Royal Society of London* by William Henly, a linen draper and electrical experimenter who has been called "the Royal Society's most prolific Franklinist."[9] Having difficulty with one particular experiment, Henly discussed it with Franklin, who gave him some useful advice. Henly explained: "On mentioning this circumstance to my worthy friend Dr. Franklin; he desired me to try whether having electrified the air *in one room*, I could by introducing the end of such an insulated rod into that air, make the balls diverge, when hanging at the opposite end of it, *in another room*."[10] Henly followed Franklin's advice and successfully performed the experiment. No doubt Franklin offered similarly useful advice to others engaged in scientific research.

The correspondence of the Quaker physician John Coakley Lettsom provides some additional information concerning Franklin's scientific experimentation in England. R. Howdell, one of Lettsom's correspondents, wrote about his impression of Franklin after spending the day with him. He began his description by comparing an engraved portrait with his actual appearance:

> The likeness of Dr. Franklin is a very good one; but the Cassius-like sternness is left out. I passed one day with him at Spithead, with Sir J. Banks and the late Dr. Solander (one of the most pleasant men I ever met with); when they went to smooth the water with oil. — Lord Loughborough was of the party. I remember there was but little conversation, except from Solander, and a laughable scene between an officer on board the ship and Dr. Franklin, on the properties of thunder and lightning. The officer continually contradicted the Doctor with saying, "Sir, you are quite wrong in your opinion; Dr. Franklin says so and so; the Doctor and you are quite contrary in your ideas. I never will allow, Sir, that Dr. F. is wrong. No, Sir; I am sure he is right, and you are wrong, begging your pardon." The Doctor never altered a feature at the conversation. All the company enjoyed a laugh except the disputants.[11]

Howdell's reminiscence, written in 1790, is mistaken in some of its detail. Surely, Lord Loughborough, then Alexander Wedderburn, was not among the party; he was Franklin's greatest enemy in the British government.

Franklin related his habit of stripping down to the skin and taking airbaths to William Reynolds-Highmore, a medical student at Edinburgh who incorporated what Franklin said in his dissertation, *De frigoris in corpus humanum potestate* (1778). Like all medical students at Edinburgh, Reynolds-Highmore wrote his dissertation in Latin, so the part describing Franklin in the nude appears decorously in the language of Cicero. When *Gentleman's Magazine* reviewed the published dissertation, however, it translated the relevant Latin passage into English:

> Dr. Highmore recommends to persons of a robust, not a delicate habit, Dr. Franklin's air-bath, which is thus described by the inventor: "Every morning at day break I get out of bed, and pass half an hour or an hour in my chamber, according to the season, in writing or reading, without any cloaths; and this seems rather pleasant than otherwise; and if I return to bed, as is sometimes the case, before I dress myself, I have an addition to my night's rest of one or two hours sleep sweeter than you can imagine." [12]

Then, as now, it seems, magazines loved to catch celebrities in the nude.

On Thursday evenings in London, Franklin usually dined with the Club of Honest Whigs, an informal group consisting of scientists, dissenting ministers, and American sympathizers.[13] James Boswell occasionally attended the club, and his writings provide a vivid account of the experience: "It consists of clergymen, physicians and some other professions . . . we have wine and punch upon the table. Some of us smoke a pipe, conversation goes on pretty formally, sometimes sensibly and sometimes furiously: At nine there is a sideboard with Welsh rabbits and apple-puff, porter and beer."[14] Joseph Priestley was one of the most prominent members of the club, and his writings elaborate their friendship. Franklin related his kite experiment to Priestley, who described it in *The History and Present State of Electricity.*[†] Priestley's writings also contain an excellent firsthand account of the meeting of the Privy Council in 1774 when Solicitor General Alexander Wedderburn denounced Franklin. Priestley's keen memory brings the experience alive.

When Franklin returned to America in 1775, the Pennsylvania Assembly

The Declaration Committee. (Left to right: Thomas Jefferson, Roger Sherman, Benjamin Franklin, Robert R. Livingston, and John Adams.) Lithograph by Currier & Ives, 1876. Library of Congress, Prints and Photographs Division (reproduction number LC-USZ62-820).

chose him as a delegate to the Continental Congress. Many of the other delegates were anxious to meet him, but their letters, surprisingly, provide few personal details about him. In 1766, Franklin had visited Europe with his friend Sir John Pringle. In Hanover, he and Pringle had toured the saltpeter works. Given the Revolutionaries' need for gunpowder in the aftermath of Lexington and Concord, the manufacture of saltpeter — an essential ingredient of gunpowder — was of the utmost importance. Robert Treat Paine, a delegate from Massachusetts, spoke with Franklin about what he had witnessed in Hanover, but Paine said little about their conversation in his correspondence, remarking only that what Franklin said was "much the same as is mentioned in one of the first of American Magazines."[15]

In his correspondence, Silas Deane, a delegate from Connecticut who would later serve with Franklin as a commissioner to Paris, mentioned Franklin's presence in Congress but found that he said little during the debates. Deane wrote his wife: "Doctr. Franklin is with Us but he is not a Speaker tho' We have I think his hearty Approbation of and assent To every Measure."[16] Of all of Franklin's fellow delegates to the Continental Congress, John Adams provides the fullest remarks about him. Adams was quite impressed with Franklin. His comments confirm what Silas Deane said, that Franklin was fairly quiet during the debates in Congress, but Adams admired Franklin's willingness to serve on many different committees.

Some of his committee work gave Franklin the opportunity to travel. In October 1775, he served on a committee to confer with George Washington at his headquarters in Massachusetts. While there, he took the opportunity to meet Adams's wife, Abigail, who recorded her impressions of him.[†] In September 1776, Congress appointed John Adams and Benjamin Franklin to travel to Staten Island and meet with Lord Howe in an effort to reconcile the differences between America and Great Britain. The attempted reconciliation failed, but the journey from Philadelphia gave Adams a chance to get to know Franklin further. Adams related the experience in his autobiography,[†] which constitutes one of its most delightful episodes.

In 1776, Congress elected Benjamin Franklin, Silas Deane, and Arthur Lee commissioners to negotiate a treaty between the United States and France. Their mission was fraught with conflict, as Arthur Lee's journal[†] indicates. In April 1778, John Adams came to France to replace Deane. Adams's autobiography records his uneasy indoctrination into French society. The experience gave Abigail Adams an opportunity to renew her friendship with Franklin, as well. Neither John nor Abigail was as impressed with him this second time around as they had been the first.

Franklin made many friends among French men as well as French women, and three left detailed reminiscences. The three Frenchmen who wrote detailed recollections of Franklin have much more in common than their acquaintance with the famous American diplomat. All three lived for many years in the house of Madame Anne-Catherine de Ligniville d'Autricourt Helvétius, known to her friends as Minette. On the death of her husband, the philosopher Claude-Adrien Helvétius, Mme. Helvétius left her townhouse on rue Sainte-Anne in Paris, and moved to Auteuil, a village just outside Paris, on the right bank of the river Seine. Auteuil was southwest of the village of Passy, where Benjamin Franklin lived during his stay in France; Auteuil was a short carriage drive from Passy. Franklin often chose to walk the two-thirds of a mile between the two villages. (Both Auteuil and Passy are now districts of the sixteenth arrondissement of

Franklin's Reception at the Court of France, 1778. Lithograph published in Philadelphia by John Smith after a painting by Anton Hohenstein, 186-. Library of Congress, Prints and Photographs Division (reproduction number LC-DIG-pga-01591).

Paris.) Pierre Jean Georges Cabanis and the two abbés, Abbé Morellet and Abbé Lefebvre de La Roche, lived in her house as guests. Such long-term hospitality was made possible by Mme. Helvétius's prosperity—her husband had been a fermier-général, a collector of taxes, then a remunerative avocation. Some people—John Adams among them—remarked on the unconventionality of this household, in which an aging but still attractive woman lived surrounded by three younger men, but there was never any suggestion of impropriety, and Franklin was unfazed.

Mme. Helvétius, in Auteuil as in Paris, ran one of the most famous, indeed glamorous, salons. All the leading philosophes, the leaders of the French Enlightenment, attended it. Helvétius had been a controversial philosophe; in a book he had published in 1758, entitled *De l'Esprit* (*Of the Mind*), he upheld a materialist conception of the mind based on Lockean epistemology, which led to the book's condemnation by both the Sorbonne and the pope. Not all visitors to Mme. Helvétius's salon were atheists, but many were deists and freethinkers of one stripe or another. Indeed, the two clergymen living at Madame Helvétius's had distanced themselves considerably from religious orthodoxy. Abbé André Morellet, a secular priest, had a living (which he lost at the time of the French Revolution), but was not active in the Church. He was probably a deist, whereas Abbé Pierre-Louis Lefebvre de La Roche was not far removed from atheism. As for Cabanis, the ideas he expressed in his most famous work, *Rapports du physique et du moral de l'homme* (*The Relations between the Physical and the Moral in Man*, 1802), which also relied on Lockean epistemology, were intrinsically materialist; late in life, however, he wrote an essay—unpublished in his lifetime—in which he admitted the existence of a supreme wisdom accounting for primary causes and stated the immortality of the soul. Madame Helvétius had occasional dealings with a masonic lodge, the Loge des Neuf Soeurs (Lodge of the Nine Sisters—a reference to the muses), which Cabanis and Franklin joined, the latter becoming affiliated in 1778.

In her salon in Auteuil, known as La Société d'Auteuil (The Auteuil Assembly), at the beginning of her residence there she entertained the Encyclopaedists, D'Alembert, Diderot, Condorcet, d'Holbach, Condillac, Chamfort, and, later, the younger generation of the Idéologues, which included Cabanis, Volney, and Destutt de Tracy. Turgot, the economist and politician was also a regular visitor; he had never married, out of devotion to Mme. Helvétius who, as a young woman, had turned down a proposal from him, and rejected him again once she was widowed; they remained close friends, however. Of all those visitors, those who lived up to 1789 all supported the French Revolution in its earlier stages, but suffered in various ways under the Reign of Terror of 1792–1794, Condorcet being led to commit suicide to escape the guillotine. It is notable that Mme. Helvétius's salon was the only one to go on meeting until the Reign of Terror.

Thus, Benjamin Franklin, when he was entertained in Auteuil or Passy, consorted with some of the most brilliant men and women in France and with people who supported the cause of the American patriots that Franklin had come to Europe to uphold and promote. Mme. Helvétius was more brilliant as a hostess than as an intellectual; she was not deeply interested in the advanced ideas of the Enlighteners, but enjoyed listening to their conversation; to all her guests (save John and Abigail Adams) she was charming and generous (her generosity, especially to the poor of her village earned her from Franklin the nickname of Our Lady of Auteuil). Franklin may have been romantically attached to her, though there is no firm evi-

Dr. Franklin erhält, als Gesandter des Americanischen FreyStaats, seine erste Audienz in Frankreich, zu Versailles, am 20ten Märtz 1778. Etching by Daniel Chodowiecki, 1784. Library of Congress, Prints and Photographs Division (reproduction number LC-USZ62-19420).

dence that he proposed to her; the notes they exchanged always remained lighthearted.

By no means was Mme. Helvétius the only French woman captivated by Franklin's charm. When he received word that Congress had granted him permission to return to America in 1785, many were sad to see him go. Thomas Jefferson, Franklin's successor as minister plenipotentiary to France, was astonished by and maybe a little jealous of the attention Franklin received from the ladies of France. As Jefferson witnessed Franklin saying good-bye to his French friends, he noticed several women smother him with embraces. When Franklin introduced his successor to them, Jefferson, referring to their affectionate embraces, wished that Franklin "would transfer these privileges to me." Franklin responded, "You are too young a man."[17]

When he landed at Philadelphia on September 14, Franklin was met with great fervor. The following month he was elected to the Supreme Executive Council of Pennsylvania for a three-year term, serving as its president throughout that time. His new governmental responsibilities did not stop him from making domestic improvements. His home on Market Street, known as Franklin Court, where his daughter Sarah, her husband, and their six children lived, now seemed somewhat cramped, so he decided to build a new addition, partly to accommodate the great personal library he brought back from France.

Franklin's Philadelphia home became an important destination for distinguished visitors to the city. Many were anxious to meet him, as the accounts of Andrew Ellicott,[†] Winthrop Sargent,[†] and Manessah Cutler[†] indicate. Cutler's account also presents the most detailed description of the library at Franklin Court. He describes the layout of the library, the

The Reception of Benjamin Franklin in France. Chromolithograph published by Charles Bros., 1882. Library of Congress, Prints and Photographs Division (reproduction number LC-DIG-pga-00475.

location of the books, and the gadgets Franklin invented to make the library more convenient. His account also shows the pride Franklin took in his library. Brissot de Warville, who was traveling through America, also stopped to visit Franklin. He, too, commented on Franklin and his library. Though brief, his comments are charming. He observed, "I have just been to see him, and enjoy his conversation, in the midst of his books, which he still calls his best friends. The pains of his cruel infirmity change not the serenity of his countenance, nor the calmness of his conversation."[18]

Old friends also renewed their acquaintance with Franklin. Dr. Benjamin Rush, another Edinburgh-trained physician, had known Franklin since medical school and even dedicated his dissertation to him. They served together in the Continental Congress: both were signers of the Declaration of Independence. Despite his own distinguished career, Rush realized he could still learn much from Franklin and attentively listened to what the great man had to say, as his writings[†] demonstrate. Samuel Vaughan also enjoyed Franklin's company as much as he could. He wrote their mutual friend Dr. Richard Price, another member of the Club of Honest Whigs:

> I spend many agreeable evenings with our good friend Doctor Franklin, who except for the stone, which prevents his using exercise, except in walking in the house up and down stairs, and sometime to the State-house (which is one eighth of a mile distant) still retains his health, spirits and memory beyond all conception, insomuch that there are few transactions, subjects or publications, ancient or modern, that are of any note but what he retains and when necessary in conversation will repeat and retain with wonderful facility. He bathes twice a week statedly (for hours) in a hot bath and, instead of relaxation, he enjoys and finds benefit from it. He desires his kind remembrance to you and the members of the Club.[19]

When the Federal Constitutional Convention began, Franklin was there to represent Pennsylvania. James Madison, the leading figure at the Constitutional Convention, came to know Franklin then and appreciate his wisdom. Madison retained fond memories of him and later recorded them. Franklin's conversation, Madison wrote, "was always a feast to me." He, too, would meet Franklin outside of the convention, sometimes visiting Franklin Court to speak with him there. Madison's notes on their conversations[†] show that though the old sage's body was slowly giving out, his mind remained sharp.

Le tombeau de Voltaire. Etched and engraved print showing the continents of Europe, Asia, Africa, and America personified, respectively, as d'Alembert, Catherine II, Prince Oronoco, and Benjamin Franklin; they are about to honor the tomb of Voltaire when the personification of the Prejudice of Ignorance rushes in from the right to disrupt the proceedings, 1778? Library of Congress, Prints and Photographs Division (reproduction number LC-USZ62-45436).

Charles Carroll of Carrollton, a fellow signer of the Declaration of Independence, had known Franklin at least since 1776. In the late 1780s, Carroll was in Philadelphia representing his native Maryland in the U.S. Senate. He visited Franklin Court to renew their friendship but found Franklin confined to his couch in a recumbent position. Franklin did not let his infirmity hinder either his conviviality or his hospitality. He insisted Carroll stay for dinner, observing, "I cannot *sit with you* at table, but I can *see* you."[20]

Mary Stevenson Hewson, whom Franklin had known since she was a girl, said that he retained his great mental capacity, even on his deathbed. She often read to him during his final weeks. Sometimes what she read stimulated his memory and prompted him to discuss a variety of subjects, as her touching account of his final days reveals.† Dr. John Jones, Franklin's physician, published a detailed account† of Franklin's death on the evening of April 17, 1790.

Numerous reminiscences of Franklin appeared after his death. With the publication of his autobiography during the 1790s, however, sorting out genuine reminiscences from those influenced by the autobiography becomes difficult. The accounts of Lefebvre de La Roche[†] and Cabanis,[†] both written after the French edition of the autobiography appeared, sound like their authors are retelling episodes from the autobiography. But both men knew Franklin when he was in Paris writing parts of his autobiography. Perhaps Franklin tested out his material on them before recording it in his autobiography. Cabanis, for one, was quick to point out that though some of the anecdotes he retold resemble episodes from the autobiography, they actually stemmed from Franklin's conversation.

Nineteenth-century writings that contain important personal information about Franklin can be divided into two basic categories: history and reminiscence. The historians understood that many people still living in the early nineteenth century possessed firsthand knowledge of Franklin, and they actively sought information from Franklin's surviving friends. Some of Franklin's old friends, in turn, recorded their reminiscences of him for posterity. Thomas Jefferson provides a major example.

In the second decade of the nineteenth century, Robert Walsh approached Jefferson, asking him for personal information about Franklin. In the process of writing a lengthy biographical article for *Delaplaine's*, Walsh anxiously sought whatever Jefferson could give him. Jefferson graciously supplied several Franklin anecdotes.[†] Jefferson himself incorporated further Franklin anecdotes in his own autobiography,[†] which was inspired by Franklin's.[21] Similarly, John Adams incorporated memories of Franklin in his autobiography.[†] Further anecdotes occur in the correspondence between Adams and Jefferson. Retelling one anecdote he had heard secondhand, Adams wrote Jefferson:

> In 1775, Franklin made a morning visit at Mrs. Yard's, to Sam Adams and John. He was unusually loquacious. "Man, a rational creature!" said Franklin. "Come, let us suppose a rational man. Strip him of all his appetites, especially his hunger and thirst. He is in his chamber, engaged in making experiments, or in pursuing some problem. He is highly entertained. At this moment a servant knocks. 'Sir, dinner is on the table.' 'Dinner! pox! pough! but what have you for dinner?' 'Ham and chickens.' 'Ham, and must I break the chain of my thoughts to go down and gnaw a morsel of damned hog's arse? Put aside your ham; I will dine to-morrow.'"[22]

D. Benjamin Franklin, et vita inter Americanos acta, et magnis electricitatis periculis clarus. Mezzotint engraved by Johann Elias Haid, 1780. Library of Congress, Prints and Photographs Division (reproduction number LC-DIG-ppmsca-09853).

Ezra Pound enjoyed this anecdote so well that he made it part of his *Cantos*.[23]

John F. Watson, an indefatigable chronicler, gathered much original information about early Philadelphia. Upon speaking with Deborah Logan, the widow of Franklin's friend Dr. George Logan, Watson realized she had much firsthand knowledge of Franklin herself. She told Watson about how the yellow willow tree came to North America: "All in our State came originally from some wicker-work found sprouting in a basket-state in Dock creek. It was seen by Dr. Franklin, who took it out and gave the cuttings to Charles Morris of that day, who reared them at the grounds now the site of the Bank of the United States, where they grew to great stature."[24] A scrupulous historian, Watson sought to verify this story; others confirmed what Deborah Logan told him. Perhaps inspired by Watson, Deborah Logan drafted a memoir of her husband, which included her memories of Franklin. In a footnote, she added another of her personal anecdotes of Franklin.[†]

As the middle third of the nineteenth century neared its end, Robert Carr may have been the last remaining person who knew Franklin personally. As an adolescent living in the neighborhood of Franklin Court in the late 1780s, Carr came to know Franklin after he returned to Philadelphia from France. Carr remembered him vividly all his life and, with the encouragement of history-minded friends, finally wrote down his memories of Franklin in 1864.[†]

With Robert Carr's death in 1866, the opportunities to gain information from people who had known Franklin personally had reached an end. Stories about Franklin still circulated orally, in manuscript, and in the periodical press — they had throughout the century — but these stories became increasingly removed from their sources. Two examples of the same anecdote included here demonstrate how a story can change through successive retellings. Both anecdotalists directly trace their versions of the "Sawdust Pudding Supper" to people who knew Franklin, Hugh Roberts, who was a member of Franklin's junto in the 1720s, and John Vaughan, the son of Franklin's friend Samuel. The version attributed to Roberts is more accurate in its detail, but neither bear the evidentiary weight of the firsthand accounts.

Numerous other stories about Franklin unattributed to any source circulated in the newspapers, magazines, and jestbooks. None appear here. Though these popular anecdotes cannot really be used as evidence to re-

Benjamin Franklin: The Statesman and Philosopher. Lithograph published by
N. Currier, 1847. Library of Congress, Prints and Photographs Division (reproduction number LC-USZ62-28235).

construct the story of Franklin's life, they are valuable for understanding
the story of Franklin's enduring reputation. In his lifetime, as the reminiscences of his friends clearly demonstrate, Franklin always had amusing
anecdotes to suit any occasion, and he never hesitated to tell them. Since
his death these anecdotes have been closely associated with him and have
helped to make Benjamin Franklin one of the best loved figures in American history.

Except where noted, the texts in this volume appear exactly as in their original sources — bibliographic information for which is listed as unnumbered notes at the end of each selection. The editors have not made silent corrections. Where they have added explanatory material, it appears within brackets; only the brackets in the House of Commons selection actually appear in the original source. Ellipses indicate places where passages have been left out.

Notes

Throughout this introduction, a superscript dagger (†) is used to indicate that a directly or indirectly referenced text is printed in this volume.

1. Thomas Jefferson, *Memoir, Correspondence, and Miscellanies from the Papers of Thomas Jefferson*, ed. Thomas Jefferson Randolph, 4 vols. (Charlottesville: F. Carr, 1829), 1: 44.

2. P. M. Zall, ed., *Ben Franklin Laughing: Anecdotes from Original Sources by and about Benjamin Franklin* (Berkeley: University of California Press, 1980), p. 70.

3. J. A. Leo Lemay, "The Theme of Vanity in Franklin's *Autobiography*," *Reappraising Benjamin Franklin: A Bicentennial Perspective*, ed. J. A. Leo Lemay (Newark: University of Delaware Press, 1993), p. 381.

4. J. A. Leo Lemay, "Franklin's *Autobiography* and the American Dream," *Benjamin Franklin's Autobiography*, ed. J. A. Leo Lemay and P. M. Zall (New York: Norton, 1986), pp. 349–360.

5. Dr. Alexander Hamilton, *The History of the Ancient and Honorable Tuesday Club*, ed. Robert Micklus, 3 vols. (Chapel Hill: University of North Carolina Press for the Institute of Early American History and Culture, 1990), 3: 214–215.

6. Elaine G. Breslaw, ed., *Records of the Tuesday Club of Annapolis, 1745–1756* (Urbana: University of Illinois Press, 1988), p. 447.

7. [Stephen Sayre], *The Englishman Deceived; A Political Piece: Wherein Some Very Important Secrets of State Are Briefly Recited, and Offered to the Consideration of the Public* (London: for G. Kearsly, 1768), p. 19.

8. William Strahan to David Hall, 10 May 1766, "Correspondence between William Strahan and David Hall, 1763–1777," *Pennsylvania Magazine of History and Biography* 10 (1886): 220–221.

9. J. L. Heilbron, *Electricity in the 17th and 18th Centuries: A Study of Early Modern Physics* (Berkeley: University of California Press, 1979), p. 421.

10. William Henly, "An Account of Some New Experiments in Electricity," *Philosophical Transactions of the Royal Society of London* 64 (1774): 429.

11. R. Howdell to John Coakley Lettsom, 12 January 1790, *Memoirs of the Life and Writings of the Late John Coakley Lettsom*, ed. Thomas Joseph Pettigrew, 3 vols. (London: for Longman, Hurst, Rees, Orme, and Brown, 1817), 1: 175–176.

12. "List of Books, — With Remarks," *Gentleman's Magazine* 49 (1779): 86–87.

Introduction

13. Verner W. Crane, "The Club of Honest Whigs: Friends of Science and Liberty," *William and Mary Quarterly*, 3d ser. 23 (April 1966): 210–233; William P. Griffith, "Priestley in London," *Notes and Records of the Royal Society of London* 38 (1983): 1–16.

14. James Boswell, *Boswell in Search of a Wife, 1766–1769*, ed. Frank Brady and Frederick A. Pottle (New York: McGraw-Hill, 1956), p. 300.

15. Robert Treat Paine to Elbridge Gerry, 10 June 1775, *Letters of Delegates to Congress, 1774–1789*, ed. Paul Hubert Smith and Ronald M. Gephart, 26 vols. (Washington: Library of Congress, 1976–2000), 1: 478.

16. Silas Deane to Elizabeth Deane, 1 July 1775, *Letters of Delegates to Congress*, 1: 567.

17. Margaret Bayard Smith to Susan B. Smith, March 1809, *The First Forty Years of Washington Society, Portrayed by the Family Letters of Mrs. Samuel Harrison Smith (Margaret Bayard) from the Collection of Her Grandson, J. Henley Smith*, ed. Gaillard Hunt (New York: C. Scribner's Sons, 1906), p. 59.

18. J.-P. Brissot de Warville, *New Travels in the United States of America, Performed in M.DCC.LXXXVIII*, 2 vols., 2d ed. (London: for J. S. Jordan, 1794), 1: 179.

19. Samuel Vaughan to Richard Price, 4 November 1786, *Letters to and from Richard Price, D.D., F.R.S.* (Cambridge, MA: John Wilson and Son, 1903), p. 96.

20. Robert Gilmor, "The Album of Robert Gilmor of Baltimore," ed. F. L. Pleadwell, *American Collector* 6 (1928): 22–23.

21. Kevin J. Hayes, *The Road to Monticello: The Life and Mind of Thomas Jefferson* (New York: Oxford University Press, 2008), p. 595.

22. John Adams to Thomas Jefferson, 15 November 1813, *The Adams-Jefferson Letters: The Complete Correspondence between Thomas Jefferson and Abigail and John Adams*, ed. Lester J. Cappon (1959; reprinted, Chapel Hill: University of North Carolina Press for the Institute of Early American History and Culture, 1988), p. 399.

23. Ezra Pound, *The Cantos* (New York: New Directions, 1970), pp. 155–156.

24. John F. Watson, *Annals of Philadelphia, Being a Collection of Memoirs, Anecdotes, and Incidents of the City and Its Inhabitants from the Days of the Pilgrim Founders* (Philadelphia: E. L. Carey and A. Hart, 1830), p. 719.

Chronology

1706	17 January	Benjamin Franklin born in Boston, the youngest son of Josiah Franklin, a tallow-chandler, and Abiah Folger Franklin
1714–1715		Attends Boston Grammar School, but his father withdraws him at the end of the school year because of its expense
1715–1716		Attends George Brownell's English school
1716–1717		Works with his father making candles and soap
1718–1721		Apprenticed to his brother James in the printing business
1722	April	The first of BF's "Silence Dogood" essays appears in the *New-England Courant*; the essay, fourteen in number, series would continue through October
	12 June	James Franklin is imprisoned by the Massachusetts Assembly for implying collusion between pirates and local officials, where he remains until July 7; BF manages the *Courant* in his absence
1723	24 January	James Franklin goes into hiding after provoking the ire of the Massachusetts Assembly by publishing the *Courant* without its censorship; BF manages the paper in his absence until February 12
	25 September	Leaves Boston secretly, breaking his indenture
	6 October	Reaches Philadelphia and finds work with Samuel Keimer as a journeyman printer

1724	5 November	Sails for London with his friend James Ralph and Quaker merchant Thomas Denham
	24 December	Reaches London, where he obtains work at Samuel Palmer's printing office
1725	*ca.* March	Writes *A Dissertation on Liberty and Necessity, Pleasure and Pain*
	Autumn	Leaves Palmer's to work for John Watts, another printer
1726	21 July	Sails for Philadelphia with Thomas Denham, for whom he works upon returning to Philadelphia
1727	March–April	Suffers pleurisy; his employer Denham is also critically ill
	June	Returns to work for Keimer
	Autumn	Forms Junto with several intelligent and ambitious Philadelphia friends
1728	June	Quits Keimer and forms printing partnership with Hugh Meredith
1729	4 February	Begins "Busy-Body" essay series in *American Weekly Mercury*
	10 April	Publishes *A Modest Enquiry into the Nature and Necessity of a Paper Currency*
	25 September	Buys *Pennsylvania Gazette* from Keimer, transforming it into the finest newspaper in colonial America; later this year or early the next BF's son William is born out of wedlock to an unknown mother
1730	1 September	Forms common-law union with Deborah Read Rogers, who agrees to take William into their household
1731	January	Joins Freemasons
	1 July	Forms the Library Company of Philadelphia, the first subscription library in America

	13 September	Sponsors business partnership with Thomas Whitemarsh to establish a print shop in South Carolina, the first of several such financial partnerships BF would establish
1732	19 December	First publishes *Poor Richard's Almanack*, which he would continue annually until 1757
1733	1 July	Begins keeping ledger of personal faults on an erasable ivory table-book
1734	24 June	Elected grand master of Masons of Pennsylvania
1736	15 October	Appointed clerk of Pennsylvania Assembly
1737	5 October	Begins serving as postmaster of Philadelphia
1739	2 November	George Whitefield arrives in Philadelphia; BF befriends him and agrees to publish his journals and sermons by subscription
1741	Winter	Designs Pennsylvania fireplace
	16 February	Issues *General Magazine and Historical Chronicle*
1743	14 May	Publishes *A Proposal for Promoting Useful Knowledge*, which is considered the founding document of the American Philosophical Society
	31 August	Daughter Sarah is born
1744	15 November	Publishes *An Account of the New Invented Pennsylvania Fire-Places*
1745		Begins electrical experiments
1747	25 May	Sends first account of electrical experiments to Peter Collinson, who presents it to Royal Society of London
	December	Publishes *Plain Truth*, which warns of Pennsylvania's vulnerability to naval attack
1748	1 January	Retires as printer to devote himself to scientific and civic affairs

	4 October	Elected to Common Council of Philadelphia
1749	Autumn	Writes *Proposals Relating to the Education of Youth in Pensilvania*, which establishes the Philadelphia Academy (now University of Pennsylvania)
1751	7 February	Founds Pennsylvania Hospital
	April	Publishes *Experiments and Observations on Electricity*
	9 May	Elected to Pennsylvania Assembly
1752	June	Conducts kite experiment, proving that lightning is electrical in nature; designs lightning rods to protect homes
1753	March	Publishes *Supplemental Experiments and Observations*
	26 September	Negotiates treaty with Ohio Indians at Carlisle, Pennsylvania, through October 4
	30 November	Royal Society of London awards BF Copley Medal for his research on electricity
1754	9 May	Concerned with French presence on the Pennsylvania frontier, BF creates and publishes the "Join or Die" political cartoon
	June–July	Attends Albany Congress, during which representatives from seven colonies arrange to defend the frontier against French
	September	Publishes *New Experiments and Observations on Electricity*
1755	April–May	Supplies Major-General Edward Braddock's forces with wagons for their march against the French at Fort Duquesne
	18 December	Leaves Philadelphia to travel to frontier to build forts and organize defenses
1756	5 February	Returns to Philadelphia

	29 April	Elected to Royal Society of London
1757	3 February	Pennsylvania Assembly chooses Franklin to serve as its London agent to negotiate dispute with the Proprietors of Pennsylvania
	23 June	Leaves for England from New York; aboard ship writes "Father Abraham's Speech" (*The Way to Wealth*)
	26 July	Reaches London
	30 July	Takes lodging with Margaret Stevenson at No. 7 Craven Street
1759	12 February	Receives honorary doctorate from the University of St. Andrews in Scotland and becomes known as Dr. Franklin
	8 August	Begins an extensive tour through northern England and Scotland, which continues to November 2
1760	17 April	Publishes *The Interest of Great Britain Considered*, which emphasizes the economic and strategic importance of Canada to Great Britain
1761	August	Travels through the Netherlands
	22 September	Witnesses the coronation of George III
1762	30 April	Receives honorary degree of civil law from Oxford
	1 November	Returns to Philadelphia
1763	7 June	Leaves Philadelphia on a tour of New Jersey, New York, and New England to inspect post offices; the trip lasts until the first week of November
1764	30 January	Publishes *A Narrative of the Late Massacres*, denouncing the "Paxton Boys," a frontier mob that massacred friendly Christian Indians
	26 May	Elected Speaker of Pennsylvania Assembly

	7 November	Leaves Philadelphia to represent the Pennsylvania Assembly as its London agent
	10 December	Reaches London
1765	2 February	Meets First Minister George Grenville to protest the proposed stamp duties
	27 February	House of Commons passes the Stamp Act, which will go into effect November 1
1766	13 February	Examined by House of Commons regarding the Stamp Act; BF's eloquent defense prompts the act's repeal
1767	29 October	Daughter Sarah marries Richard Bache in Philadelphia
1768	7 January	Publishes *Causes of the American Discontents before 1768*
1769	2 January	Elected president of American Philosophical Society, a position he holds until his death
	12 August	Grandson Benjamin Franklin Bache is born
1771	July–August	Writes the first part of his autobiography
	25 August	Tours Ireland and Scotland through November 30
1773	September	Publishes "Rules by Which a Great Empire May Be Reduced to a Small One" and "Edict by the King of Prussia"
1774	January	Denounced by Solicitor General Alexander Wedderburn before the Privy Council
	September	Attempts negotiations to settle differences between Great Britain and America
1775	20 March	Leaves London
	5 May	Arrives in Philadelphia
	6 May	Is chosen delegate to the Continental Congress by the Pennsylvania Assembly

	July	Drafts Articles of Confederation
1776	1 June	Appointed by Congress to the Committee of Five to draft the Declaration of Independence
	September	Congress elects BF commissioner to France
	27 October	Leaves Philadelphia, taking two grandsons with him, William Temple Franklin and Benjamin Franklin Bache
1778	April	Embraces Voltaire at a meeting of the French Academy of Sciences
1779	December	Benjamin Vaughan publishes Franklin's *Political, Miscellaneous, and Philosophical Pieces*
1783	September	Signs definitive treaty of peace between Great Britain and the United States
1784	Spring	Writes second part of autobiography
1785	July	Leaves France for the last time
	14 September	Reaches Philadelphia
	October	Elected to the presidency of the Supreme Executive Council of Pennsylvania
1786		Builds addition on to his Philadelphia home to house his large personal library
1787	23 April	Named president of the Pennsylvania Society for Promoting the Abolition of Slavery and devotes much effort to abolition
1790	17 April	Dies quietly at home

Franklin in His Own Time

[Speaking about Natural History, 1748]

PEHR KALM

Pehr Kalm (1716–1779), a Swedish botanist, received an excellent education at the University of Uppsala, where he studied with both Anders Celsius and Linnaeus. After taking his doctorate in economics and natural history at Åbo Academy, Kalm became its first professor of economics the following year. With the Academy's support, he visited North America in 1748 and traveled around the continent for three years. During his sojourn, he met many notable Americans, including Benjamin Franklin. Kalm's record of their time together in November 1748 presents a vivid portrayal of Franklin in his forties. Recognizing Kalm's dedication to the study of natural history, Franklin shaped his conversation accordingly and related many pertinent stories about minerals and animal life. Greatly impressed with Franklin, Kalm became an important correspondent of his as he continued exploring North America upon leaving Philadelphia. In a letter to Franklin dated September 2, 1750, Kalm wrote one of the earliest descriptions of Niagara Falls. Returning to Sweden in 1751, he resumed his academic duties and prepared his American diary for publication. It appeared as *En Resa til Norra America* (1753–1761), which Franklin's friend Johann Reinhold Forster translated into English as *Travels into North America* (1770–1771). Recognized as a major contribution to the study of natural history, Kalm's *Travels* has since been reprinted numerous times.

MR. FRANKLIN TOLD ME that in that part of *New England*, where his father lived, two rivers fell into the sea, in one of which they caught great numbers of herrings, and in the other not one. Yet the places where these rivers discharged themselves into the sea, were not far asunder. They had observed that when the herrings came in spring to deposit their spawn, they always swam up the river where they used to catch them, but never came into the other. This circumstance led Mr. *Franklin*'s father who was settled between the two rivers, to try whether it was not possible to make the herrings likewise live in the other river. For that purpose he put out his nets, as they were coming up for spawning, and he caught some. He took the spawn out of them, and carefully carried it across the land into the other river.

It was hatched, and the consequence was, that every year afterwards they caught more herrings in that river; and this is still the case. This leads one to believe that the fish always like to spawn in the same place where they were hatched, and from whence they first put out to sea; being as it were accustomed to it.

The following is another peculiar observation. It has never formerly been known that codfish were to be caught at Cape *Hinlopen*: they were always caught at the mouth of the *Delaware*; but at present they are numerous in the former place. From hence it may be concluded, that fish likewise change their place of abode of their own accord.

A captain of a ship who had been in *Greenland*, asserted from his own experience, that on passing the seventieth deg. of north lat. the summer heat was there much greater, than it is below that degree. From hence he concluded, that the summer heat at the pole itself, must be still more excessive, since the sun shines there for such a long space of time, without ever setting. The same account with similar consequences drawn from thence, Mr. *Franklin* had heard of the ship captains in *Boston*, who had sailed to the most northern parts of this hemisphere. But still more astonishing is the account he got from Captain *Henry Atkins*, who still lives at *Boston*. He had for some time been upon the fishery along the coasts of *New England*. But not catching as much as he wished, he sailed north, as far as *Greenland*. At last he went so far, that he discovered people, who had never seen *Europeans* before (and what is more astonishing) who had no idea of the use of fire, which they had never employed; and if they had known it, they could have made no use of their knowledge, as there were no trees in the country. But they eat the birds and fish which they caught quite raw. Captain *Atkins* got some very scarce skins in exchange for some trifles. . . .

Mr. Franklin related, that he had, when a boy, seen two of the animals which they call *Moose-deer*, but he well remembered that they were not near of such a size as they must have been, if the horns found in *Ireland* were to fit them: the two animals which he saw, were brought to *Boston*, in order to be sent to *England* to Queen *Ann*. The height of the animal up to the back was that of a pretty tall horse; but the head and its horns were still higher. . . .

Mr. *Franklin* gave me a piece of a stone, which on account of its indestructibility in the fire, is made use of in *New England* for making melting furnaces and forges.

It consists of a mixture of *Lapis Ollaris*, or Serpentine stone, and of

Asbest. The greatest part of it is a grey Serpentine stone, which is fat and smooth to the touch, and is easily cut and worked. Here and there are some glittering speckles of that sort of asbest, whose fibres come from a center like rays, or *Star Asbest.* This stone is not found in strata or solid rocks, but here and there scattered on the fields. . . .

The *mountain flax*, or that kind of stone, which Bishop [Johan] Browallius calls *Amiantus fibris separabilibus molliusculis*, in his lectures on mineralogy, which were published in 1739, or the amiant with soft fibres which can easily be separated, is found abundantly in Pensylvania. Some pieces are very soft, others pretty tough: Mr. *Franklin* told me that twenty and some odd years ago, when he made a voyage to *England*, he had a little purse with him, made of the mountain flax of this country, which he presented to Sir *Hans Sloane.* I have likewise seen paper made of this stone: and I have likewise received some small pieces of it, which I keep in my cabinet. Mr. *Franklin* had been told by others, that, on exposing this mountain flax to the open air in winter, and leaving it in the cold and wet, it would grow together, and more fit for spinning. But he did not venture to determine how far this opinion was grounded. On this occasion he related a very pleasant accident which happened to him with this mountain flax: he had, several years ago, got a piece of it, which he gave to one of his journeymen printers, in order to get it made into a sheet at the paper mill. As soon as the fellow brought the paper, Mr. *Franklin* rolled it up, and threw it into the fire, telling the journeyman he would see a miracle, a sheet of paper which did not burn: the ignorant fellow asserted the contrary, but was greatly astonished, upon seeing himself convinced. Mr. *Franklin* then explained to him, though not very clearly, the peculiar qualities of the paper. As soon as he was gone, some of his acquaintance came in, who immediately knew the paper. The journeyman thought he would shew them a great curiosity and astonish them. He accordingly told them that he had curiously made a sheet of paper, which would not burn, though it was thrown into the fire. They pretended to think it impossible, and he as strenuously maintained his assertion. At last they laid a wager about it; but whilst he was busy with stirring up the fire, the others slyly besmeared the paper with fat: the journeyman, who was not aware of it, threw it into the fire, and that moment it was all in flames: this astonished him so much, that he was almost speechless; upon which they could not help laughing, and so discovered the whole artifice.

In several houses of the town, a number of little *Ants* run about, living under ground, and in holes in the wall. The length of their bodies is one geometrical line. Their colour is either black or dark red: they have the custom of carrying off sweet things, if they can come at them, in common with the ants of other countries. Mr. *Franklin* was much inclined to believe that these little insects could by some means communicate their thoughts or desires to each other, and he confirmed his opinion by some examples. When an ant finds some sugar, it runs immediately under ground to its hole, where having stayed a little while, a whole army comes out, unites and marches to the place where the sugar is, and carries it off by pieces: or if an ant meets with a dead fly, which it cannot carry alone, it immediately hastens home, and soon after some more come out, creep to the fly, and carry it away. Some time ago Mr. *Franklin* put a little earthen pot with treacle into a closet. A number of ants got into the pot and devoured the treacle very quickly. But as he observed it, he shook them out, and tied the pot with a thin string to a nail which he had fastened in the ceiling; so that the pot hung down by the string. A single ant by chance remained in the pot: this ant eat till it was satisfied; but when it wanted to get off, it was under great concern to find its way out: it ran about the bottom of the pot, but in vain: at last it found after many attempts the way to get to the ceiling by the string. After it was come there, it ran to the wall, and from thence to the ground. It had hardly been away for half an hour, when a great swarm of ants came out, got up to the ceiling, and crept along the string into the pot, and began to eat again: this they continued till the treacle was all eaten: in the mean time one swarm running down the string, and the other up.

From *Travels into North America*, trans. Johann Reinhold Forster, 3 vols. (Warrington: William Eyres, 1770–1771), 1: 293–299, 303–306.

[Extracts from the Diary, 1755]

DANIEL FISHER

Upon emigrating from England in 1750, Daniel Fisher (*fl.* 1720–1755) settled in Williamsburg, Virginia, where he entered the mercantile trade, selling groceries, imported tea, and other general merchandise. He also briefly operated a tavern. Fisher kept his retail store going through 1752 with little success. In May 1755, he left Williamsburg for Philadelphia in search of work. Given his experience, he hoped to find employment in the Philadelphia mercantile trade. Initially thwarted in his quest, he wrote Franklin to ask for help. Such self-introductions violated contemporary etiquette; ideally a mutual friend should have introduced two unacquainted parties. Unphased by Fisher's breach in etiquette, Franklin magnanimously invited him to tea and offered to do what he could. He hired him to do some clerical and secretarial work in June, which Fisher continued sporadically into early August. Franklin also suggested the possibility of a teaching position at the English school of the Academy of Philadelphia, which never materialized. The last week of July Fisher began lodging and boarding with the Franklins. As his diary reveals, he was impressed with Benjamin Franklin's kindness and indulgence. He was less taken with Deborah Franklin, whom he found petty, jealous, and vindictive. Fisher's portrayal is one of the fullest yet least flattering depictions of Mrs. Franklin, which, as J. A. Leo Lemay suggests in his *Life of Benjamin Franklin*, must be tempered with recourse to other contemporary accounts of her. Fisher left Philadelphia to return to Virginia in August. Before leaving, he purchased some clothing, several yards of fine linen, and other goods to sell in Williamsburg, but the hapless Fisher was robbed on the road to Virginia (*Virginia Gazette*, 5 September 1755).

Excerpts from Fisher's diary appeared in the *Pennsylvania Magazine of History and Biography* in 1893, which has been an important source for Franklin's biographers. But actually, Louise Pecquet du Bellet edited and printed the entire diary as part of her four-volume opus, *Some Prominent Virginia Families* (1907). The complete diary helps to correct several errors that Franklin's biographers have perpetuated. Lemay, for example, depicts Fisher as a young man at the start of his career, but the full diary shows that Fisher was married with children and had operated his own business in Williamsburg for many years. Pecquet du Bellet's edition provides the source for the present text, which has been silently modernized and regularized to make it more reader friendly.

JUNE 1ST AND 2ND I SPENT very melancholy hearing nothing from Col. [William] Hunter whom I was cautious of teasing, til on the 3d. I was informed he that morning set out to Virginia. So whether he had any talk with Mr. [William] Allen convinced was I never. The circumstances, in a kind of despair, entered my romantic head to communicate my unhappy condition to Mr. Franklin, a Gentleman in good esteem here and well known to the philosophical world. I without reserve laid the whole of my affairs before him, requesting his aid if such a thing might be without inconvenience to himself. This in writing I sent to him June 4th. Early in the morning, about the same day I received a note by a servant under a wafer in these words, "Mr. Franklin Compliments to Mr. Fisher and desire the favor of his Company to drink tea at five o'clock this afternoon." I went at the time; and in my imagination met with a humane, kind reception. He expressed a concern for my affliction, and promised to assist me into some business provided it was in his power. In returning from Mr. Franklin's, a silversmith in the neighborhood to Mr. Franklins, Seeing me come out that Gentleman House, Spoke to me as I was passing his door, and invited me to sit down. This man's name was [Samuel] Soumien. I had been several times in his Company at My Inn, and Considered him as a very inquisitive Person, Craving a knowledge of other Peoples affairs, tho' no ways concerning himself. I accepted his offer of sitting at his door, and he soon began to fish for my business with Mr. Franklin by asking whether I had any previous knowledge or acquaintance with him; not obtaining a thorough information of all he wanted to know, and knowing I wanted a private Lodging, he made me an offer of his, which I gladly accepted. We agreed at Twelve shillings a week, and I came thither the same Evening. The Family consisted of, himself, his Wife, and a daughter of hers, a Young Woman about 13 years of age, a Negro Man, and two Negro Wenches. I was very well pleased to observe that this Family seemed to be acquainted with Mr. Franklin's.

June 5th: Thursday—As I was coming down from my chamber this afternoon, a Gentlewoman was sitting upon one of the lowest Stairs which was but narrow, and there not being room enough to pass, She arose up and threw herself immediately upon the Floor and sat there. Mr. Soumien and his Wife greatly entreated her to arise and take a Chair, but in vain; She would keep her Seat, and kept it I think the longer for their entreaty. This Gentlewoman whom (tho' I had seen before) I did not know, appeared to be Mrs. Franklin. She assumed the Airs of extraordinary Freedom, and great humility. Lamented heartily the misfortune of those who were unhappily infected with a too tender or benevolent disposition, said she believed all the world claimed a privilege of troubling her Pappey (So she usually Calls Mr. Franklin) with their Calamities and distresses, giving us a general history of many Such wretches and their impertinent applications to him.

Mr. Franklin's moral character is good, and he and Mrs. Franklin live irreproachably as Man and Wife.

Friday June 6th: I kept my Chamber, being very ill with my old disorder the cholic but was relieved by taking some drops of Castor and laudanum the next morning. The first rain fell last night that had been since a long time, which greatly refreshed the Earth.

Received an invitation from Mr. Franklin to dine with him to morrow.

Sunday June 8th about half an hour after nine this morning, I went to the Quakers' meeting on Society Hill. It proved a Silent one, except one old Man in the Gallery, who spoke about two minutes. What he said was not very edifying, nor had it the approbation of the Friends themselves. Some of them in my hearing, esteeming him a Babbler.

I dined to day with Mr. Franklin and went afterwards to the Dutch Churches.

The Lutheran Church has an Organ and a good Performer. The Calvinist Church has an Organ and a good Performer, both 9th and 10th Employed in writing Letters to my Wife and Mr. [Nathaniel] Walthoe.

Wednesday 11th so very cold for this two nights past, that many People required Fires in their Parlours as in Winter.

Thursday the 12th This morning about Nine Mr. Franklin sent for me to copy a pretty long Letter from General [Edward] Braddock, acknowledging the care of the Pennsylvanians in sending Provisions etc to the Forces. Mr. Franklin in particular; and complaining of the neglect of the Governments of Virginia and Maryland especially; in speaking of which the Colonies, he says, They have promised everything and had performed nothing;

and of the Pennsylvanian, he said They had promised nothing, and had performed everything. That even the small supply she had received from the first two Colonys even in general so decayed or damaged, as to be of no use, and in a letter before this, of which I only saw a Copy, the General acknowledges she had been greatly imposed on in the character given him of the People of Pennsylvania; but that he would in long take an opportunity of doing ample Justice, to the Ministry at Home. When I finished several hasty Copies for which the Post then waited, he desired I would breakfast with him the next morning, and he would then give me more work. June 13th and 14th I was closely employed in several Copys of a Manuscript Treatise entitled the "Observations concerning the Increase of Mankind, Peopling of Countries, etc."

From June 15th to July 10th employed generally in writing or Sorting of Papers at the Printing office. On July 11th I wrote long Letters to my Wife and Mr. Walthoe giving them an exact account of my Situation. I should have observed that on St. John the Baptist Day (June 24th) There was the Greatest Procession of Free Masons to the Church and their Lodge in Second Street, that was ever seen in America. No less than 160 being in the Procession in Gloves, Aprons etc. attended by a band of music. Mr. Allin the Grand Master honouring them with his Company, as did the Deputy Grand Master Mr. Benjamin Franklin, and his Son Mr. Wm. Franklin who walked as the next Chief Officer—a sword Bearer with a naked sword drawn, headed the Procession. They dined together elegantly, as it is said at their Hall upon Turtle etc. Perceiving I had nothing ever to hope or expect from Mr. Allin I rarely went near him unless twice for a supply of money; Mr. [William] Nelson in case of need, having given me a Bill of credit for Twelve Pistoles.

Friday July 18th This afternoon about Three Oclock we were terribly alarmed by an Express by way of Maryland from Coln. [James] Innes, dated at Wills Creek or Port Cumberland July 11th giving an account that the Forces under Gen'l Braddock were entirely defeated by the French on the 9th on the River Monongahela. The General, Sr. John St. Clair and a number of the Officers killed, and all our fine artillery taken. The Consternation that this City upon the occasion is hardly to be expressed. The next day we received other accounts less terrible, but none very authentic or particular, and on the 20th Some Indian Traders from the upper parts of the country, tho' not from the Camp brought still more flattering accounts, and Reports were various till Wednesday July 23rd when about noon arrived the following Paragraph by the Lancaster Post Dated Carlile 21st July 1755 — "It is now reduced to a certainty; that our Army under General Braddock is defeated; The General and St. John St. Clair dangerously wounded — about a Thousand men lost, with the Train of Artillery and Baggage. The remaining part of the Army Under Col. [Thomas] Dunbar have destroyed all their Baggage except two six Pounders and Provision necessary for their retreat to Wills Creek, where I expect they are by this time." This account was credited and afterward more particularly Confirmed by Mr. [Robert] Orme Aid a Camp to the Gen'l. The Mobb here upon this occasion, were very unruly; assembling in great numbers with an intention of demolishing the Mass House belonging to the Roman Catholics, wherein they were underhand excited and encouraged by some People of a Higher Rank. But the peaceable Quakers insisting that the Catholics as well as Christians of other denominations, were settled upon the faith of the Constitution, or Wm. Penn's Charter, and that the Government were bound to protect them, so long at least, as they remained inoffensive and paid a dutiful regard to the establishment. The Magistrates met, and with a good deal of difficulty, prevailed with the Mobb to desist. Having as yet made no settled agreement with Mr. Franklin, and being not certain that he had any real occasion for my Services, having several Days together nothing for me to do, I happened to have a very slender acquaintance with one Captain [James] Coultas, who lived at the upper Ferry on the River Schuilkil, and who it was generally believed would be elected Sheriff of Philadelphia at the ensuing Election. A Person of Sense and Character, and to my apprehension, of no less generosity and good nature. To this Gentleman I wrote a few lines, imparting, that if the business he was entering upon required any such aid as it was in my power to administer, I should be very glad to serve him; I apprehending the frequent auctions or Sales which a Sheriff was necessarily concerned in might, require Some Such assistance. In a Day or Two after this, meeting with Captn. Coultas at "Indian King," he called me aside, acknowledged the receipt of my Letter, Said that it would not have a decent book to dispose of my part of an office which he was not then possessed of; not but he said, from the assurance of his Friends, he believed could depend on it; But this he would assure me, if it so happened, I might rely upon any Act of Friendship or kindness in his power to Serve me. Extremely pleased with the humanly rational generosity of this Sensible man,

I immediately flew to my Friend Mr. Franklin with the news, that he might participate in my Satisfaction, but was some what surprised that he did not consider what I had done, in the same view with myself. He allowed Capn. Coultas was a very worthy man, and would Sincerely perform everything I was encouraged to expect or hope for; but could not apprehend that any thing he could do for me would be worthy my acceptance. That he had himself thought of several ways of serving me. and has rejected them only, because he esteemed them too mean. Particularly he said, He could immediately put me into the Academy, in the Capacity of English School Master, a Place of 60 a year, with some other advantages; but refrained mentioning it to me in hopes of having it soon in his power of doing better for me. I assured him with the utmost gratitude, the employ did not appear in so mean a light to me; and the only reason I had for declining the favour, was the diffidence of my ability in doing Justice to his recommendation, a thing which he said, he was not in the least apprehensive of. However, presuming it gave him no offence, I craved his leave to decline the kind offer, and he declared himself very well satisfied.

Having informed him that I should prefer Serving him as a Clerk provided he had any occasion for me; On Monday Morning July 28th I received the following Letter from him.

"Monday morning July 28th Sir till our building is finished which I hope will be in 2 or 3 weeks, I have no more to accommodate a Clerk. But it is my intention to have one, tho' my business is so small that I cannot afford to give more than I have always given Vizt, Diet at my own Table, with Lodging and washing and 25 per annum. I could never think this worth offering to you, but if you think fit to accept of it, till something better shall fall in the way, you shall be very welcome to it, etc E B Franklin P. S. I may commence from the time you first began to write for me, in which case, I discharge your Board etc at Mr. Soumien's; or from the present time, and then I pay for the writing done, or if you choose it, I will get you into the Charity School as I mentioned before."

Without the least hesitation I gave the preference to his service, and he let me know that it should not hinder his endeavours of Serving me further.

Mr. Soumien had often informed me of great uneasiness and dissatisfactions in Mr. Franklin's family in a manner no way pleasing to me, and which in truth I was unwilling to Credit; but as Mrs. Franklin and I, of late, began to be very Friendly and Sociable, I discerned great grounds, for Mr. Soumien's Reflections, arising solely from jealousy of her disposition; She suspecting Mr. Franklin for having too great an esteem for his Son in prejudice of herself and Daughter, a young woman of about 12 or 13 years of age, for whom it was visible Mr. Franklin had no less esteem than for his Son. In this situation I was, when on August the 7th I received a most kind letter from Mr. Walthoe informing me that Mr. Mitchelson, the Person who rented his store was become a Bankrupt, and that as it was unlikely I should ever remain in quiet under Mr. [Henry] Wetherburn, If I thought his House would be of service to me, I should have the preference to any Person whatever, and that I might rest assured of any other friendly aid in his Power; My Family too he assured me, had now manifested an entire conformity to my will, either to embrace the opportunity and trying here for our Friends at York would assist us, or if I was better pleased with the prospect that Philadelphia afforded, they would remove thither upon the first notice. The uncertainty of my situation together with reflecting upon what might be the consequence of General Braddock's defeat brought me to a resolution of Seeing my Family and Mr. Walthoe at Williamsburg before I came to any Certain determination of a settlement; Yet I showed Mr. Franklin my letter, and craved his opinion, who very readily came into mine, assuring me also he would wait a considerable space for the result of our Conferences before he supplied himself with a Clerk or the School with a Master. So I fixed upon Sunday the 10th for setting out on my journey to Williamsburg. Being not determined which Road I should take (there being several) Mr. Franklin said, if I went the upper, he would get me to take an order for a small matter of Money on Mr. Mercer in Virginia, with whom he had had no settlement for Nine years, upon which I told him, I did not regard a few miles of riding to serve him, and he might depend upon my making Mr. Mercers in my way. He gave me also Six Pistol[e]s, asking if that was sufficient for the trouble he had given me. I told him it was. The evening (Saturday) before I set out, I was with him till after eleven oclock, when he pressed me to accept of Two Guineas more, which I refused and I said that in case of accidents, from my horse failing, or any other misfortune, I had a Gold Watch in my pocket which would give me some Credit. It was near Twelve when we parted with mutual good wishes.

From "The Fisher History," in *Some Prominent Virginia Families*, ed. Louise Pecquet du Bellet, 4 vols. (Lynchburg: J. P. Bell, 1907), 2: 803–808.

The Examination of Doctor Benjamin Franklin (1767)

House of Commons

The Stamp Act forms the subject of Franklin's fullest interview. After the law passed in 1765, protests erupted throughout colonial America. Parliament had greatly underestimated colonial opposition to the Stamp Act. In February 1766, the House of Commons met to consider what to do. They called several witnesses, the principal one being Benjamin Franklin, who came before the House to testify on February 13. The clerk assistant kept a detailed transcription of the legislators' questions and Franklin's responses. By law the publication of such proceedings was illegal, but they were often leaked to the press. Franklin's testimony was published in 1767 as *The Examination of Doctor Benjamin Franklin*. This document presents a different view of Franklin than most of the others. Unlike the jovial jokester he appears to be elsewhere, Franklin comes off in this document as informed, serious, and dedicated to the cause of colonial American rights. Strongly influenced by Franklin's testimony, Parliament repealed the Stamp Act. Franklin's friend William Strahan observed: "The House of Commons examined several Merchants and others, to procure what Light they could into the Nature of the Objections which were made to it with you; among whom was Dr Franklin. His Examination lasted three Hours; and, I find, from all Hands, that the Answers he gave to the many Questions asked him, threw more Light upon the Subject than all the other Informations they had put together. They were indeed manly, distinct, clear, and satisfactory" (96). The reviewer for *Gentleman's Magazine* (37 [July 1767]: 368–369) offered a fine appreciation of the published pamphlet:

> From this examination of Dr. *Franklin*, the reader may form a clearer and more comprehensive idea of the state and disposition of *America*, of the expediency or inexpediency of the measure in question, and of the character and conduct of the minister who proposed it, than from all that has been written upon the subject in news papers and pamphlets, under the

titles of essays, letters, speeches, and considerations, from the first moment of its becoming the object of public attention till now.

The questions in general are put with great subtilty and judgment, and they are answered with such deep and familiar knowledge of the subject, such precision and perspicuity, such temper and yet such spirit, as do the greatest honour to Dr. *Franklin*, and justify the general opinion of his character and abilities.

WHAT IS YOUR NAME, and place of abode?

A. Franklin, of Philadelphia.

Q. Do the Americans pay any considerable taxes among themselves?

A. Certainly many, and very heavy taxes.

Q. What are the present taxes in Pennsylvania, laid by the laws of the Colony?

A. There are taxes on all estates real and personal, a poll tax, a tax on all offices, professions, trades and businesses, according to their profits; an excise on all wine, rum, and other spirits; and a duty of Ten Pounds per head on all Negroes imported, with some other duties.

Q. For what purposes are those taxes laid?

A. For the support of the civil and military establishments of the country, and to discharge the heavy debt contracted in the last war.

Q. How long are those taxes to continue?

A. Those for discharging the debt are to continue till 1772, and longer, if the debt should not be then all discharged. The others must always continue.

Q. Was it not expected that the debt would have been sooner discharged?

A. It was, when the peace was made with France and Spain — But a fresh war breaking out with the Indians, a fresh load of debt was incurred, and the taxes, of course, continued longer by a new law.

Q. Are not all the people very able to pay those taxes?

A. No. The frontier counties, all along the continent, having been frequently ravaged by the enemy, and greatly impoverished, are able to pay very little tax. And therefore, in consideration of their distresses, our late tax laws do expressly favour those counties, excusing the sufferers; and I suppose the same is done in other governments.

Q. Are not you concerned in the management of the Post-Office in America?

A. Yes. I am Deputy Post-Master General of North-America.

Q. Don't you think the distribution of stamps, by post, to all the inhabitants, very practicable, if there was no opposition?

A. The posts only go along the sea coasts; they do not, except in a few instances, go back into the country; and if they did, sending for stamps by post would occasion an expence of postage, amounting, in many cases, to much more than that of the stamps themselves.

Q. Are you acquainted with Newfoundland?

A. I never was there.

Q. Do you know whether there are any post roads on that island?

A. I have heard that there are no roads at all; but that the communication between one settlement and another is by sea only.

Q. Can you disperse the stamps by post in Canada?

A. There is only a post between Montreal and Quebec. The inhabitants live so scattered and remote from each other, in that vast country, that posts cannot be supported among them, and therefore they cannot get stamps per post. The English Colonies too, along the frontiers, are very thinly settled.

Q. From the thinness of the back settlements, would not the stamp-act be extreamly inconvenient to the inhabitants, if executed?

A. To be sure it would; as many of the inhabitants could not get stamps when they had occasion for them, without taking long journeys, and spending perhaps Three or Four Pounds, that the Crown might get Sixpence.

Q. Are not the Colonies, from their circumstances, very able to pay the stamp duty?

A. In my opinion, there is not gold and silver enough in the Colonies to pay the stamp duty for one year.

Q. Don't you know that the money arising from the stamps was all to be laid out in America?

A. I know it is appropriated by the act to the American service; but it will be spent in the conquered Colonies, where the soldiers are, not in the Colonies that pay it.

Q. Is there not a ballance of trade due from the Colonies where the troops are posted, that will bring back the money to the old Colonies?

[14]

A. I think not. I believe very little would come back. I know of no trade likely to bring it back. I think it would come from the Colonies where it was spent directly to England; for I have always observed, that in every Colony the more plenty the means of remittance to England, the more goods are sent for, and the more trade with England carried on.

Q. What number of white inhabitants do you think there are in Pennsylvania?

A. I suppose there may be about 160,000.

Q. What number of them are Quakers?

A. Perhaps a third.

Q. What number of Germans?

A. Perhaps another third; but I cannot speak with certainty.

Q. Have any number of the Germans seen service, as soldiers, in Europe?

A. Yes, — many of them, both in Europe and America.

Q. Are they as much dissatisfied with the stamp duty as the English?

A. Yes, and more; and with reason, as their stamps are, in many cases, to be double.

Q. How many white men do you suppose there are in North-America?

A. About 300,000, from sixteen to sixty years of age.

Q. What may be the amount of one year's imports into Pennsylvania from Britain?

A. I have been informed that our merchants compute the imports from Britain to be above 500,000 Pounds.

Q. What may be the amount of the produce of your province exported to Britain?

A. It must be small, as we produce little that is wanted in Britain. I suppose it cannot exceed 40,000 Pounds.

Q. How then do you pay the ballance?

A. The Ballance is paid by our produce carried to the West-Indies, and sold in our own islands, or to the French, Spaniards, Danes and Dutch; by the same carried to other colonies in North-America, as to New-England, Nova-Scotia, Newfoundland, Carolina and Georgia; by the same carried to different parts of Europe, as Spain, Portugal and Italy. In all which places we receive either money, bills of exchange, or commodities that suit for remittance to Britain; which, together with all the profits on the industry of our merchants and mariners, arising in those circuitous voyages, and the freights made by their ships, center finally in Britain, to discharge the ballance, and pay for British manufactures continually used in the province, or sold to foreigners by our traders.

Q. Have you heard of any difficulties lately laid on the Spanish trade?

A. Yes, I have heard that it has been greatly obstructed by some new regulations, and by the English men of war and cutters stationed all along the coast in America.

Q. Do you think it right that America should be protected by this country, and pay no part of the expence?

A. That is not the case. The Colonies raised, cloathed and paid, during the last war, near 25000 men, and spent many millions.

Q. Were you not reimbursed by parliament?

A. We were only reimbursed what, in your opinion, we had advanced beyond our proportion, or beyond what might reasonably be expected from us; and it was a very small part of what we spent. Pennsylvania, in particular, disbursed about 500,000 Pounds, and the reimbursements, in the whole, did not exceed 60,000 Pounds.

Q. You have said that you pay heavy taxes in Pennsylvania; what do they amount to in the Pound?

A. The tax on all estates, real and personal, is Eighteen Pence in the Pound, fully rated; and the tax on the profits of trades and professions, with other taxes, do, I suppose, make full Half a Crown in the Pound.

Q. Do you know any thing of the rate of exchange in Pennsylvania, and whether it is fallen lately?

A. It is commonly from 170 to 175. I have heard that it has fallen lately from 175 to 162 and a half, owing, I suppose, to their lessening their orders for goods; and when their debts to this country are paid, I think the exchange will probably be at par.

Q. Do not you think the people of America would submit to pay the stamp duty, if it was moderated?

A. No, never, unless compelled by force of arms.

Q. Are not the taxes in Pennsylvania laid on unequally, in order to burthen the English trade, particularly the tax on professions and business?

A. It is not more burthensome in proportion than the tax on lands. It is intended, and supposed to take an equal proportion of profits.

Q. How is the assembly composed? Of what kinds of people are the members, landholders or traders?

A. It is composed of landholders, merchants and artificers.

Q. Are not the majority landholders?

A. I believe they are.

Q. Do not they, as much as possible, shift the tax off from the land, to ease that, and lay the burthen heavier on trade?

A. I have never understood it so. I never heard such a thing suggested. And indeed an attempt of that kind could answer no purpose. The merchant or trader is always skilled in figures, and ready with his pen and ink. If unequal burthens are laid on his trade, he puts an additional price on his goods; and the consumers, who are chiefly landholders, finally pay the greatest part, if not the whole.

Q. What was the temper of America towards Great-Britain before the year 1763?

A. The best in the world. They submitted willingly to the government of the Crown, and paid, in all their courts, obedience to acts of parliament. Numerous as the people are in the several old provinces, they cost you nothing in forts, citadels, garrisons or armies, to keep them in subjection. They were governed by this country at the expence only of a little pen, ink and paper. They were led by a thread. They had not only a respect, but an affection, for Great-Britain, for its laws, its customs and manners, and even a fondness for its fashions, that greatly increased the commerce. Natives of Britain were always treated with particular regard; to be an Old England-man was, of itself, a character of some respect, and gave a kind of rank among us.

Q. And what is their temper now?

A. O, very much altered.

Q. Did you ever hear the authority of parliament to make laws for America questioned till lately?

A. The authority of parliament was allowed to be valid in all laws, except such as should lay internal taxes. It was never disputed in laying duties to regulate commerce.

Q. In what proportion hath population increased in America?

A. I think the inhabitants of all the provinces together, taken at a medium, double in about 25 years. But their demand for British manufactures increases much faster, as the consumption is not merely in proportion to their numbers, but grows with the growing abilities of the same numbers to pay for them. In 1723, the whole importation from Britain to Pennsylvania, was but about 15,000 Pounds Sterling; it is now near Half a Million.

[17]

Q. In what light did the people of America use to consider the parliament of Great-Britain?

A. They considered the parliament as the great bulwark and security of their liberties and privileges, and always spoke of it with the utmost respect and veneration. Arbitrary ministers, they thought, might possibly, at times, attempt to oppress them; but they relied on it, that the parliament, on application, would always give redress. They remembered, with gratitude, a strong instance of this, when a bill was brought into parliament, with a clause to make royal instructions laws in the Colonies, which the house of commons would not pass, and it was thrown out.

Q. And have they not still the same respect for parliament?

A. No; it is greatly lessened.

Q. To what causes is that owing?

A. To a concurrence of causes; the restraints lately laid on their trade, by which the bringing of foreign gold and silver into the Colonies was prevented; the prohibition of making paper money among themselves; and then demanding a new and heavy tax by stamps; taking away, at the same time, trials by juries, and refusing to receive and hear their humble petitions.

Q. Don't you think they would submit to the stamp-act, if it was modified, the obnoxious parts taken out, and the duty reduced to some particulars, of small moment?

A. No; they will never submit to it.

Q. What do you think is the reason that the people of America increase faster than in England?

A. Because they marry younger, and more generally.

Q. Why so?

A. Because any young couple that are industrious, may easily obtain land of their own, on which they can raise a family.

Q. Are not the lower rank of people more at their ease in America than in England?

A. They may be so, if they are sober and diligent, as they are better paid for their labour.

Q. What is your opinion of a future tax, imposed on the same principle with that of the stamp act; how would the Americans receive it?

A. Just as they do this. They would not pay it.

Q. Have you not heard of the resolutions of this house, and of the house of lords, asserting the right of parliament relating to America, including a power to tax the people there?

A. Yes, I have heard of such resolutions.

Q. What will be the opinion of the Americans on those resolutions?

A. They will think them unconstitutional, and unjust.

Q. Was it an opinion in America before 1763, that the parliament had no right to lay taxes and duties there?

A. I never heard any objection to the right of laying duties to regulate commerce; but a right to lay internal taxes was never supposed to be in parliament, as we are not represented there.

Q. On what do you found your opinion, that the people in America made any such distinction?

A. I know that whenever the subject has occurred in conversation where I have been present, it has appeared to be the opinion of every one, that we could not be taxed in a parliament where we were not represented. But the payment of duties laid by act of parliament, as regulations of commerce, was never disputed.

Q. But can you name any act of assembly, or public act of any of your governments, that made such distinction?

A. I do not know that there was any; I think there was never an occasion to make any such act, till now that you have attempted to tax us; that has occasioned resolutions of assembly, declaring the distinction, in which I think every assembly on the continent, and every member in every assembly, have been unanimous.

Q. What then could occasion conversations on that subject before that time?

A. There was in 1754 a proposition made (I think it came from hence) that in case of a war, which was then apprehended, the governors of the Colonies should meet, and order the levying of troops, building of forts, and taking every other necessary measure for the general defence; and should draw on the treasury here for the sums expended, which were afterwards to be raised in the Colonies by a general tax, to be laid on them by act of parliament. This occasioned a good deal of conversation on the subject, and the general opinion was, that the parliament neither would nor could lay any tax on us, till we were duly represented in parliament, because it was not just, nor agreeable to the nature of an English constitution.

Q. Don't you know there was a time in New-York, when it was under consideration to make an application to parliament to lay taxes on that Colony, upon a deficiency arising from the assembly's refusing or neglecting to raise the necessary supplies for the support of the civil government?

A. I never heard of it.

Q. There was such an application under consideration in New-York; and do you apprehend they could suppose the right of parliament to lay a tax in America was only local, and confined to the case of a deficiency in a particular Colony, by a refusal of its assembly to raise the necessary supplies?

A. They could not suppose such a case, as that the assembly would not raise the necessary supplies to support its own government. An assembly that would refuse it must want common sense, which cannot be supposed. I think there was never any such case at New-York, and that it must be a misrepresentation, or the fact must be misunderstood. I know there have been some attempts, by ministerial instructions from hence, to oblige the assemblies to settle permanent salaries on governors, which they wisely refused to do; but I believe no assembly of New-York, or any other Colony, ever refused duly to support government by proper allowances, from time to time, to public officers.

Q. But in case a governor, acting by instruction, should call on an assembly to raise the necessary supplies, and the assembly should refuse to do it, do you not think it would then be for the good of the people of the colony, as well as necessary to government, that the parliament should tax them?

A. I do not think it would be necessary. If an assembly could possibly be so absurd as to refuse raising the supplies requisite for the maintenance of government among them, they could not long remain in such a situation; the disorders and confusion occasioned by it must soon bring them to reason.

Q. If it should not, ought not the right to be in Great-Britain of applying a remedy?

A. A right only to be used in such a case, I should have no objection to, supposing it to be used merely for the good of the people of the Colony.

Q. But who is to judge of that, Britain or the Colony?

A. Those that feel can best judge.

Q. You say the Colonies have always submitted to external taxes, and object to the right of parliament only in laying internal taxes; now can you shew that there is any kind of difference between the two taxes to the Colony on which they may be laid?

A. I think the difference is very great. An external tax is a duty laid on commodities imported; that duty is added to the first cost, and other charges on the commodity, and when it is offered to sale, makes a part of the price. If the people do not like it at that price, they refuse it; they are not obliged to pay it. But an internal tax is forced from the people without their consent, if not laid by their own representatives. The stamp-act says, we shall have no commerce, make no exchange of property with each other, neither purchase nor grant, nor recover debts; we shall neither marry, nor make our wills, unless we pay such and such sums, and thus it is intended to *extort* our money from us, or ruin us by the consequences of refusing to pay it.

Q. But supposing the external tax or duty to be laid on the necessaries of life imported into your Colony, will not that be the same thing in its effects as an internal tax?

A. I do not know a single article imported into the Northern Colonies, but what they can either do without, or make themselves.

Q. Don't you think cloth from England absolutely necessary to them?

A. No, by no means absolutely necessary; with industry and good management, they may very well supply themselves with all they want.

Q. Will it not take a long time to establish that manufacture among them? and must they not in the mean while suffer greatly?

A. I think not. They have made a surprising progress already. And I am of opinion, that before their old clothes are worn out, they will have new ones of their own making.

Q. Can they possibly find wool enough in North-America?

A. They have taken steps to increase the wool. They entered into general combinations to eat no more lamb, and very few lambs were killed last year. This course persisted in, will soon make a prodigious difference in the quantity of wool. And the establishing of great manufactories, like those in the clothing towns here, is not necessary, as it is where the business is to be carried on for the purposes of trade. The people will all spin, and work for themselves, in their own houses.

Q. Can there be wool and manufacture enough in one or two years?

A. In three years, I think, there may.

Q. Does not the severity of the winter, in the Northern Colonies, occasion the wool to be of bad quality?

A. No; the wool is very fine and good.

Q. In the more Southern Colonies, as in Virginia; don't you know that the wool is coarse, and only a kind of hair?

A. I don't know it. I never heard it. Yet I have been sometimes in Virginia. I cannot say I ever took particular notice of the wool there, but I believe it is good, though I cannot speak positively of it; but Virginia, and the Colonies south of it, have less occasion for wool; their winters are short, and not very severe, and they can very well clothe themselves with linen and cotton of their own raising for the rest of the year.

Q. Are not the people, in the more Northern Colonies, obliged to fodder their sheep all the winter?

A. In some of the most Northern Colonies they may be obliged to do it some part of the winter.

Q. Considering the resolutions of parliament, as to the right, do you think, if the stamp-act is repealed, that the North Americans will be satisfied?

A. I believe they will.

Q. Why do you think so?

A. I think the resolutions of right will give them very little concern, if they are never attempted to be carried into practice. The Colonies will probably consider themselves in the same situation, in that respect, with Ireland; they know you claim the same right with regard to Ireland, but you never exercise it. And they may believe you never will exercise it in the Colonies, any more than in Ireland, unless on some very extraordinary occasion.

Q. But who are to be the judges of that extraordinary occasion? Is it not the parliament?

A. Though the parliament may judge of the occasion, the people will think it can never exercise such right, till representatives from the Colonies are admitted into parliament, and that whenever the occasion arises, representatives will be ordered.

Q. Did you never hear that Maryland, during the last war, had refused to furnish a quota towards the common defence?

A. Maryland has been much misrepresented in that matter. Maryland, to my knowledge, never refused to contribute, or grant aids to the Crown. The assemblies every year, during the war, voted considerable sums, and formed bills to raise them. The bills were, according to the constitution of that province, sent up to the council, or upper house, for concurrence, that they might be presented to the governor, in order to be enacted into laws. Unhappy disputes between the two houses arising, from the defects of that constitution principally, rendered all the bills but one or two abortive. The proprietary's council rejected them. It is true Maryland did not contribute its proportion, but it was, in my opinion, the fault of the government, not of the people.

Q. Was it not talked of in the other provinces as a proper measure to apply to parliament to compel them?

A. I have heard such discourse; but as it was well known, that the people were not to blame, no such application was ever made, nor any step taken towards it.

Q. Was it not proposed at a public meeting?

A. Not that I know of.

Q. Do you remember the abolishing of the paper currency in New England, by act of assembly?

A. I do remember its being abolished, in the Massachusett's Bay.

Q. Was not Lieutenant Governor Hutchinson principally concerned in that transaction?

A. I have heard so.

Q. Was it not at that time a very unpopular law?

A. I believe it might, though I can say little about it, as I lived at a distance from that province.

Q. Was not the scarcity of gold and silver an argument used against abolishing the paper?

A. I suppose it was.

Q. What is the present opinion there of that law? Is it as unpopular as it was at first?

A. I think it is not.

Q. Have not instructions from hence been sometimes sent over to governors, highly oppressive and unpolitical?

A. Yes.

Q. Have not some governors dispensed with them for that reason?

A. Yes, I have heard so.

Q. Did the Americans ever dispute the controlling power of parliament to regulate the commerce?

A. No.

Q. Can any thing less than a military force carry the stamp-act into execution?

A. I do not see how a military force can be applied to that purpose.

Q. Why may it not?

A. Suppose a military force sent into America, they will find nobody in arms; what are they then to do? They cannot force a man to take stamps who chooses to do without them. They will not find a rebellion; they may indeed make one.

Q. If the act is not repealed, what do you think will be the consequences?

A. A total loss of the respect and affection the people of America bear to this country, and of all the commerce that depends on that respect and affection.

Q. How can the commerce be affected?

A. You will find, that if the act is not repealed, they will take very little of your manufactures in a short time.

Q. Is it in their power to do without them?

A. I think they may very well do without them.

Q. Is it their interest not to take them?

A. The goods they take from Britain are either necessaries, mere conveniences, or superfluities. The first, as cloth, &c. with a little industry they can make at home; the second they can do without, till they are able to provide them among themselves; and the last, which are much the greatest part, they will strike off immediately. They are mere articles of fashion, purchased and consumed, because the fashion in a respected country, but will now be detested and rejected. The people have already struck off, by general agreement, the use of all goods fashionable in mournings, and many thousand pounds worth are sent back as unsaleable.

Q. Is it their interest to make cloth at home?

A. I think they may at present get it cheaper from Britain, I mean of the same fineness and neatness of workmanship; but when one considers other circumstances, the restraints on their trade, and the difficulty of making remittances, it is their interest to make every thing.

Q. Suppose an act of internal regulations, connected with a tax, how would they receive it?

A. I think it would be objected to.

Q. Then no regulation with a tax would be submitted to?

A. Their opinion is, that when aids to the Crown are wanted, they are to be asked of the several assemblies, according to the old established usage, who will, as they always have done, grant them freely. And that their money ought not to be given away without their consent, by persons at a distance, unacquainted with their circumstances and abilities. The granting aids to the Crown, is the only means they have of recommending themselves to their sovereign, and they think it extremely hard and unjust, that a body of men, in which they have no representatives, should make a merit to itself of giving and granting what is not its own, but theirs, and deprive them of a right they esteem of the utmost value and importance, as it is the security of all their other rights.

Q. But is not the post-office, which they have long received, a tax as well as a regulation?

A. No; the money paid for the postage of a letter is not of the nature of a tax; it is merely a quantum meruit for a service done; no person is compellable to pay the money, if he does not chuse to receive the service. A man may still, as before the act, send his letter by a servant, a special messenger, or a friend, if he thinks it cheaper and safer.

Q. But do they not consider the regulations of the post-office, by the act of last year, as a tax?

A. By the regulations of last year the rate of postage was generally abated near thirty per cent. through all America; they certainly cannot consider such abatement as a tax.

Q. If an excise was laid by parliament, which they might likewise avoid paying, by not consuming the articles excised, would they then not object to it?

A. They would certainly object to it, as an excise is unconnected with any service done, and is merely an aid which they think ought to be asked of them, and granted by them, if they are to pay it, and can be granted for them by no others whatsoever, whom they have not impowered for the purpose.

Q. You say they do not object to the right of parliament in laying duties on goods to be paid on their importation; now, is there any kind of difference between a duty on the importation of goods, and an excise on their consumption?

A. Yes; a very material one; an excise, for the reasons I have just mentioned, they think you can have no right to lay within their country. But the sea is yours; you maintain, by your fleets, the safety of navigation in it; and keep it clear of pirates; you may have therefore a natural and equitable right to some toll or duty on merchandizes carried through that part of your dominions, towards defraying the expence you are at in ships to maintain the safety of that carriage.

Q. Does this reasoning hold in the case of a duty laid on the produce of their lands exported? and would they not then object to such a duty?

A. If it tended to make the produce so much dearer abroad as to lessen the demand for it, to be sure they would object to such a duty; not to your right of laying it, but they would complain of it as a burthen, and petition you to lighten it.

Q. Is not the duty paid on the tobacco exported a duty of that kind?

A. That, I think, is only on tobacco carried coastwise from one Colony to another, and appropriated as a fund for supporting the college at Williamsburgh, in Virginia.

Q. Have not the assemblies in the West-Indies the same natural rights with those in North America?

A. Undoubtedly.

Q. And is there not a tax laid there on their sugars exported?

A. I am not much acquainted with the West-Indies, but the duty of four and a half per cent. on sugars exported, was, I believe, granted by their own assemblies.

Q. How much is the poll-tax in your province laid on unmarried men?

A. It is, I think, Fifteen Shillings, to be paid by every single freeman, upwards of twenty-one years old.

Q. What is the annual amount of all the taxes in Pennsylvania?

A. I suppose about 20,000 Pounds sterling.

Q. Supposing the stamp-act continued, and enforced, do you imagine that ill humour will induce the Americans to give as much for worse manufactures of their own, and use them, preferably to better of ours?

A. Yes, I think so. People will pay as freely to gratify one passion as another, their resentment as their pride.

[26]

Q. Would the people at Boston discontinue their trade?

A. The merchants are a very small number, compared with the body of the people, and must discontinue their trade, if nobody will buy their goods.

Q. What are the body of the people in the Colonies?

A. They are farmers, husbandmen or planters.

Q. Would they suffer the produce of their lands to rot?

A. No; but they would not raise so much. They would manufacture more, and plough less.

Q. Would they live without the administration of justice in civil matters, and suffer all the inconveniences of such a situation for any considerable time, rather than to take the stamps, supposing the stamps were protected by a sufficient force, where every one might have them?

A. I think the supposition impracticable, that the stamps should be so protected as that every one might have them. The act requires sub-distributors to be appointed in every county town, district and village, and they would be necessary. But the principal distributors, who were to have had a considerable profit on the whole, have not thought it worth while to continue in the office, and I think it impossible to find sub-distributors fit to be trusted, who, for the trifling profit that must come to their share, would incur the odium, and run the hazard that would attend it; and if they could be found, I think it impracticable to protect the stamps in so many distant and remote places.

Q. But in places where they could be protected, would not the people use them rather than remain in such a situation, unable to obtain any right, or recover, by law, any debt?

A. It is hard to say what they would do. I can only judge what other people will think, and how they will act, by what I feel within myself. I have a great many debts due to me in America, and I had rather they should remain unrecoverable by any law, than submit to the stamp-act. They will be debts of honour. It is my opinion the people will either continue in that situation, or find some way to extricate themselves, perhaps by generally agreeing to proceed in the courts without stamps.

Q. What do you think a sufficient military force to protect the distribution of the stamps in every part of America?

A. A very great force; I can't say what, if the disposition of America is for a general resistance.

Q. What is the number of men in America able to bear arms, or of disciplined militia?

A. There are, I suppose, at least—

[Question objected to. He withdrew. Called in again.]

Q. Is the American stamp-act an equal tax on that country?

A. I think not.

Q. Why so?

A. The greatest part of the money must arise from law suits for the recovery of debts, and be paid by the lower sort of people, who were too poor easily to pay their debts. It is therefore a heavy tax on the poor, and a tax upon them for being poor.

Q. But will not this increase of expence be a means of lessening the number of law suits?

A. I think not; for as the costs all fall upon the debtor, and are to be paid by him, they would be no discouragement to the creditor to bring his action.

Q. Would it not have the effect of excessive usury?

A. Yes, as an oppression of the debtor.

Q. How many ships are there laden annually in North-America with flax-seed for Ireland?

A. I cannot speak to the number of ships, but I know that in 1752, 10,000 hogsheads of flax-seed, each containing 7 bushels, were exported from Philadelphia to Ireland. I suppose the quantity is greatly increased since that time; and it is understood that the exportation from New York is equal to that from Philadelphia.

Q. What becomes of the flax that grows with that flax-seed?

A. They manufacture some into coarse, and some into a middling kind of linen.

Q. Are there any slitting mills in America?

A. I think there are, but I believe only one at present employed. I suppose they will all be set to work, if the interruption of the trade continues.

Q. Are there any fulling mills there?

A. A great many.

Q. Did you never hear that a great quantity of stockings were contracted for for the army during the war, and manufactured in Philadelphia?

A. I have heard so.

Q. If the stamp act should be repealed, would not the Americans think they could oblige the parliament to repeal every external tax law now in force?

A. It is hard to answer questions of what people at such a distance will think.

Q. But what do you imagine they will think were the motives of repealing the act?

A. I suppose they will think that it was repealed from a conviction of its inexpediency; and they will rely upon it, that while the same inexpediency subsists, you will never attempt to make such another.

Q. What do you mean by its inexpediency?

A. I mean its inexpediency on several accounts; the poverty and inability of those who were to pay the tax; the general discontent it has occasioned; and the impracticability of enforcing it.

Q. If the act should be repealed, and the legislature should shew its resentment to the opposers of the stamp-act, would the Colonies acquiesce in the authority of the legislature? What is your opinion they would do?

A. I don't doubt at all, that if the legislature repeal the stamp-act, the Colonies will acquiesce in the authority.

Q. But if the legislature should think fit to ascertain its right to lay taxes, by any act laying a small tax, contrary to their opinion, would they submit to pay the tax?

A. The proceedings of the people in America have been considered too much together. The proceedings of the assemblies have been very different from those of the mobs, and should be distinguished, as having no connection with each other. — The assemblies have only peaceably resolved what they take to be their rights; they have taken no measures for opposition by force; they have not built a fort, raised a man, or provided a grain of ammunition, in order to such opposition. — The ringleaders of riots they think ought to be punished; they would punish them themselves, if they could. Every sober sensible man would wish to see rioters punished; as otherwise peaceable people have no security of person or estate. But as to any internal tax, how small soever, laid by the legislature here on the people there, while they have no representatives in this legislature, I think it will never be submitted to. — They will oppose it to the last. They do not consider it as at all necessary for you to raise money on them by your taxes, because they are, and always have been, ready to raise money by taxes among themselves, and to grant large sums, equal to their abilities, upon requisition from the Crown. — They have not only granted equal to their abilities, but, during all the last war, they granted far beyond their abilities, and beyond their proportion with this country, you yourselves being judges, to the amount of many hundred thousand pounds, and this they did freely and readily, only on a sort of promise from the secretary of state, that it should be recommended to parliament to make them compensation. It was accordingly recommended to parliament, in the most honourable manner, for them. America has been greatly misrepresented and abused here, in papers, and pamphlets, and speeches, as ungrateful, and unreasonable, and unjust, in having put this nation to immense expence for their defence, and refusing to bear any part of that expence. The Colonies raised, paid and clothed, near 25000 men during the last war, a number equal to those sent from Britain, and far beyond their proportion; they went deeply into debt in doing this, and all their taxes and estates are mortgaged, for many years to come, for discharging that debt. Government here was at that time very sensible of this. The Colonies were recommended to parliament. Every year the King sent down to the house a written message to this purpose, That his Majesty, being highly sensible of the zeal and vigour with which his faithful subjects in North-America had exerted themselves, in defence of his Majesty's just rights and possessions, recommended it to the house to take the same into consideration, and enable him to give them a proper compensation. You will find those messages on your own journals every year of the war to the very last, and you did accordingly give 200,000 Pounds annually to the Crown, to be distributed in such compensation to the Colonies. This is the strongest of all proofs that the Colonies, far from being unwilling to bear a share of the burthen, did exceed their proportion; for if they had done less, or had only equalled their proportion, there would have been no room or reason for compensation. — Indeed the sums reimbursed them, were by no means adequate to the expence they incurred beyond their proportion; but they never murmured at that; they esteemed their Sovereign's approbation of their zeal and fidelity, and the approbation of this house, far beyond any other kind of compensation; therefore there was no occasion for this act, to force money from a willing people; they had not refused giving money for the purposes of the act; no requisition had been made; they were always willing and ready to do what could reasonably be expected from them, and in this light they wish to be considered.

Q. But suppose Great-Britain should be engaged in a war in Europe, would North-America contribute to the support of it?

A. I do think they would, as far as their circumstances would permit. They consider themselves as a part of the British empire, and as having one common interest with it; they may be looked on here as foreigners, but they do not consider themselves as such. They are zealous for the honour and prosperity of this nation, and, while they are well used, will always be ready to support it, as far as their little power goes. In 1739 they were called upon to assist in the expedition against Carthagena, and they sent 3000 men to join your army. It is true Carthagena is in America, but as remote from the Northern Colonies, as if it had been in Europe. They make no distinction of wars, as to their duty of assisting in them. I know the last war is commonly spoke of here as entered into for the defence, or for the sake of the people of America. I think it is quite misunderstood. It began about the limits between Canada and Nova-Scotia, about territories to which the Crown indeed laid claim, but were not claimed by any British Colony; none of the lands had been granted to any Colonist; we had therefore no particular concern or interest in that dispute. As to the Ohio, the contest there began about your right of trading in the Indian country, a right you had by the treaty of Utrecht, which the French infringed; they seized the traders and their goods, which were your manufactures; they took a fort which a company of your merchants, and their factors and correspondents, had erected there, to secure that trade. Braddock was sent with an army to re-take that fort (which was looked on here as another incroachment on the King's territory) and to protect your trade. It was not till after his defeat that the Colonies were attacked. They were before in perfect peace with both French and Indians; the troops were not therefore sent for their defence. The trade with the Indians, though carried on in America, is not an American interest. The people of America are chiefly farmers and planters; scarce any thing that they raise or produce is an article of commerce with the Indians. The Indian trade is a British interest; it is carried on with British manufactures, for the profit of British merchants and manufacturers; therefore the war, as it commenced for the defence of territories of the Crown, the property of no American, and for the defence of a trade purely British, was really a British war — and yet the people of America made no scruple of contributing their utmost towards carrying it on, and bringing it to a happy conclusion.

Q. Do you think then that the taking possession of the King's territorial rights, and strengthening the frontiers, is not an American interest?

A. Not particularly, but conjointly a British and an American interest.

Q. You will not deny that the preceding war, the war with Spain, was entered into for the sake of America; was it not occasioned by captures made in the American seas?

A. Yes; captures of ships carrying on the British trade there, with British manufactures.

Q. Was not the late war with the Indians, since the peace with France, a war for America only?

A. Yes; it was more particularly for America than the former, but it was rather a consequence or remains of the former war, the Indians not having been thoroughly pacified, and the Americans bore by much the greatest share of the expence. It was put an end to by the army under General Bouquet; there were not above 300 regulars in that army, and above 1000 Pennsylvanians.

Q. Is it not necessary to send troops to America, to defend the Americans against the Indians?

A. No, by no means; it never was necessary. They defended themselves when they were but an handful, and the Indians much more numerous. They continually gained ground, and have driven the Indians over the mountains, without any troops sent to their assistance from this country. And can it be thought necessary now to send troops for their defence from those diminished Indian tribes, when the Colonies are become so populous, and so strong? There is not the least occasion for it; they are very able to defend themselves.

Q. Do you say there were no more than 300 regular troops employed in the late Indian war?

A. Not on the Ohio, or the frontiers of Pennsylvania, which was the chief part of the war that affected the Colonies. There were garrisons at Niagara, Fort Detroit, and those remote posts kept for the sake of your trade; I did not reckon them, but I believe that on the whole the number of

[32]

Americans, or provincial troops, employed in the war, was greater than that of the regulars. I am not certain, but I think so.

Q. Do you think the assemblies have a right to levy money on the subject there, to grant to the Crown?

A. I certainly think so; they have always done it.

Q. Are they acquainted with the declaration of rights? And do they know that, by that statute, money is not to be raised on the subject but by consent of parliament?

A. They are very well acquainted with it.

Q. How then can they think they have a right to levy money for the Crown, or for any other than local purposes?

A. They understand that clause to relate to subjects only within the realm; that no money can be levied on them for the Crown, but by consent of parliament. The Colonies are not supposed to be within the realm; they have assemblies of their own, which are their parliaments, and they are in that respect, in the same situation with Ireland. When money is to be raised for the Crown upon the subject in Ireland, or in the Colonies, the consent is given in the parliament of Ireland, or in the assemblies of the Colonies. They think the parliament of Great-Britain cannot properly give that consent till it has representatives from America; for the petition of right expressly says, it is to be by common consent in parliament, and the people of America have no representatives in parliament, to make a part of that common consent.

Q. If the stamp-act should be repealed, and an act should pass, ordering the assemblies of the Colonies to indemnify the sufferers by the riots, would they obey it?

A. That is a question I cannot answer.

Q. Suppose the King should require the Colonies to grant a revenue, and the parliament should be against their doing it, do they think they can grant a revenue to the King, without the consent of the parliament of G. Britain?

A. That is a deep question. — As to my own opinion, I should think myself at liberty to do it, and should do it, if I liked the occasion.

Q. When money has been raised in the Colonies, upon requisitions, has it not been granted to the King?

A. Yes, always; but the requisitions have generally been for some service expressed, as to raise, clothe and pay troops, and not for money only.

Q. If the act should pass, requiring the American assemblies to make compensation to the sufferers, and they should disobey it, and then the parliament should, by another act, lay an internal tax, would they then obey it?

A. The people will pay no internal tax; and I think an act to oblige the assemblies to make compensation is unnecessary, for I am of opinion, that as soon as the present heats are abated, they will take the matter into consideration, and, if it is right to be done, they will do it of themselves.

Q. Do not letters often come into the post-offices in America, directed to some inland town where no post goes?

A. Yes.

Q. Can any private person take up those letters, and carry them as directed?

A. Yes; any friend of the person may do it, paying the postage that has occurred.

Q. But must he not pay an additional postage for the distance to such inland town?

A. No.

Q. Can the post-master answer delivering the letter, without being paid such additional postage?

A. Certainly he can demand nothing, where he does no service.

Q. Suppose a person, being far from home, finds a letter in a post-office directed to him, and he lives in a place to which the post generally goes, and the letter is directed to that place, will the post-master deliver him the letter, without his paying the postage receivable at the place to which the letter is directed?

A. Yes; the office cannot demand postage for a letter that it does not carry, or farther than it does carry it.

Q. Are not ferrymen in America obliged, by act of parliament, to carry over the posts without pay?

A. Yes.

Q. Is not this a tax on the ferrymen?

A. They do not consider it as such, as they have an advantage from persons travelling with the post.

Q. If the stamp-act should be repealed, and the Crown should make a requisition to the Colonies for a sum of money, would they grant it?

A. I believe they would.

[34]

Q. Why do you think so?

A. I can speak for the Colony I live in; I had it in instruction from the assembly to assure the ministry, that as they always had done, so they should always think it their duty to grant such aids to the Crown as were suitable to their circumstances and abilities, whenever called upon for the purpose, in the usual constitutional manner; and I had the honour of communicating this instruction to that honourable gentleman then minister.

Q. Would they do this for a British concern; as suppose a war in some part of Europe, that did not affect them?

A. Yes, for any thing that concerned the general interest. They consider themselves as a part of the whole.

Q. What is the usual constitutional manner of calling on the Colonies for aids?

A. A letter from the secretary of state.

Q. Is this all you mean, a letter from the secretary of state?

A. I mean the usual way of requisition, in a circular letter from the secretary of state, by his Majesty's command, reciting the occasion, and recommending it to the Colonies to grant such aids as became their loyalty, and were suitable to their abilities.

Q. Did the secretary of state ever write for money for the Crown?

A. The requisitions have been to raise, clothe and pay men, which cannot be done without money.

Q. Would they grant money alone, if called on?

A. In my opinion they would, money as well as men, when they have money, or can make it.

Q. If the parliament should repeal the stamp-act, will the assembly of Pennsylvania rescind their resolutions?

A. I think not.

Q. Before there was any thought of the stamp-act, did they wish for a representation in parliament?

A. No.

Q. Don't you know that there is, in the Pennsylvania charter, an express reservation of the right of parliament to lay taxes there?

A. I know there is a clause in the charter, by which the King grants that he will levy no taxes on the inhabitants, unless it be with the consent of the assembly, or by act of parliament.

Q. How then could the assembly of Pennsylvania assert, that laying a tax on them by the stamp-act was an infringement of their rights?

A. They understand it thus; by the same charter, and otherwise, they are intitled to all the privileges and liberties of Englishmen; they find in the great charters, and the petition and declaration of rights, that one of the privileges of English subjects is, that they are not to be taxed but by their common consent; they have therefore relied upon it, from the first settlement of the province, that the parliament never would, nor could, by colour of that clause in the charter, assume a right of taxing them, till it had qualified itself to exercise such right, by admitting representatives from the people to be taxed, who ought to make a part of that common consent.

Q. Are there any words in the charter that justify that construction?

A. The common rights of Englishmen, as declared by Magna Charta, and the petition of right, all justify it.

Q. Does the distinction between internal and external taxes exist in the words of the charter?

A. No, I believe not.

Q. Then may they not, by the same interpretation, object to the parliament's right of external taxation?

A. They never have hitherto. Many arguments have been lately used here to shew them that there is no difference, and that if you have no right to tax them internally, you have none to tax them externally, or make any other law to bind them. At present they do not reason so, but in time they may possibly be convinced by these arguments.

Q. Do not the resolutions of the Pennsylvania assembly say all taxes?

A. If they do, they mean only internal taxes; the same words have not always the same meaning here and in the Colonies. By taxes they mean internal taxes; by duties they mean customs; these are their ideas of the language.

Q. Have you not seen the resolutions of the Massachusett's Bay assembly?

A. I have.

Q. Do they not say, that neither external nor internal taxes can be laid on them by parliament?

A. I don't know that they do; I believe not.

Q. If the same Colony should say neither tax nor imposition could be laid, does not that province hold the power of parliament can hold neither?

[36]

A. I suppose that by the word imposition, they do not intend to express duties to be laid on goods imported, as regulations of commerce.

Q. What can the Colonies mean then by imposition as distinct from taxes?

A. They may mean many things, as impressing of men, or of carriages, quartering troops on private houses, and the like; there may be great impositions, that are not properly taxes.

Q. Is not the post-office rate an internal tax laid by act of parliament?

A. I have answered that.

Q. Are all parts of the Colonies equally able to pay taxes?

A. No, certainly; the frontier parts, which have been ravaged by the enemy, are greatly disabled by that means, and therefore, in such cases, are usually favoured in our tax-laws.

Q. Can we, at this distance, be competent judges of what favours are necessary?

A. The parliament have supposed it, by claiming a right to make tax laws for America; I think it impossible.

Q. Would the repeal of the stamp-act be any discouragement of your manufactures? Will the people that have begun to manufacture decline it?

A. Yes, I think they will; especially if, at the same time, the trade is opened again, so that remittances can be easily made. I have known several instances that make it probable. In the war before last, tobacco being low, and making little remittance, the people of Virginia went generally into family manufacturers. Afterwards, when tobacco bore a better price, they returned to the use of British manufactures. So fulling mills were very much disused in the last war in Pennsylvania, because bills were then plenty, and remittances could easily be made to Britain for English cloth and other goods.

Q. If the stamp-act should be repealed, would it induce the assemblies of America to acknowledge the rights of parliament to tax them, and would they erase their resolutions?

A. No, never.

Q. Is there no means of obliging them to erase those resolutions?

A. None that I know of; they will never do it unless compelled by force of arms.

Q. Is there a power on earth that can force them to erase them?

A. No power, how great soever, can force men to change their opinions.

Q. Do they consider the post-office as a tax, or as a regulation?

A. Not as a tax, but as a regulation and conveniency; every assembly encouraged it, and supported it in its infancy, by grants of money, which they would not otherwise have done; and the people have always paid the postage.

Q. When did you receive the instructions you mentioned?

A. I brought them with me, when I came to England, about 15 months since.

Q. When did you communicate that instruction to the minister?

A. Soon after my arrival, while the stamping of America was under consideration, and before the bill was brought in.

Q. Would it be most for the interest of Great-Britain, to employ the hands of Virginia in tobacco, or in manufactures?

A. In tobacco to be sure.

Q. What used to be the pride of the Americans?

A. To indulge in the fashions and manufactures of Great-Britain.

Q. What is now their pride?

A. To wear their old cloaths over again, till they can make new ones.

Withdrew.

The Examination of Doctor Benjamin Franklin, Relative to the Repeal of the American Stamp Act, In MDCCLXVI (London: J. Almon, 1767).

[Science, Religion, and Politics in London, 1769, 1795, 1802]

JOSEPH PRIESTLEY

Joseph Priestley (1733–1804), a prolific writer, brilliant scientist, and founder of the Unitarian Church, was one of Benjamin Franklin's best friends in England. The two shared a similar educational philosophy. Both recognized the importance of books and reading. In terms of religion, both refused to accept the dogma of the past and sought new ways of looking at fundamental belief, though Priestley did find Franklin's skepticism unsettling. Both shared a scientific curiosity that led to many new discoveries. And both men enjoyed debate, seeing the clash of ideas as the best way to reach the truth. Priestley first developed his interest in scientific research upon meeting Franklin and other men of science in London during the winter of 1765–1766. Franklin's electrical research fascinated him, and the two spoke about the subject at great length. Priestley decided to write the history of electricity but his new scientific friends insisted he perform experiments himself before writing history, which he did. Franklin related the story of his kite experiment, which Priestley included in his *History of Electricity* (1767), which provides virtually all that is known about Franklin's experiment. Priestley himself contributed many important, original experiments to the history of science. He isolated and identified seven different gases, including oxygen. In terms of politics, Priestley sympathized with the Americans during the Revolutionary War, and he supported the French Revolution, as well. In 1791, rioters burned his home, partly because of his support for the French Revolution but also because of his outspoken religious views, which challenged the hegemony of the Anglican Church and, indeed, challenged the whole notion of the Holy Trinity. Ostracized in England, he emigrated to the United States in 1794, settling in Northumberland, Pennsylvania.

From *The History and Present State of Electricity* (1769)

To demonstrate, in the completest manner possible, the sameness of the electric fluid with the matter of lightning, Dr. Franklin, astonishing as it must have appeared, contrived actually to bring lightning from the heavens, by means of an electrical kite, which he raised when a storm of thunder was perceived to be coming on. This kite had a pointed wire fixed upon it, by which it drew the lightning from the clouds. This lightning descended by the hempen string, and was received by a key tied to the extremity of it; that part of the string which was held in the hand being of silk, that the electric virtue might stop when it came to the key. He found that the string would conduct electricity even when nearly dry, but that when it was wet, it would conduct it quite freely; so that it would stream out plentifully from the key, at the approach of a person's finger.

At this key he charged phials, and from electric fire thus obtained, he kindled spirits, and performed all other electrical experiments which are usually exhibited by an excited globe or tube.

As every circumstance relating to so capital a discovery as this (the greatest, perhaps, that has been made in the whole compass of philosophy, since the time of Sir Isaac Newton) cannot but give pleasure to all my readers, I shall endeavour to gratify them with the communication of a few particulars which I have from the best authority.

The Doctor, after having published his method of verifying his hypothesis concerning the sameness of electricity with the matter of lightning, was waiting for the erection of a spire in Philadelphia to carry his views into execution; not imagining that a pointed rod, of a moderate height, could answer the purpose; when it occurred to him, that, by means of a common kite, he could have a readier and better access to the regions of thunder than by any spire whatever. Preparing, therefore, a large silk handkerchief, and two cross sticks, of a proper length, on which to extend it; he took the opportunity of the first approaching thunder storm to take a walk into a field, in which there was a shed convenient for his purpose. But dreading the ridicule which too commonly attends unsuccessful attempts in science, he communicated his intended experiment to no body but his son, who assisted him in raising the kite.

The kite being raised, a considerable time elapsed before there was any appearance of its being electrified. One very promising cloud had passed over it without any effect; when, at length, just as he was beginning to despair of his contrivance, he observed some loose threads of the hempen string to stand erect, and to avoid one another, just as if they had been suspended on a common conductor. Struck with this promising appearance, he immediately presented his knucle to the key, and (let the reader judge of the exquisite pleasure he must have felt at that moment) the discovery was complete. He perceived a very evident electric spark. Others succeeded, even before the string was wet, so as to put the matter past all dispute, and when the rain had wet the string, he collected electric fire very copiously. This happened in June 1752, a month after the electricians in France had verified the same theory, but before he had heard of anything that they had done.

Besides this kite, Dr. Franklin had afterwards an insulated iron rod to draw the lightning into his house, in order to make experiments whenever there should be a considerable quantity of it in the atmosphere; and that he might not lose any opportunity of that nature, he connected two bells with this apparatus, which gave him notice, by their ringing, whenever his rod was electrified.

The Doctor being able, in this manner, to draw the lightning into his house, and make experiments with it at his leisure; and being certain that it was in all respects of the same nature with electricity, he was desirous to know if it was of the positive or negative kind. The first time he succeeded in making an experiment for this purpose was the 12th of April 1753, when it appeared that the lightning was negative. Having found that the clouds electrified negatively in eight successive thunder gusts, he concluded they were always electrified negatively, and formed a theory to account for it. But he afterwards found he had concluded too soon. For, on the sixth of June following, he met with one cloud which was electrified positively; upon which he corrected his former theory, but did not seem able perfectly to satisfy himself with any other. The Doctor sometimes found the clouds would change from positive to negative electricity several times in the course of one thunder gust, and he once observed the air to be strongly electrified during a fall of snow, when there was no thunder at all.

But the grand practical use which Dr. Franklin made of his discovery of the sameness of electricity and lightning, was to secure buildings from being damaged by lightning, a thing of vast consequence in all parts of the world, but more especially in several parts of North America, where thunder storms are more frequent, and their effects, in that dry air, more dreadful, than they are ever known to be with us.

From *Memoirs of Dr. Joseph Priestley, to the Year 1795*

It is much to be lamented, that a man of Dr. Franklin's general good character, and great influence, should have been an unbeliever in Christianity, and also have done so much as he did to make others unbelievers. To me, however, he acknowledged that he had not given so much attention as he ought to have done to the evidences of Christianity, and desired me to recommend to him a few treatises on the subject, such as I thought most deserving of his notice, but not of great length, promising to read them, and give me his sentiments on them. Accordingly, I recommended to him [David] Hartley's evidences of Christianity in his *Observations on Man*, and what I had then written on the subject in my *Institutes of Natural and Revealed Religion*. But the American war breaking out soon after, I do not believe that he ever found himself sufficiently at leisure for the discussion.

"Letter from Dr. Priestley" (1802)

I have just read in the *Monthly Review*, vol. 36, p. 357, that the late Mr. [Thomas] Pennant said of Dr. Franklin, that, "living under the protection of our mild Government, he was secretly playing the incendiary, and too successfully inflaming the minds of our fellow-subjects in America, till that great explosion happened, which for ever disunited us from our once happy colonies."

As it is in my power, as far as my testimony will be regarded, to refute this charge, I think it due to our friendship to do it. It is probable that no person now living was better acquainted with Dr. Franklin and his sentiments on all subjects of importance, than myself, for several years before the American war. I think I knew him as well as one man can generally know another. At that time I spent the winters in London, in the family of the Marquis of Landsdown [i.e., William Petty, second earl of Shelburne and first marquess of Lansdowne] and few days passed without my seeing more or less of Dr. Franklin; and the last day that he passed in England, having given out that he should depart the day before, we spent together, without any interruption, from morning until night.

Now he was so far from wishing for a rupture with the colonies, that he did more than most men would have done to prevent it. His constant Advice to his countrymen, he always said, was "to bear every thing from England, however unjust" saying, that "it could not last long, as they would soon outgrow all their hardships." On this account Dr. [Richard] Price, who then corresponded with some of the principal persons in America, said, he began to be very unpopular there. He always said, "If there must be a war, it will be a war of ten years, and I shall not live to see the end of it." This I have heard him say many times.

It was at his request, enforced by that of Dr. [John] Fothergil, that I wrote an anonymous pamphlet, calculated to shew the injustice and impolicy of a war with the Colonies, previous to the meeting of a new Parliament. As I then lived at Leeds, he corrected the press himself; and, to a passage in which I lamented the attempt to establish arbitrary power in so large a part of the British Empire, he added the following clause, "To the imminent hazard of our most valuable commerce, and of that national strength, security, and felicity, which depend on union and on liberty."

The unity of the British Empire in all its parts was a favourite idea of his. He used to compare it to a beautiful China vase, which, if once broken, could never be put together again: and so great an admirer was he at that time of the British Constitution, that he said he saw no inconvenience from its being extended over a great part of the globe. With these sentiments he left England; but when, on his arrival in America, he found the war begun, and that there was no receding, no man entered more warmly into the interests of what he then considered as *his country*, in opposition to that of Great Britain. Three of his letters to me, one written immediately on his landing, and published in the collection of his *Miscellaneous Works*, p. 365, 552, and 555, will prove this.

By many persons Dr. Franklin is considered as having been a cold-hearted man, so callous to every feeling of humanity, that the prospect of all the horrors of a civil war could not affect him. This was far from being the case. A great part of the day above-mentioned that we spent together, he was looking over a number of American newspapers, directing me what to extract from them for the English ones; and, in reading them, he was frequently not able to proceed for the tears literally running down his cheeks. To strangers he was cold and reserved; but where he was intimate, no man indulged more to pleasantry and good-humour. By this he was the delight of a club, to which he alludes in one of the letters above referred to, called the Whig Club, that met at the London Coffee-house, of which Dr. Price,

Dr. [Andrew] Kippis, Mr. John Lee, and others of the same stamp, were members.

Hoping that this vindication of Dr. Franklin will give pleasure to many of your readers, I shall proceed to relate some particulars relating to his behaviour, when Lord Loughborough, then Mr. Wedderburn, pronounced his violent invective against him at the Privy Council, on his presenting the complaints of the Province of Massachusetts (I think it was) against their governor. Some of the particulars maybe thought amusing.

On the morning of the day on which the cause was to be heard, I met Mr. [Edmund] Burke in Parliament-street, accompanied by Dr. [John] Douglas, afterwards Bishop of Carlisle; and after introducing us to each other, as men of letters, he asked me whither I was going; I said, I could tell him whither I *wished* to go. He then asking me where that was, I said to the Privy Council, but that I was afraid I could not get admission. He then desired me to go along with him. Accordingly I did, but when we got to the anti-room, we found it quite filled with persons as desirous of getting admission as ourselves. Seeing this, I said, we should never get through the crowd. He said, "Give me your arm"; and, locking it fast in his, he soon made his way to the door of the Privy Council. I then said, Mr. Burke, you are an excellent leader; he replied, "I wish other persons thought so too."

After waiting a short time, the door of the Privy Council opened, and we entered the first; when Mr. Burke took his stand behind the first chair next to the President, and I behind that the next to his. When the business was opened, it was sufficiently evident, from the speech of Mr. [Alexander] Wedderburn, who was Counsel for the Governor, that the real object of the Court was to insult Dr. Franklin. All this time he stood in a corner of the room, not far from me, without the least apparent emotion.

Mr. [John] Dunning, who was the leading Counsel on the part of the Colony, was so hoarse that he could hardly make himself heard; and Mr. [John] Lee, who was the second, spoke but feebly in reply; so that Mr. Wedderburn had a complete triumph. — At the sallies of his sarcastic wit, all the members of the Council, the President himself (Lord Gower) not excepted, frequently laughed outright. No person belonging to the Council behaved with decent gravity, except Lord North, who, coming late, took his stand behind the chair opposite to me.

When the business was over, Dr. Franklin, in going out, took me by the hand in a manner that indicated some feeling. I soon followed him, and, going through the anti-room, saw Mr. Wedderburn there surrounded with a circle of his friends and admirers. Being known to him, he stepped forward as if to speak to me; but I turned aside, and made what haste I could out of the place.

The next morning I breakfasted with the Doctor, when he said, "He had never before been so sensible of the power of a good conscience; for that if he had not considered the thing for which he had been so much insulted, as one of the best actions of his life, and what he should certainly do again in the same circumstances, he could not have supported it."

He was accused of clandestinely procuring certain letters, containing complaints against the Governor, and sending them to America, with a view to excite their animosity against him, and thus to embroil the two countries. But he assured me, that he did not even know that such letters existed, till they were brought to him as agent for the Colony, in order to be sent to his constituents; and the cover of the letters, on which the direction had been written, being lost, he only guessed at the person to whom they were addressed by the contents.

That Dr. Franklin, notwithstanding he did not shew it at the time, was much impressed by the business, of the Privy Council, appeared from this circumstance: — When he attended there, he was dressed in a suit of Manchester velvet; and Silas Deane told me, that, when they met at Paris to sign the treaty between France and America, he purposely put on that suit.

Hoping that this communication will be of some service to the memory of Dr. Franklin, and gratify his friends, I am, Sir, your's &c.

J. Priestley
Northumberland, Nov. 10, 1802.

From *The History and Present State of Electricity, with Original Experiments* (London: for J. Dodsley, J. Johnson, J. Payne, and T. Cadell, 1769), pp. 169–175.

From *Memoirs of Dr. Joseph Priestley, to the Year 1795* (Northumberland, PA: John Binns, 1806), pp. 88–90.

"Letter from Dr. Priestley," *Monthly Magazine* 15 (1 February 1803): 1–2.

[Franklin in London, 1774–1775]

Josiah Quincy, Jr.

The son of Benjamin Franklin's friend Josiah Quincy (1710–1784), Josiah Quincy, Jr. (1744–1775) was a prominent young radical in Revolutionary Boston. He graduated with his Bachelor's degree from Harvard College in 1763. The Stamp Act crisis in 1765 radicalized Quincy. When he took his master's degree at Harvard the following year, he delivered the commencement address, choosing patriotism as his subject. He soon became a member of Samuel Adams's inner circle, writing many pseudonymous newspaper articles defending the American cause. Quincy furthered his education by reading law with the prominent Boston attorney Oxenbridge Thacher and eventually took over his practice. He solidified his reputation as a lawyer and a patriot by assisting John Adams in his defense of the British soldiers charged with murder in the 1770 Boston Massacre.

Quincy contracted tuberculosis in the early 1770s. On the advice of his physicians, he visited South Carolina, returning overland to Boston and thus giving himself an excellent perspective on colonial America as a whole. In May 1774, he published his most famous work, *Observations on the Act of Parliament Commonly Called the Boston Port-Bill; with Thoughts on Civil Society and Standing Armies*, a scathing indictment of British policy in colonial America made all the more powerful when Quincy signed his own name to it. This pamphlet was reprinted in Philadelphia, and Edward and Charles Dilly reprinted it in London. Moses Coit Tyler, who provided some brief comments on the work in *The Literary History of the American Revolution* (1897), greatly enjoyed its "hectic intensity of style" (1: 272). Quincy's *Observations* deserves a more extensive critical appreciation.

Massachusetts friends sent Quincy to London in September 1774, partly to gather political intelligence and possibly to negotiate with British officials. He carried with him letters of introduction from such figures as James Bowdoin, one of Franklin's longtime friends and correspondents. Given their shared intellectual interests and their passion for American democracy, Quincy and Franklin became good friends, regardless of the nearly forty-year difference in age. From London, Quincy wrote his father, "Your friend Dr. Franklin is a *truely* great and good Man" (*Papers* 21: 513). Franklin, in turn, appreciated Quincy's intellect and enthusiasm but worried about his health. As he told Bowdoin, "I am much pleased with Mr. Quincy. 'Tis a thousand Pities his Strength of Body is not equal to his Strength of Mind. His Zeal for the Public (like that of David for God's House) will I fear eat him up" (*Papers* 21: 507). As the following excerpt from his journal demonstrates, Quincy actively sought out prominent figures in British politics and enjoyed meeting Franklin's scientific friends, yet his increasingly poor health took its toll. He left London on March 16 but died on board a ship within sight of Massachusetts.

NOVEMBER 17. PROCEEDED TO LONDON, where I arrived about eleven o'clock A.M.

The numbers, opulence etc. of this great city far surpass all I had imagined.

My ideas are upon the rack, my astonishment amazing.

Was waited upon by Messrs. Th[omas]. Bromfield, E. and C. Dilly and Mr. Jno. Williams — from all of whom I received many civilities. Waited upon Dr. B. Franklin and drank tea with him. He appears in good health and spirits, and seems warm in our cause, and confident of our ultimate success.

I find many friends to liberty and America rejoined on notice of my arrival.

One of the Sons of Liberty (unknown to me) informed Mr. B[romfield] that he heard one in the coffee-house to-day say, "Yes, he has been *blowing up* the *seeds* of sedition in America and has now come to do the same here."

I desired Mr. B. to convey word that if I had done nothing but *blow up seeds*, they would probably be very harmless, as they would never take root but if I should have the good fortune to *sow any here* and they should afterwards *ripen*, he or the ministry might *blow them about* at their leisure.

I find among a certain set of Americans there was great wonderment made at the N. E. [New England] Coffee-house about what brought me to London. My *Observations* have been reprinted here with approbation, as I hear. . . .

November 18. This morning Jno. Williams, Esqr., Inspector of the Customs in the M[assachusett]s Bay waited upon me and we had more than an hour's private conversation together. He informed me that Governor [Thomas] Hutchinson had repeatedly assured the Ministry that a union of the Colonies was utterly impracticable, that the people were greatly divided among themselves in every colony, and that there could be no doubt that all America would *submit*, and that they *must*, and moreover would, *soon*.

It is now not five minutes since Mr. W. left me, and these I think were his very words; he added, moreover, that Governor H. had not only repeatedly told the Ministry so, as several of the Lords had informed him, but that Governor Hutchinson had more than once said the same to persons in the Ministry in his presence.

Mr. Williams desired to wait upon me to see Lords North and Dartmouth, but as it was not at their Lordships' desire he made the request, I declined going for the present.

Mr. Williams also presented the complements of Corbin Morris, Esqr. (one of the Commissioners of the Customs, and a gentleman high in the sentiments of Administration) with a request that I would come and dine with him to-day; but being engaged to dine out this and several succeeding days, I was obliged to decline the invitation.

Dined with Dr. Franklin in company with Dr. [Edward] Bancroft and Mr. Williams.

Dr. Franklin confirmed the account given by John Williams, Esqr., relative to Governor H[utchinson], so far as that several of the nobility and Ministry had assured him of the same facts. . . .

[November 24.] Was introduced by Drs. Franklin and [Richard] Price and spent part of the afternoon and evening with the Royal Society.

Spent the residue of the evening with a club of friends of Liberty at the London Coffee[-house]. Was there introduced by Drs. Franklin and Price to Mr. Alderman [Richard] Oliver, Mr. [Samuel] Vaughan, eight or nine dissenting clergymen, and several other gentlemen.

I found the most sanguine hopes of good from the spirit of the Americans, and the most ardent wishes for their success.

Dr. Franklin acknowledged to me that he was the author of the "Way to make a great Empire a little one," and the "Edict of the King of Prussia." . . .

[November 27.] Dined with Dr. Franklin and spent the evening with him and his friends. . . .

December 1. Dined with Mr. Roger of the Treasury in company with a Commissioner of the Treasury, two members of Parliament and others.

Went at six with Dr. Franklin to Samuel Vaughan, Esqr.'s seat at Wanstead, where we spent our time very happily till Saturday night. . . .

December 9. Returned from Mr. Thornton's, dined at home, and spent the afternoon and evening with Dr. Franklin alone.

December 10. Dined with Mr. Allyne [i.e., John Alleyne] an eminent Counsellor at Law, and spent evening with him and Dr. Franklin, Messrs. Lees, Galloway [i.e., William Monkton, Lord Galway], a member of Parliament, and others. . . .

December 13. Dined with Mr. [Thomas Brand] Hollis (brother to the late benefactor of Harvard Colledge [Thomas Hollis]) with a large circle of friends to liberty, and spent the evening with Dr. Franklin.

[December 14.] Spent the evening with Mr. [Stephen] Sayre in company with Dr. F. and others.

In the course of conversation Dr. F. said that more than sixteen years ago, long before any dispute with America, the present Lord Camden, then Mr. [Charles] Pratt, said to him, "For all what you Americans say of your loyalty and all that, I know you will one day throw off your dependance upon this country, and notwithstanding your boasted affection to this country, you will set up for independence."

Dr. F. said that he assured him no such idea was entertained in the mind of the Americans, and no such idea will ever enter their heads unless you grossly abuse them.

Very true, replied Mr. Pratt, that is one of the main causes I see will happen, and will produce the event. . . .

[January 16.] Dined with Mr. Brand Hollis in company with Dr. Priestly, Dr. Franklin, Price and others.

January 17. Dined with Mrs. [Margaret] Stevenson with a number of American gentlemen and British ladies in celebration of Dr. Franklin's birthday who made one of the festive company, though he this day enters the [seventieth] year of his age. . . .

January 19. Attended H[ouse] of Commons and heard debates between North, Burke and Mr. [William] Eden.

Spent the evening at the London Coffee house with Drs. Franklin, [Joseph] Priestly, Price, [John] Calder and many others. . . .

January 24. Visited by Dr. [John] Fothergill who prescribed for my disorder.

Was this day to have dined at Mr. Towgood's with Franklin, Dr. Price, Dr. [Joseph] Jeffries and Dr. Priestly, but my illness prevented that pleasure.

January 25. Visited by Dr. Fothergill, who peremptorily refused his fee, saying, *quem Deus vult perdere prius dementat* [whom God will ruin He first deprives of his senses].

Received invitation to dine on Friday at Mrs. Huson's [i.e., Mary Stevenson Hewson's], Kensington, and Sunday with Mr. Hollis, — health obliged me to decline both.

Dined at Lord Shelburne's in company with Lord Tankerville, Drs. Franklin, Price, Priestly, Counsellors Dunning, Lee, Leigh and several others.

After a very elegant entertainment his Lordship laid before us copies of the papers from America now lying before the two Houses for their consideration. . . .

February 26. Rode out for the fourth time on horseback about twelve or fourteen miles. Evidently better when I am in the open air, and the motion of the horse not fatiguing.

My friends redouble in number and frequency their visits, as the time of my departure for America draws nigh. Among many others this past week, often visited by Dr. Price, Priestly, Franklin, Rogers, Towgood, Sh[eri]ff Lee, Arthur Lee, etc. . . .

March 1. Went to London in order to go to the British Museum with Dr. Franklin. When we came there we found it was Ash Wednesday and no day of exhibition. I returned with Dr. Franklin to his house, who obligingly gave me a letter to Dr. [Charles] Morton for my introduction to that world of curiosities on the morrow.

On this day I had about an hour and a half's private conversation with Dr. Franklin on the subject of the present situation of American affairs, and what course America and especially New England ought now and during the spring and summer to hold.

I opened the discourse by telling of him the opinions of Dr. Price, Dr. Priestly, William Lee, Arthur Lee and others on those subjects: The Dr. utterly dissented from them all: he entered largely into the subject, and spoke the most substantial good sense and solid wisdom for near an hour.

I wish I might with propriety enter his discourse: it would do lasting honor to his sagacity, judgment, morality and benevolence. I was charmed: I renounced my own opinion: I became a convert to his. I feel a kind of enthusiasm which leads me to believe that it was something almost supernatural which induced this discourse and prompted the Dr. to speak so fully and divinely upon the subject. This interview may be a means of preventing much calamity and producing much good to Boston and the M. Bay, and in the end to all America. . . .

March 3. This day (being the day before my departure) I dined with Dr. Franklin, and had three hours private conversation with him. Disswades from France or Spain or Hereditary Prince of B[runswick]. Intimate with both the Spanish and French Ambassadors: the latter a great shrewd man.

By no means take any step of great consequence (unless on a sudden emergency) without advice of the Continental Congress, and explicitly and in so many words said, that only New England could hold for ages against this country, and if they were firm and united in seven years would conquer them.

Said he had the best intelligence that the manufacturers were bitterly feeling and loudly complaining of the loss of the American trade.

Let your adherence be to the non-importation and non-exportation agreement, a year from next September, or to the next sessions of Parliament, and the day is won.

From "Journal of Josiah Quincy, Jun., During His Voyage and Residence in England from September 28th, 1774, to March 3d, 1775," ed. Mark Antony DeWolfe Howe, *Proceedings of the Massachusetts Historical Society* 50 (1917): 437–469.

[Franklin as a Congressman and a Diplomat, 1775–1778]

John Adams

As a delegate to the Continental Congress, John Adams (1735–1826) finally had the opportunity to meet Benjamin Franklin. Though Adams had heard much about Franklin beforehand, he was not disappointed upon meeting him. In the letters he wrote during the time he and Franklin worked together in the Continental Congress, Adams had nothing but praise for him. To James Warren, Adams wrote, "Dr Franklyn needs nothing to be said. There is no abler or better American that I know of." Speaking about a congressional committee chosen to go to Canada in February 1776, Adams wrote Warren again, elaborating his impressions: "Franklins Character you know. His masterly Acquaintance with the French Language, his extensive Correspondence in France, his great Experience in Life, his Wisdom, Prudence, Caution, his engaging Address, united to his unshaken Firmness in the present American System of Politicks and War, point him out as the fittest Character for this momentous Undertaking" (*Letters of Delegates to Congress*, 2: 80; 3: 275). Adams subsequently worked with Franklin on the committee to draft the Declaration of Independence and found nothing in their working relationship to shake his lofty opinion of Franklin.

When Adams went to Paris to take over the position vacated by Silas Deane and serve with Franklin and Arthur Lee as joint commissioners to France, he began to question Franklin's abilities, however. It seemed to Adams that Franklin's mastery of the French language was not as great as he previously had supposed. Also, the always prim and proper Adams took offense at Franklin's flirtatious manner among the ladies of French society. Not only does Adams's autobiography possess great documentary value, it also marks a major contributor to the literary history of American autobiography.

From John Adams to Abigail Adams, 23 July 1775

My Dear

You have more than once in your Letters mentioned Dr. Franklin, and in one intimated a Desire that I should write you something concerning him.

Dr. Franklin has been very constant in his Attendance on Congress from the Beginning. His Conduct has been composed and grave and in the Opinion of many Gentlemen very reserved. He has not assumed any Thing, nor affected to take the lead; but has seemed to choose that the Congress should pursue their own Principles and sentiments and adopt their own Plans: Yet he has not been backward: has been very usefull, on many occasions, and discovered a Disposition entirely American. He does not hesitate at our boldest Measures, but rather seems to think us, too irresolute, and backward. He thinks us at present in an odd State, neither in Peace nor War, neither dependent nor independent. But he thinks that We shall soon assume a Character more decisive.

He thinks, that We have the Power of preserving ourselves, and that even if We should be driven to the disagreable Necessity of assuming a total Independency, and set up a separate state, We could maintain it. The People of England, have thought that the Opposition in America, was wholly owing to Dr. Franklin: and I suppose their scribblers will attribute the Temper, and Proceedings of this Congress to him: but there cannot be a greater Mistake. He has had but little share farther than to co-operate and assist. He is however a great and good Man. I wish his Colleagues from this City were All like him, particularly one [John Dickinson], whose Abilities and Virtues, formerly trumpeted so much in America, have been found wanting.

From *Diary and Autobiography of John Adams*

Monday, September 9, 1776.

Resolved, that in all Continental Commissions and other Instruments where heretofore the Words "United Colonies," have been used, the Stile be altered for the future to the United States.

The Board of War brought in a report, which was read.

On this day, Mr. Franklin, Mr. Edward Rutledge, and Mr. John Adams, proceeded on their Journey to Lord [Richard] Howe, on Staten Island, the two former in Chairs, and the last on Horseback. The first night We lodged at an Inn, in New Brunswick. On the Road, and at all the public Houses, We saw such Numbers of Officers and Soldiers, straggling and loytering, as gave me at least, but a poor Opinion of the Discipline of our forces and excited as much indignation as anxiety. Such thoughtless dissipation at a time so critical, was not calculated to inspire very sanguine hopes or give great Courage to Ambassadors: I was nevertheless determined that it should not dishearten me. I saw that We must and had no doubt but We should be chastised into order in time.

The Taverns were so full We could with difficulty obtain Entertainment. At Brunswick, but one bed could be procured for Dr. Franklin and me, in a Chamber little larger than the bed, without a Chimney, and with only one small Window. The Window was open, and I, who was an invalid and afraid of the Air in the night, shut it close. "Oh!" says Franklin, "don't shut the Window, We shall be suffocated." I answered I was afraid of the Evening Air. Dr. Franklin replied, "The Air within this Chamber will soon be, and indeed is now worse than that without Doors: come! open the Window and come to bed, and I will convince you: I believe you are not acquainted with my Theory of Colds. Opening the Window, and leaping into Bed, I said I had read his Letters to Dr. [Samuel] Cooper in which he had advanced, that Nobody ever got cold by going into a cold Church, or any other cold Air: but the Theory was so little consistent with my experience, that I thought it a Paradox: However I had so much curiosity to hear his reasons, that I would run the risque of a cold. The Doctor then began a harangue upon Air and cold and Respiration and Perspiration, with which I was so much amused that I soon fell asleep, and left him and his Philosophy together: but I believe they were equally sound and insensible within a few minutes after me, for the last Words I heard were pronounced as if he was more than half asleep. — I remember little of the Lecture, except, that the human Body, by Respiration and Perspiration, destroys a gallon of Air in a Minute: that two such Persons as were now in that Chamber, would consume all the Air in it, in an hour or two: that by breathing over again the matter thrown off, by the Lungs and the Skin, We should imbibe the real Cause of Colds, not from abroad but from within. I am not inclined to introduce here a dissertation on this Subject. There is much Truth I believe, in some things he advanced: but they warrant not the assertion that a Cold is never taken from cold air. I have often conversed with him since on the same subject: and I believe with him that Colds are often taken in foul Air, in close Rooms; but they are often taken from cold Air, abroad too. I have often asked him, whether a Person heated with Exercise, going suddenly into cold Air, or standing still in a current of it, might not have his Pores suddenly contracted, his Perspiration stopped, and that matter thrown into the Circulations or cast upon the Lungs, which he acknowledged was the Cause of Colds. To this he never could give me a satisfactory Answer. And I have heard that in the Opinion of his own able Physician Dr. [John] Jones he fell a Sacrifice at last, not to the Stone, but to his own Theory, having caught the violent Cold which finally choaked him, by sitting for some hours at a Window, with the cool Air blowing upon him.

The next Morning We proceeded on our Journey, and the Remainder of this Negotiation, will be related from the Journals of Congress, and from a few familiar Letters, which I wrote to my most intimate Friends before and after my Journey. The abrupt uncouth freedom of these, and all others of my Letters, in those days require an Apology. Nothing was farther from my Thoughts, than that they would ever appear before the Public. Oppressed with a Load of Business, without an Amanuensis, or any Assistance, I was obliged to do every Thing myself. For seven Years before this I had never been without three Clerks in my Office as a Barrister; but now I had no Secretary nor servant whom I could trust to write: and every thing must be copied by myself, or be hazarded without any. The few that I wrote upon this Occasion I copied; merely to assist my memory as Occasion might demand.

There were a few Circumstances which appear neither in the Journals of Congress nor in my Letters, which may be thought by some worth preserving. Lord Howe had sent over an Officer as an Hostage for our Security. I said to Dr. Franklin, it would be childish in Us to depend upon such a Pledge, and insisted on taking him over with Us, and keeping our Surety on the same side of the Water with Us. My Colleagues exulted in the Proposition and agreed to it instantly. We told the Officer, if he held himself under our direction he must go back with Us. He bowed Assent, and We all embarked in his Lordships Barge. As We approached the Shore, his Lordship, observing Us, came down to the Waters Edge to receive Us, and looking at the Officer, he said, Gentlemen, you make me a very high Compliment, and you may depend upon it, I will consider it as the most sacred of Things. We walked up to the House between Lines of Guards of Grenadiers, looking as fierce as ten furies, and making all the Grimaces and Gestures and motions of their Musquets, with Bayonets fixed, which I suppose military Etiquette requires but which We neither understood nor regarded.

The House had been the Habitation of military Guards, and was as dirty as a stable: but his Lordship had prepared a large handsome Room, by spreading a Carpet of Moss and green Spriggs from Bushes and Shrubs in the Neighbourhood, till he had made it not only wholesome but romantically elegant, and he entertained Us with good Claret, good Bread, cold Ham, Tongues, and Mutton. . . .

Two or three Circumstances, which are omitted in this report, and indeed not thought worth notice in any of my private Letters, I afterwards found circulated in Europe, and oftener repeated than any other Part of this whole Transaction. Lord Howe was profuse in his Expressions of Gratitude to the State of Massachusetts, for erecting a marble Monument in Westminster Abbey to his Elder Brother Lord [George Augustus] Howe who was killed in America in the last French War, saying, "he esteemed that Honour to his Family *above all Things in this World.* That such was his Gratitude and affection to this Country, on that Account, that he felt for America as for a Brother, and if America should fall, he should feel and lament it, like the Loss of a Brother." Dr. Franklin, with an easy Air and a collected Countenance, a Bow, a Smile, and all that Naivetee, which sometimes appeared in his Conversation and is often observed in his Writings, replied "My Lord, We will do our Utmost Endeavours, to save your Lordship that mortification." His Lordship appeared to feel this, with more Sensibility than I could expect: but he only returned "I suppose you will endeavour to give Us employment in Europe." To this Observation, not a Word, nor a look from which he could draw any Inference, escaped any of the Committee. . . .

April 9. Thursday. 1778. Though the City was very silent and still in the latter part of the night, the Bells, Carriages and Cries in the Street, were noisy enough in the morning.

Went in a Coach to Passy with Dr. [Nicolas] Noel and my Son [John Quincy Adams]. [We visited] Dr. Franklin with whom I had served the best part of two Years in Congress in great Harmony and Civility, and there had grown up between Us that kind of Friendship, which is commonly felt between two members of the same public Assembly, who meet each other every day not only in public deliberations, but at private Breakfasts, dinners and Suppers, and especially in secret confidential Consultations, and who always agreed in their Opinions and Sentiments of public affairs. This had been the History of my Acquaintance with Franklin and he received me accordingly with great apparent Cordiality. Mr. [Silas] Deane was gone to Marseilles to embark with D'Estaing [Charles Henri Théodat, comte d'Estaing] for America. Franklin undertook the care of Jesse Deane, as I suppose had been agreed between him and the Childs Father before his departure. And he was soon sent, with my Son and Dr. Franklins Grandson Benjamin Franklin Bache, whom as well as William [Temple] Franklin whom he called his Grandson, the Dr. had brought with him from America, to the Pension of Mr. Le Coeur at Passy.

Dr. Franklin presented to me the Compliments of Mr. Turgot [Anne Robert Jacques Turgot, baron de l'Aulne] the late Controuler of the Finances and a very pressing Invitation to dine with him. Though I was not very well accoutrered to appear in such Company I was persuaded and concluded to go. I went with Dr. Franklin and Mr. [Arthur] Lee, and dined with this Ex Minister. The Dutchess D'Anville [Marie Louise Nicole Elisabeth de La Rochefoucauld, duchesse d'Anville] the Mother of the Duke de la Rochefoucauld, and twenty others of the Great People of France were there. I thought it odd that the first Lady I should dine with in France should happen to be the Widow of our Great Ennemy who commanded a kind of Armada against Us, within my Memory: but I was not the less pleased with her Conversation for that. She appeared to be venerable for her Years, and several of her Observations at Table, full as I thought of bold, masculine and original Sense were translated to me. The House, Gardens, Library, Furniture, and Entertainment of the Table, appeared very magnificent to me, who had yet seen but little of France, and nothing at all of any other part of Europe. Mr. Turgot had the Appearance and deportment of a grave, wise and amiable Man. I was very particularly examined by the Company through my Colleagues and Interpriters Franklin and Lee concerning American Affairs. I should have been much better pleased to have been permitted to remain less conspicuous: but I gave to all their Inquiries the most concise and clear Answer I could and came off, for the first time I thought, well enough. Returned and supped with Franklin on Cheese and Beer.

Dr. Franklin had shewn me the Apartements and Furniture left by Mr. Deane, which were every Way more elegant, than I desired, and comfortable and convenient as I could wish. Although Mr. Deane in Addition to these had a House, furniture and Equipage in Paris, I determined to put my Country to no further expence on my Account but to take my Lodgings under the same Roof with Dr. Franklin and to Use no other Equipage than his, if I could avoid it. This House was called The Basse Court de Monsieur Le Ray de Chaumont, which was to be sure, not a Title of great Dignity for the Mansion of Ambassadors though they were no more than American Ambassadors. Nevertheless it had been nothing less than the famous Hotel de Vallentinois, with a Motto over the Door Si sta bene, non se move, which I thought a good rule for my Conduct. If you stand well do not move; or stand still.

April 10. Fryday. 1778. The first moment Dr. Franklin and I happened to be alone, he began to complain to me of the Coolness as he very coolly called it, between the American Ministers. He said there had been disputes between Mr. Deane and Mr. Lee. That Mr. Lee was a Man of an anxious uneasy temper which made it disagreable to do business with him: that he seemed to be one of those Men of whom he had known many in his day, who went on through Life quarrelling with one Person or another till they commonly ended in the loss of their reason. He said Mr. [Ralph] Izard was there too, and joined in close friendship with Mr. Lee. That Mr. Izard was a Man of violent and ungoverned Passions. That each of these had a Number of Americans about him, who were always exciting disputes and propagating Stories that made the Service very disagreable. That Mr. Izard [also spelled Izzard], who as I knew had been appointed a Minister to the Grand Duke of Tuscany, instead of going to Italy remained there with his Lady and Children at Paris, and instead of minding his own Business, and having nothing else to do he spent his time in consultations with Mr. Lee and in interfering with the Business of the Commission to this Court. That they had made strong Objections to the Treaty, and opposed several Articles of it. That neither Mr. Lee nor Mr. Izard were liked by the French. That Mr. William Lee his Brother, who had been appointed to the Court of Vienna, had been lingering in Germany and lost his Papers, that he called upon the Ministers at Paris for considerable Sums of Money, and by his Connection with Lee and Izard and their party, increased the Uneasiness &c. &c. &c.

I heard all this with inward Grief and external patience and Composure. I only answered, that I was personally much a Stranger to Mr. Izard and both the Lees. That I was extreamly sorry to hear of any misunderstanding among the Americans and especially among the public Ministers, that it would not become me to take any part in them. That I ought to think of nothing in such a Case, but Truth and Justice, and the means of harmonizing and composing all Parties: But that I foresaw I should have a difficult, dangerous and disagreable part to Act, but I must do my duty as well as I could.

When Mr. Lee arrived at my Lodgings one Morning, it was proposed that a Letter should be written to Mr. [Charles William Frederic] Dumas at the Hague to inform him of my Arrival and my Colleagues proposed that I should write it. I thought it an awkward thing for me to write an Account of myself, and asked Dr. Franklin to write it, after We had considered and agreed upon what should be written, which I thought the more proper as he was the only one of Us who had been acquainted with Mr. Dumas. . . .

It so happened or had been so contrived, that We Were invited to dine at Monsieur Brillons [also sometimes spelled Brillions], a Family in which Mr. Franklin was very intimate, and in which he spent much of his Time. Here We met a large Company of both Sexes and among them were Monsieur Le Vailliant [i.e., Louis Guillaume Le Veillard] and his Lady. Madam Brillion [Mme. d'Hardancourt Brillon] was one of the most beautifull Women in France, a great Mistress of Musick, as were her two little Daughters. The Dinner was Luxury, as usual in that Country. A large Cake was brought in with three flaggs flying. On one of them "Pride subdued": on another "Haec dies, in qua fit Congressus, exultemus et potemus in eâ." Mr. Brillon was a rough kind of Country Squire. His Lady all softness, sweetness and politeness. I saw a Woman in Company, as a Companion of Madam Brillon who dined with her at Table, and was considered as one of the Family. She was very plain and clumzy. When I afterwards learned both from Dr. Franklin and his Grandson, and from many other Persons, that this Woman was the Amie of Mr. Brillion and that Madam Brillion consoled herself by the Amitie of Mr. Le Vailliant, I was astonished that these People could live together in such apparent Friendship and indeed without cutting each others throats. But I did not know the World. I soon saw and heard so much of these Things in other Families and among allmost all the great People of the Kingdom that I found it was a thing of course. It was universally understood and Nobody lost any reputation by it. Yet I must say that I never knew an Instance of it, without perceiving that all their Complaisancy was external and ostensible only: a mere conformity to the fashion: and that internally there was so far from being any real friendship or conjugal Affection that their minds and hearts were full of Jealousy, Envy, revenge and rancour. In short that it was deadly poison to all the calm felicity of Life. There were none of the delightful Enjoyments of conscious Innocence and mutual Confidence. It was mere brutal pleasure. . . .

April 11. Saturday 1778. Went to Versailles with Dr. Franklin and Mr. Lee, visited the Secretary of State for foreign Affairs, the Count de Vergennes and was politely received. He hoped I should stay long enough in France, to acquire the French Language perfectly. — Assured me that every Thing should be done to make France agreable to me. Hoped the Treaty would be agreable, and the Alliance lasting. Although the Treaty had gone somewhat farther than the System I had always advocated in Congress and further than my Judgment could yet perfectly approve, it was now too late to make any Objections, and I answered that I thought the Treaty liberal and generous, as indeed it was upon the whole, and that I doubted not of its speedy ratification. I communicated to him the resolution of Congress respecting the Suspension of Burgoins embarkation, which he read through and pronounced "Fort bon." We were then conducted to the Count Maurepas, the Prime Minister or the Kings Mentor, as he was often called. I was presented to him by Dr. Franklin as his New Colleague, and again politely received. This Gentleman was near fourscore Years of Age, with a fresh rosy Countenance, and apparently in better health and greater Vigour than Dr. Franklin himself. He had been dismissed from Office and exiled to his Lands by Lewis the fifteenth in 1748 and in his retirement if not before had obtained the Reputation of a Patriot, for which reason he had been recalled to Court by Lewis 16th, and placed at the head of Affairs. . . .

[April 13, 1778.] Dr. Franklin, Mr. Lee and myself went to Versailles, were introduced to the Levee of Mr. De Sartine [Antoine Raymond Jean Gualbert Gabriel de Sartine, comte d'Alby], a vast number of Gentlemen were Attending, in one room after another, and We found the Minister at last, entrenched as deep as We had on a former day seen the Count de Maurepas. The Minister of the Marine, received Us very politely, and shewed Us into his Cabinet, where were all the Books and Papers of his Office. After he had finished the Business of his Levee, he came into the Cabinet to Us, and asked whether I spoke French, and whether I understood French? I should have answered malheureusement (miserably), or point du tout (not at all), but Mr. Franklin answered Un Peu, si l'on parle lentement et doucement (a little if one speaks slowly or moderately). — He then made an Apology to each of Us, seperately in the name of his Lady, for her Absence, being gone into Paris to visit a sick relation. We were soon conducted down to dinner, which appeared [to] me as splendid as any I had seen, all Elegance and Magnificence. The Company of Gentlemen was numerous, and only four Ladies. During the dinner many other Gentlemen came in who I suppose had dined elsewhere, walked the room, leaned over the Chairs of the Ladies and Gentlemen at Table and conversed with them. After dinner the Company all arose as was usual in France, and went into another room, where a great Additional Number of Gentlemen came in. After some time We retired and went to make a Visit to Madam De Maurepas, the Lady of the prime Minister. The Countess was not at home, and Count Laurigais [Louis Léon Félicité de Brancas, comte de Lauraguais], who had conducted Us to her Apartments, wrote our Card for Us in the Porters Book "Messrs. Franklin, Lee and Adams, pour avoir l'honneur de voir (to have the honor to see) Madame De Maurepas." This I believe was the only time that I saw Laurigais. He spoke our Language so well, and seemed to have so much information that I wished for more Acquaintance with him: but finding that he was not a favourite at court and especially with those Ministers who had the principal management of our American Affairs, and hearing from Dr. Franklin and Dr. [Edward] Bancroft that Mr. Lee and Mr. Izzard had given Offence by too much familiarity with him, I declined any farther Enquiry concerning him. And I never heard that those Gentlemen had any intercourse with him, after that time. . . .

April 14. Tuesday 1778. I returned the Visits which had been made me by the American Gentlemen. This I found was an indispensable Punctilio, with my Countrymen in France. Great Offence had been taken by some of them, because Dr. Franklin had not very exactly performed this important Ettiquette, especially by those of them who had come over to Paris from England.

April 15. Wednesday. 1778. Dined with Madam Helvetius One Gentleman and one Lady, besides Dr. Franklin, his Grandson and myself, made the Company. An elegant Dinner. This was a Lady of established Reputation also: The Widow of the famous Helvetius, who, as Count Sarsefield [Guy Claude, comte de Sarsfield] once said to me, if he had made a few millions of Livres the more as one of the Farmers General, and written a few Books the less as a Philosopher it might have been better for France and the World. . . .

Dr. Franklin was reported to speak french very well, but I found upon attending critically to him that he did not speak it, grammatically, and upon my asking him sometimes whether a Phrase he had used was correct, he acknowledged to me, that he was wholly inattentive to the grammar. His pronunciation too, upon which the French Gentlemen and Ladies complemented him very highly and which he seemed to think pretty well, I soon found was very inaccurate, and some Gentlemen of high rank afterwards candidly told me that it was so confused, that it was scarcely possible to understand him. Indeed his Knowledge of French, at least his faculty of speaking it, may be said to have commenced with his Embassy to France. He told me that when he was in France some Years before, Sir John Pringle was with him, and did all his conversation for him, as his Interpreter, and that he understood and spoke French, with great difficulty, untill his present Residence, although he read it. . . .

This day We dined at Mr. La Fretés. A splendid House, Gardens and Furniture. The Family were fond of Paintings and exhibited a Variety of exquisite Pieces, but none of them struck me more than one Picture of a Storm and another of a Calm at Sea. I had not forgotten the Gulph Stream, the English Channel nor the Bay of Biscay.

At this dinner the Conversation turned upon the Infrequency of Marriage in France. Go into any company they said and you would find very few who were married, and upon Examination of the numerous Company at Table I was found the only married Person in Company except the Heads of the Family. Here We were shewn a manuscript History of the Revolution in Russia in the Year 1762. The Author was asked why he did not publish it. He answered that he had no mind to be assassinated as he certainly should be if he printed it and was known to be the Writer. Mr. Franklin retired to another room and read it. When he returned it to the Author he made many Eulogies of the Style, Arrangement, Perspicuity &c. and added "You have followed the manner of Sallust, and you have surpassed him." — I thought this as good a french Compliment as the best of the Company could have made.

At Table there was much conversation about the Education of daughters at the Convents, and I found the discreetest people, especially among the Ladies, had a very bad Opinion of such Education. They were very bad Schools for Morals. It was then News to me that they were thought such in France.

The greatest part of the Conversation was concerning Voltaire. He was extolled to the Skies as a Prodigy. His Eminence in History, Epick Poetry, Dramatick Poetry, Phylosophy, even the Neutonian Phylosophy: His Prose and Verse were equally admirable. No Writer had ever excelled in so many Branches of Science and Learning, besides that astonishing multitude of his fugitive Pieces. He was the grand Monarch of Science and Litterature. If he should die the Republick of Letters would be restored. But it was now a Monarchy &c. &c. &c. . . .

[April 18, 1778.] On our return [from dinner] called and drank Tea, at Madam Brillions. We then made a Visit to M. [Henri] Boulainvilliers, who is Lord of the Manor of Passi and a descendant of the celebrated Boulain-villiers who wrote many Books particularly on the States General and a Life of Mahomet &c. He had just come out with his Lady and daughter to his Country Seat at Passi, for the Season. His Daughter bore the Title of Mademoiselle De Passi, and was certainly one of the most beautiful young Ladies, I ever saw in France. She afterwards married The Marquis De Tonnere [Stanislas Marie Adélaïomte de Clermont-Tonnerre], a Gentle-man of great Quality and fortune, since so famous for his tragical Catastro-phy in the beginning of the Revolution. This Noblemans Character was as amiable as that of his Father in Law was otherwise. Boulainvilliers held a superb hereditary office under the Crown which gave him very high Rank and great Emolument. But although he was very rich he was represented as oppressive, tyrannical and cruel as well as avaricious to a great degree. Mr. Franklin who at the age of seventy odd, had neither lost his Love of Beauty nor his Taste for it called Mademoiselle De Passy his favourite and his flame and his Love and his Mistress, which flattered the Family and did not displease the young Lady. . . .

April 21. Tuesday. 1778. Dined at Mr. [Jacques Donatien Le Ray de] Chaumonts, with the largest collection of great Company, that I had yet seen. . . . But these incessant Dinners, and dissipations were not the Ob-jects of my Mission to France. My Countrymen were suffering in America, and their Affairs were in great confusion in Europe. With much Grief and concern, I received daily and almost hourly information, of the disputes be-tween the Americans in France. The bitter Animosities between Mr. Deane and Mr. Lee: between Dr. Franklin and Mr. Lee: between Dr. Franklin and Mr. Izzard: between Dr. Bancroft and Mr. Lee and Mr. Izzard: and between Mr. Charmichael [William Carmichael] and all them. Sir James Jay was there too, a Brother of Mr. John Jay, and an able Physician as well as a Man of Letters and information. He had lately come over from England, and although he seemed to have no Animosity against any of the Gentlemen, he confirmed many of the Reports that I had heard from several Persons before, such as that Mr. Deane had been at least as attentive to his own Interest, in dabbling in the English funds, and in trade, and in fitting out Privateers as to the Public, and said that he would give Mr. Deane fifty thousand Pounds Sterling for the fortune he had made here. That Dr. Bancroft too had made a fortune here, by speculating in the English Stocks and by gambling Policies in London. Mr. McCrery [Willian McCreery] too, had adopted the Cry of Mr. Lees Ennemies, and said that the Lees were selfish, and that this was a Family misfortune. Dr. Franklin, Mr. Deane and Dr. Bancroft were universally considered as indissoluble Friends. The Lees and Mr. Izzard were equally attached in friendship to each other. The Friends and followers of each party both among the french and Americans were equally bitter against each other. Mr. Deane appeared to me, to have made himself agreable here, to Mr. De Chaumont, Mr. [Pierre Augustin Caron de] Beaumarchais, Mr. [John Joseph] Monthieu, and Mr. [John] Holker, Persons of importance and influence at that time, and with that Ministry, particularly the Count de Vergennes and Mr. De Sartine. Mr. Deane was gone home in great Splendor, with Compliments, Certificates and Recommendations in his favour from the King and Minister, and many other Persons French and American, among whom was Dr. Franklin who shewed me his Letter of recommendation in very strong terms. Mr. Deane had been active, industrious, subtle and in some degree successfull, having accomplished some of the great purposes of his Mission. Mr. [Conrad Alexander] Gerard and Mr. Holker were also his Friends: and although he had little order in his Business public or private, had lived very expensively and spent great Sums of Money that no body could Account for, and allthough unauthorised Contracts had well nigh ruined our Army, embarrassed Congress more than any thing that had ever happened and put his Country to a great and useless expence, I was still apprehensive there would be great Altercations excited by him in America, both in and out of Congress. . . .

In this place it is necessary to introduce a few portraits of Characters that the subsequent narration may be better understood.

Dr. Franklin one of my Colleagues is so generally known that I shall not attempt a Sketch of his Character at present. That He was a great Genius, a great Wit, a great Humourist and a great Satyrist, and a great Politician is certain. That he was a great Phylosopher, a great Moralist and a great Statesman is more questionable. . . .

[April 29, 1778.] After dinner We went to the Accademy of Sciences, and heard Mr. [Jean le Rond] D'Alembert as Secretary perpetual, pronounce Eulogies on several of their Members lately deceased. Voltaire and Franklin were both present, and there presently arose a general Cry that Monsieur Voltaire and Monsieur Franklin should be introduced to each other. This was done and they bowed and spoke to each other. This was no Satisfaction. There must be something more. Neither of our Philosophers seemed to divine what was wished or expected. They however took each other by the hand. — But this was not enough. The Clamour continued, untill the explanation came out "Il faut s'embrasser, a la francoise." The two Aged Actors upon this great Theatre of Philosophy and frivolity then embraced each other by hugging one another in their Arms and kissing each others cheeks, and then the tumult subsided. And the Cry immediately spread through the whole Kingdom and I suppose over all Europe Qu'il etoit charmant. Oh! il etoit enchantant, de voir Solon et Sophocle embrassans. How charming it was! Oh! it was enchanting to see Solon and Sophocles embracing! . . .

May 6. Wednesday. 1778. Franklin told Us one of his Characteristic Stories. A Spanish Writer of certain Vissions of Hell, relates that a certain evil Spirit he met with who was civil and well bred, shewed him all the Apartments in the place. Among others that of deceased Kings. The Spaniard was much amused at so illustrious a Sight, and after viewing them for sometime, said he should be glad to see the rest of them. The rest? said the Daemon. Here are all the Kings who ever reigned upon earth from the creation of it to this day, what the Devil would the Man have?

This Anecdote was in the Spirit of those times for the Philosophers of the last Age had raised a king killing Spirit in the World. I wrote the Story down in the Evening with a Note upon it not less Characteristick of myself. It was this. This Fable is not so charitable as Dr. [Isaac] Watts, who in his view of Heaven says "here and there I see a King," which seems to imply that Kings are as good as other men, since it is but here and there that We see a King upon Earth. . . .

May 19. Tuesday. 1778. We dined with Mr. De Challut [Chalut de Vé-rin], one of the Farmers General. — We were introduced into the most superb Gallery I had yet seen. The Paintings, Statues, and Curiosities, were as rich and costly as they were innumerable. The Old Marshall Richelieu [Louis François Armand Vignerot du Plessis, duc et maréchal de Richelieu], and a vast number of other great Company dined with Us. After dinner Mr. De Challut invited Dr. Franklin and me to go to the Opera and take Seats in his Logis, which We did. The Musick and dancing were very fine. The French Opera is a very pleasing Entertainment for a few times. There is every Thing, which can please the Eye or the Ear. But the Words are unintelligible, and if they were not, they are said to be very insignificant. One always wishes in such an Amusement to learn something. The Imagination, the Passions and the Understanding have too little Employment in the Opera. . . .

[May 20, 1778.] After dinner We went and drank Tea, with Madame Foucault, and took a view of Mr. [Jean Simon David de] Foucaults House. A very grand Hotel it was, or at least appeared so to me. The Furniture, the Beds, the Curtains, the every Thing was as rich as Silk and Gold could make it. — But I was wearied to death with gazing wherever I went, at a profusion of unmeaning Wealth and Magnificence. The Adieus of Hector and Andromache, had attracted my Attention and given me more pleasure melancholly as it was, than the sight of all the Gold of Ophir could. — Gold, Marble, Silk, Velvet, Silver, Ivory and Alabaster, made up the Show every where.

I shall make no Scruple to violate my own rule of Criticism, by introducing on the same page with Hector and Andromache, a Story of Franklins which he gave Us in the same day. Franklin delighted in New Gate Anecdotes and he told us one of a Taylor who stole a horse, was detected and committed to New Gate, where he met another Felon, who had long followed the Trade of Horse Stealing. The Taylor told his Story to the other who enquired, why he had not taken such a road, and assumed such a disguise and why he had not disguised the Horse? I did not think of it. Did not think of it? Who are You? and what has been your Employment? A Taylor. — You never stole a Horse before I suppose in your Life? Never.- What Business had you with Horse Stealing? Why did not you content yourself with your Cabbage? . . .

May 26. Tuesday. 1778. Dined at the Seat in the Country of Monsieur [Henri Léonard Jean Baptiste] Bertin, a Secretary of State. Madam Bertin, the Lady of the Ministers Nephew, invited Dr. Franklin, Mr. William Temple Franklin and me to ride with her in her Coach with four Horses, which

We did. This was one of the pleasantest rides, I had seen. We rode near the Backside of Mount Calvare, which is the finest Hill near Paris, though Mont Martre is a very fine Elevation. The Gardens, Walks and Waterworks of Mr. Bertin were in a Style of magnificence, like all other Seats of the Gentlemen in this Country. He was a Batchelor. His House and Gardens were situated upon the River Seine. He shewed his Luxury, as he called it, which was a collection of misshapen Rocks, at the End of his Garden, drawn together, from great distances, at an Expence of several Thousands of Guineas. I told him I would sell him a thousand times as many for half a Guinea. His Water Works were curious, four Pumps going by means of two horses. The Mechanism was simple and ingenious. The Horses went round as in a Mill. The four Pumps empty themselves into a square Pond, which contains an Acre. From this Pond the Water flows, through Pipes, down to every Part of the Garden. . . .

July 4. 1778. This being the Anniversary of the Declaration of American Independence, We had the honour of the Company of all the American Gentlemen and Ladies, in and about Paris, to dine with Dr. Franklin and me, at Passi, together with a few of the French Gentlemen in the Neighbourhood, Mr. Chaumont, Mr. Brillon, Mr. Vaillant, Mr. [Ferdinand] Grand, Mr. Beaudoin, Mr. Gerard De Rayneval, the Abby's Challut and Arnoud &c. Mr. Izzard and Dr. Franklin were upon such Terms, that Franklin would not have invited him, and I know not that Izzard would have accepted the Invitation if he had. But I said to Mr. Franklin that I would invite him, and I believe Dr. [James] Smith and all the rest that he omitted and bring them all together and compell them if possible to forget their Animosities. Franklin consented, and I sent Cards to them in my name only. The others were invited in the Names of both of Us. The Day was passed joyously enough and no ill humour appeared from any quarter.

From *Adams Family Correspondence*, ed. L. H. Butterfield et al., 9 vols. to date. The Adams Papers, Series II. (Cambridge, MA: Belknap Press of Harvard University Press, 1963-), 1: 252-253.

From *Diary and Autobiography of John Adams*, ed. L. H. Butterfield et al., 4 vols. The Adams Papers, Series I. (Cambridge, MA: Belknap Press of Harvard University Press, 1961), 3: 417-420, 422; 4: 41-44, 46-48, 56-57, 58, 59-62, 63-64, 67-69, 80-81, 91, 104, 105, 117, 143-144.

[Franklin in Boston and Paris, 1775 and 1784]

ABIGAIL ADAMS

As a delegate to the Continental Congress, Franklin actively served on numerous committees. In October 1775, for example, he served on a committee to confer with George Washington at his Massachusetts headquarters. His responsibilities for this committee let him indulge his love of travel. While in Massachusetts, he took the opportunity to renew old friendships and make some new ones. Having worked with John Adams in Congress, he was eager to meet his wife. On October 26, 1775, he had dinner at the home of Josiah Quincy together with James Bowdoin, Samuel Cooper, and Abigail Adams (1744–1818). Before the dinner she wrote her husband, informing him that she had "a great desire to see Dr. Franklin" (*Adams Family Correspondence*, 1: 313). As the excerpt of a letter she wrote her husband after this dinner with Franklin indicates, she was generally impressed with him, though she obviously saw in him what she wanted to see. He agreed to carry some letters from her back to her husband in Philadelphia. And as she indicated in another letter, Franklin even invited her to come to Philadelphia to be with her husband while the Continental Congress was in session (*Adams Family Correspondence*, 1: 325).

The first impression she had of Franklin changed when she dined with him in Paris nine years later. Also in attendance was Anne-Catherine de Ligniville d'Autricourt Helvétius. Abigail Adams did not like Madame Helvétius, nor did she appreciate Franklin's shameless flirtations. Their daughter Abigail or "Nabby" also attended the dinner, and she felt the same way. Critiquing Madame Helvétius, she wrote a correspondent: "I could not judge of her conversation as I could not understand a word, but if it was in unison with her dress, and manners, I assure you that I consider myself fortunate that I did not" (*Adams Family Correspondence*, 5: 431–432).

From Abigail Adams to John Adams, 5 November 1775

I hope you have received several Letters from me in this fortnight past. I wrote by Mr. Linch [Thomas Lynch], and by Dr. Frankling the latter of whom I had the pleasure of dining with, and of admiring him whose character from my Infancy I had been taught to venerate. I found him social, but not talkative, and when he spoke something usefull droped from his Tongue; he was grave, yet pleasant, and affable. — You know I make some pretensions to physiognomy and I thought I could read in his countanance the Virtues of his Heart, among which patriotism shined in its full Lusture — and with that is blended every virtue of a christian, for a true patriot must be a religious Man. I have been led to think from a late Defection that he who neglects his duty to his Maker, may well be expected to be deficient and insincere in his duty towards the public. Even suppose Him to possess a large share of what is called honour and publick Spirit yet do not these Men by their bad Example, by a loose immoral conduct corrupt the Minds of youth, and vitiate the Morrals of the age, and thus injure the publick more than they can compensate by intrepidity, Generosity and Honour?

From Abigail Adams to Lucy Cranch, 5 September 1784

I have been in company with but one French Lady since I arrived, for strangers here make the first visit and nobody will know you untill you have waited upon them in form.

This Lady I dined with at Dr. Franklings. She enterd the Room with a careless jaunty air. Upon seeing Ladies who were strangers to her, she bawled out ah Mon dieu! where is Frankling, why did you not tell me there were Ladies here? You must suppose her speaking all this in French. How said she I look? takeing hold of a dressing chimise made of tiffanny which She had on over a blew Lutestring, and which looked as much upon the decay as her Beauty, for she was once a handsome woman. Her Hair was fangled, over it she had a small straw hat with a dirty half gauze hankerchief round it, and a bit of dirtyer gauze than ever my maids wore was sewed on behind. She had a black gauze Skarf thrown over her shoulders. She ran out of the room. When she returnd, the Dr. enterd at one door she at the other, upon which she ran forward to him, caught him by the hand, helas Frankling, then gave him a double kiss one upon each cheek and an other upon his forehead. When we went into the room to dine she was placed between the Dr. and Mr. Adams. She carried on the chief of the conversation at dinner, frequently locking her hand into the Drs. and sometimes spreading her Arms upon the Backs of both the Gentlemans Chairs, then throwing her Arm carelessly upon the Drs. Neck.

I should have been greatly astonished at this conduct, if the good Doctor had not told me that in this Lady I should see a genuine French Woman, wholy free from affectation or stifness of behaviour and one of the best women in the world. For this I must take the Drs. word, but I should have set her down for a very bad one altho Sixty years of age and a widow. I own I was highly disgusted and never wish for an acquaintance with any Ladies of this cast. After dinner she threw herself upon a settee where she shew more than her feet. She had a little Lap Dog who was next to the Dr. her favorite. This She kisst and when he wet the floor she wiped it up with her chimise. This is one of the Drs. most intimate Friends, with whom he dines once every week and She with him. She is rich and is my near Neighbour, but I have not yet visited her. Thus my dear you see that Manners differ exceedingly in different Countries. I hope however to find amongst the French Ladies manners more consistant with my Ideas of decency, or I shall be a mere recluse.

From Abigail Adams to Cotton Tufts, 8 September 1784

I dined the other Day with Dr. Franklin who appears to enjoy good Health. There was a Lady present who so cordially embraced him, and repeated it so often, that I think the old Gentleman cannot be averse to the example of King David, for if embraces will tend to prolong his life and promote the vigour of his circulations, he is in a fair way to live the age of an Antediluvian.

From *Adams Family Correspondence*, ed. L. H. Butterfield et al., 9 vols. to date. The Adams Papers, Series II. (Cambridge, MA: Belknap Press of Harvard University Press, 1963-), 1: 320-321; 5: 436-438, 459.

[Two Conversations with Benjamin Franklin, 1777-1778]

Philip Gibbes

The oldest son of Philip and Elizabeth Gibbes, Philip Gibbes (1731–1815) descended from a family that had settled in Barbados during the early seventeenth century. On February 1, 1753, he married Agnes Osborne, the daughter and heiress of Samuel Osborne, another prominent Barbados planter. Together they had two sons and two daughters. In 1774, Gibbes was made a Baronet of Great Britain. He may have met Franklin in London in 1774 or 1775. As a prominent West Indian planter, Gibbes felt trapped by the conflict between Great Britain and the United States. By remaining loyal to the crown, Barbados and the other Sugar Colonies had subjected themselves to the depredations of American privateers. Speaking for many West Indian planters, Gibbes admitted that they felt "innocent and helpless." He was anxious to do whatever he could to reconcile the differences between the Mother Country and the American colonies. To that end, Gibbes traveled from London to Paris in February 1777 to meet Franklin in an attempt to bring American and British negotiators together. Gibbes's initial effort was unsuccessful, but he returned to Paris eleven months later to try again. Franklin was even more adamant the second time. He knew there could be no reconciliation because the United States would insist on independence, which Great Britain refused to concede. Reporting their interview, Franklin told Arthur Lee the gist of what Gibbes had said, which Lee recorded in his diary for January 6, 1778: "The Dr. told him Sir Phil. Gibbes had been there to sound him about propositions of peace, to which he replied we had none to make, the many which congress had made were treated with contempt, and that the dependency of the colonies was gone forever, like the clouds of last year" (1: 374).

A Conversation with Doctor Franklin at Paris on the
5th of February 1777 or Some Days Before

I opened my conversation with Doctor Franklin by saying, "My first visit, Sir, was to the Philosopher and the acquaintance. I shall now address you in another stile. I feel myself so much affected by this unhappy dispute between Great Britain and her Colonies, that I determined to avail myself of the little acquaintance I once had with you, to pray you would indulge me with some conversation on the subject. I know I am not entitled to your confidence; perhaps you may think I am not entitled to your communication. I beg, Sir, at once to set you at ease, by assuring you, that if you should judge it imprudent to answer me, or improper even to hear me, I shall rest satisfied with your caution." The Doctor kept silence, but gave attention: I went on; "Give me leave here to promise, that this visit is not made at the request of, or even in consequence of any communication I have had with any man whatever. I am unconnected, uninfluenced; I feel my[self] independent, and my conduct is directed by my own Ideas of propriety. It has always been my Opinion, that no man is of so little consequence, but that he may be useful, if he will be active. Upon this Occasion I determined not to be restrained by a timid caution from offering myself as an humble instrument, if I can be used, for the general good. I have all the predeliction for America, that is consistent with my attachment to Great Britain. I wish to see peace established upon such constitutional principles, as shall secure the permanent prosperity of both Countries. United, they continue for ever formidable; separated, they soon become weakened." Here I paused. The Doctor continued silent, but I thought attentive. The interval tho' short was awkward. I then proceeded; "The work of reconciliation is become perhaps difficult; but it is far from impracticable. I cannot presume to surmise what terms the King and the Parliament of Great Britain may be inclined to grant to America. But I think I hazard nothing in assuring you, that administration is sincerely disposed to conciliate with America. I know your Abilities Sir; I know your influence in America. You owe it to your country, who confides in you. You owe it to Heaven, to whom you are accountable, to employ all your powers to facilitate a reconciliation. This unfortunate business must be terminated. It must end either in absolute conquest by the Sword, or in an equitable Union by negotiation. The first is too horrible to think of. Let me then beseech you, Sir, to devise the means of making known to Administration the terms, which will satisfy America, or of applying to administration to sollicit the conditions which would be granted to America. I want to see a communication opened. I would by no means undertake to convey any thing directly from you to any person in Administration But if I could engage so much of your confidence as to be entrusted with the great outlines of Reconciliation, I think I could find the means of conveying them to Lord G.G. [George Sackville Germain]." Here Doctor Franklin answered to this effect "I am much afraid Sir, that things are gone too far to admit of reconciliation. I am inclined to think that America would insist upon such terms, as Great Britain would not be disposed to grant." (I pass over the Doctors observations upon the harsh treatment of Great Britain to America, and the respectful conduct of America to Great Britain to a certain period. He concluded with saying) "We know that the King, the Ministry, and the people despise and hate us; that they wish the destruction, the very extirpation of the Americans. Great Britain has injured us too much ever to forgive us. We on our parts can place no confidence in Parliament; for we have no security for their engagements. We delayed the declaration of Independency as long as we hoped for justice from Great Britain. It was the people that called for it long before it was made the Act of Congress. It is made and we must maintain it if we can." Here I begged the Doctor to reflect, "that in cases not immediately within view, the ablest and best of men could only form opinions and take their measures upon the information they received. I wish Sir, said I, that you should be well informed of the sense of the people and the firmness of the Ministry. I speak to you as a man of honour, and tell it you upon the fullest persuasion, that however well inclined Administration may be, it is fixed and determined to prosecute the War with vigour, unless America will submit to reasonable terms. The resolution is taken in conformity with the temper of the people, whose liberal Grants seem to anticipate the demands of the Minister. The ministry and people look to the end, and will not withhold the means. Knowing then the power you have to contend with, Policy, Humanity, and every motive that ought to influence the human mind seem to conspire to direct America to sue for Peace." The Doctor replied, "I am not authorized to treat or to make proposals; besides this is a very improper time. Great Britain is now flushed with the Idea of victories gained in America. With respect to the power we have to contend with, we know it is formidable, but we know how far it can affect us. We have made up our Accounts in which we have stated the loss of all our towns upon the Coasts. We have already reconciled ourselves to that misfortune; but we know it is impossible to penetrate our country. Thither we are resolved to retire, and to wait events, which we trust will be favorable. We expect to be more powerfully attacked the next Campaign; but we know we shall be better prepared for our defence. What we wanted in the last campaign, we shall be fully supplied with in the next. You observed Sir, (he said) that Great Britain and America united were formidable. We feel the advantages, and wish to preserve the continuance of the union, for we know that separated both Countries must become weak; *but there is this difference, Great Britain will always remain weak; America after a time, will grow strong.*" At this pause I rose to take my leave. "I am sorry (I said) I cannot induce you to impart any thing to me, which I may hope to turn to the mutual advantage of the contending parties." He then said, "Tho, Sir, I am not impowered to say or do any thing, I can venture to declare it, as the resolution of America to treat upon no other footing than that of Independency. If Great Britain is disposed to grant Conditions, the proposal of them must come from herself. You may be sure none will ever come from America, after the repeated contempt shewn to her petitions. *A reconciliation founded upon a foederal union of the two Countries may take place.* In that Union, they may engage to make peace and war as one state, and such advantages may be granted to Great Britain in the regulation of commerce as may satisfy her." In my last reply, I took the liberty to say, "I lamented much that Parliament, tenacious of dignity, had refused to receive the demands of America, and lost the happy moment of satisfying them. I hope Sir America pleased with the sound of independency will not prolong the War by a vain struggle for the word. If she can enjoy the advantages without the name, I hope she will learn to be wise and to be satisfied."

[A Second Conversation]

Paris Jany. 5th 1778

2d. Conversation. This day Doctor Franklin came to me by appointment; when a conversation ensued to the following effect.

Sir. P. Gibbes. "I should not be candid, if I did not tell you that I communicated to a person in administration the substance of my former Conversation with you upon the Subject of American affairs. Tho' I have no reason to say it has hitherto produced any effect, I would not be discouraged from requesting another conversation with you upon the same subject. I am going to England. I wish to carry with me the present ideas of America with respect to the terms of peace. Private, nay distant, hints from one party seldom fail to produce an open communication from the other, when conciliation is equally the desire of both. This idea, I trust, will excuse me to you and justify me to my friends in England, that I presume to speak to you upon this important business. I know how far it has extended itself. I know that difficulties to the conclusion will encrease in proportion to the influence, which other powers are allowed to gain in the progress of this unfortunate affair. Permit me then Sir to desire you will consider, as the friend of America, whether you ought not to avail yourself of the offer I now make you of communicating to Administration her present sentiments. I know I presume a great deal in this interference, unauthorized by any man; But where nothing is attempted nothing can be effected. I want to see a communication opened between Great Britain and America."

Docr. Franklin. "I am of Opinion, Sir, it would do harm to communicate, even as matter of private conversation, the expectations of America. Great Britain is making preparations for a vigorous campaign, with the idea of enforcing submission. While she entertains that hope, the terms which America may think just and reasonable, she may call insolent. Proposals from America, intimated even in the manner you suggest might be supposed to arise from apprehension, and might obstruct the ends you seem desirous to promote.

"America is ready to make peace. If Great Britain desires to make peace, let her propose the terms to the Commissioners here; who are impowered to treat. But I will think of the matter and give you my thoughts."

Sir P. G. "You cannot suppose, Sir, that Administration will ever treat formally and openly with Commissioners from the Congress, at a place too, where it is the avowed policy of the people to obstruct negotiation and protract the war. I rather hoped, you would have suggested something that might have induced Administration to offer such terms, as the Generosity of a Great Nation may grant without incurring the imputation of meaness. I never presumed to conceive any mode, by which Great Britain should proceed in order to open a communication with America; But if I might be permitted to indulge the thought I would propose, "That Parliament should pass an Act to authorize the thirteen united provinces to appoint, each, one or two Representatives; who should be the Representative body

[75]

of America. That this body of Representatives should appoint and send Commissioners to London, empowered to conclude a definitive treaty with the Legislature of Great Britain: Or that Great Britain should appoint and send Commissioners to America, vested with the most ample powers, that our Constitution can repose in them to conclude a Peace."

Docr. F. "Great Britain may pass what Acts she pleases. America will not think herself bound to act in conformity to them. Besides, the distance will protract the negotiation. If Great Britain cannot enforce submission she must treat. Why then delay it? If the Ministry have personal objections to the present Commissioners, let them state their objection. If they have an objection to Paris, as the Place of Negotiation, let them name any town in Flanders. But whenever it shall please them to propose terms, it is hoped they will be clear and explicit; nothing concealed to create future discussion. They should be generous. You have expressed it happily. They should be such, and offered in such manner, that all the world may say, they were directed by a noble generosity and not compelled. If you should impart this conversation to your friends in England, it will be proper to acquaint them, *that whatever terms Great Britain may propose will be communicated to France.* We are new at treaty. Advantage may be taken of our incapacity, and it is prudent to consult those upon whose experience and friendship we can depend."

Sir P. G. "I am sorry, I much lament, Sir, that your engagements with France oblige you to submit to her the terms of peace between Great Britain and America."

Docr. Fr. "Do not mistake me. I did not say we should *submit* them to France. I said, distrusting ourselves we should consult France upon the terms that should be proposed by Great Britain. We have not engaged with France to be decided by her Opinion. America considers herself as an independent state, and will decide ultimately for herself. If she approves the terms proposed, she will accept them. I am told Lord North intends to propose something conciliatory. If it be like his former proposition, it will not avail any thing. But terms that come voluntarily, and shew generosity, will do honour to Great Britain and may engage the confidence of America."

Sir P. G. "It will be some satisfaction to me to know that I have faithfully represented our last conversation. I endeavoured to state it with exactness. And hope you will find I have not varied it. I pray you will take the trouble to read it."

Docr. Fr. "It is accurate. But to one part, I must now except. At that time America would have entered into a *federal union* to make peace and war as one Nation. Since then, it has cost her much blood and treasure to defend and strengthen her Independence. I do not imagine she would now enter into such an engagement. Great Britain charges her with ingratitude for the protection she gave her at a Great Expence, in the last war. America does not intend to involve Great Britain in wars, or to share with her in such as she may involve herself in. The system of America is universal commerce with every nation; war with none."

Sir P. G. "Permit me, Sir, to ask you as one personally, and not inconsiderably interested, what is the intention of America with respect to the *Sugar Islands*. They are innocent and helpless. They have given no provocation to America; And yet you have made war upon them, by making Captures of their property, to the injury of all, and the ruin of many of the Planters."

Docr. F. "With respect to the Sugar Islands, when this matter shall be settled, we will trade with them, as with other people. But we will have no other connection with them. If we have taken their property, we have taken it as the property of the Subjects of a Nation, who has made war upon us."

From *The Papers of Benjamin Franklin*, ed. Leonard W. Labaree, et al., 39 vols. to date (New Haven: Yale University Press, 1959-), 23: 281–285; 25: 419–423.

[Extracts from the Journal, 1777]

ARTHUR LEE

Arthur Lee (1740–1792) came from a distinguished Virginia family, several members of which became active in the American Revolution. He took his MD from the University of Edinburgh in 1764 and returned to Virginia to practice medicine. He went back to Great Britain in 1768 to read law. In 1770, he became the London agent for Massachusetts. With the establishment of the Continental Congress, Lee acted as confidential correspondent in London for the Committee of Secret Correspondence of the Continental Congress. Besides these private communiqués, Lee also wrote political articles and pamphlets for a wider audience, the most important being *An Appeal to the Justice and Interests of the People of Great Britain* (1774) and a follow-up work, *Second Appeal* (1775). In 1776, Lee left London for Paris to serve as joint commissioner to negotiate a treaty and solicit aid with Benjamin Franklin and Silas Deane. Though dedicated to the American cause, Lee's contentious nature got him into trouble. He accused Deane of embezzling congressional funds, which resulted in Deane's recall to the United States. Lee also critiqued the way Franklin carried out their commission. Convinced that the American cause was just and right, Lee became frustrated with anyone else who did not think so. He could not understand why the nations of Europe did not instantly side with the United States. Lee grew frustrated with Franklin because his diplomatic approach was more prudent and more patient. Franklin shrewdly understood what Lee had a hard time understanding, that diplomacy takes time, that the nations of Europe had to be courted, persuaded, convinced of the American cause before they would recognize or aid the United States in its war against Great Britain. Congress ultimately resolved to maintain only one minister in France. In 1779, it chose Franklin and recalled Lee.

While in Paris serving as a commissioner, Lee kept a detailed journal, expressing his concerns and complaints about both Deane and Franklin. What follows are two extracts from his journal. The first entry is atypical. It forms a lengthy account of a long conversation he and Franklin had one night. Lee recorded Franklin's conversation using indirect dialogue. It forms a powerful perspective on Franklin's attitude toward the American Revolution, which Franklin recognized as an unprecedented event in the history of man. The second entry, which expresses Lee's dissatisfaction with Franklin, is more typical and serves to represent Lee's journal as a whole.

Carping, contentious, hot tempered, jealous: Lee, it seems, refused to accept what anyone else said without question. In *The Life of Thomas Jefferson* (1837), George Tucker recorded an anecdote illustrating Arthur Lee's disputatious nature: "Dr. Lee, being once caught in a shower of rain in London, sought shelter under a shed, and a gentleman who had joined him, from the same motive, civilly remarking, 'It rains very hard, Sir'—his difficult companion immediately replied, 'It rains hard, Sir; but I don't think you can say it rains very hard'" (1: 180).

[OCTOBER] 25TH. [1777] HAVING SOME CONVERSATION with Dr. F. upon the present state of things, he seemed to agree with me in thinking that France and Spain mistook their interest and opportunity in not making an alliance with us now, when they might have better terms than they could expect hereafter. That it was well for us they left us to work out our own salvation; which the efforts we had hitherto made, and the resources we had opened, gave us the fairest reason to hope we should be able to do. He told me the manner in which the whole of this business had been conducted, was such a miracle in human affairs, that if he had not been in the midst of it, and seen all the movements, he could not have comprehended how it was effected. To comprehend it we must view a whole people for some months without any laws or government at all. In this state their civil governments were to be formed, an army and navy were to be provided by those who had neither a ship of war, a company of soldiers, nor magazines, arms, artillery or ammunition. Alliances were to be formed, for they had none. All this was to be done, not at leisure nor in a time of tranquillity and communication with other nations, but in the face of a most formidable invasion, by the most powerful nation, fully provided with armies, fleets, and all the instruments of destruction, powerfully allied and aided, the commerce with other nations in a great measure stopped up, and every power from whom they could expect to procure arms, artillery, and ammunition, having by the influence of their enemies forbade their subjects to supply them on any pretence whatever. Nor was this all; they had internal opposition to encounter, which alone would seem sufficient to have frustrated all their efforts. The Scotch, who in many places were numerous, were secret or open foes as opportunity offered. The Quakers, a powerful body in Pennsylvania, gave every opposition their art, abilities and influence could suggest. To these were added all those whom contrariety of opinion, tory principles, personal animosities, fear of so dreadful and dubious an undertaking, joined with the artful promises and threats of the enemy rendered open or concealed opposers, or timid neutrals, or lukewarm friends to the proposed revolution. It was, however, formed and established in despite of all these obstacles, with an expedition, energy, wisdom, and success of which most certainly the whole history of human affairs has not, hitherto, given an example. To account for it we must remember that the revolution was not directed by the leaders of faction, but by the opinion and voice of the majority of the people; that the grounds and principles upon which it was formed were known, weighed and approved by every individual of that majority. It was not a tumultuous resolution, but a deliberate system. Consequently, the feebleness, irresolution, and inaction which generally, nay, almost invariably attends and frustrates hasty popular proceedings, did not influence this. On the contrary, every man gave his assistance to execute what he had soberly determined, and the sense of the magnitude and danger of the undertaking served only to quicken their activity, rouse their resources, and animate their exertions. Those who acted in council bestowed their whole thoughts upon the public; those who took the field did, with what weapons, ammunition and accommodation they could procure. In commerce, such profits were offered as tempted the individuals of almost all nations, to break through the prohibition of their governments, and furnish arms and ammunition, for which they received from a people ready to sacrifice every thing to the common cause, a thousand fold. The effects of anarchy were prevented by the influence of public shame, pursuing the man who offered to take a dishonest advantage of the want of law. So little was the effects of this situation felt, that a gentleman, who thought their deliberations on the establishment of a form of government too slow, gave it as his opinion that the people were likely to find out that laws were not necessary, and might therefore be disposed to reject what they proposed, if it were delayed. Dr. Franklin assured me that upon an average he gave twelve hours in the twenty-four to public business. One may conceive what progress must be made from such exertions of such an understanding, aided by the co-operation of a multitude of others upon such business, not of inferior abilities. The consequence was, that in a few months, the governments were established; codes of law were formed, which, for wisdom and justice, are the admiration of all the wise and thinking men in Europe. Ships of war were built, a multitude of cruisers were fitted out, which have done more injury to the British commerce than it ever suffered before. Armies of offence and defence were formed, and kept the field, through all the rigours of winter, in the most rigorous climate. Repeated losses, inevitable in a defensive war, as it soon became, served only to renew exertions that quickly repaired them. The enemy was every where resisted, repulsed, or besieged. On the ocean, in the channel, in their very ports, their ships were taken, and their commerce obstructed. The greatest revolution the world ever saw, is likely to be effected in a few years; and the power that has for centuries made all Europe tremble, assisted by 20,000 German mercenaries, and favoured by the universal concurrence of Europe to prohibit the sale of warlike stores, the sale of prizes, or the admission of the armed vessels of America, will be effectually humbled by those whom she insulted and injured, because she conceived they had neither spirit nor power to resist or revenge it. . . .

[November] 2d. Going to Passy, according to the appointment, I found Mr. Deane had set out for Fontainbleau with Mr. Chaumont, to endeavour to obtain from Mons. Sartine a reversal of the above orders. Dr. F. was to open the letters, and then send them after Mr. D. All this was done without one word of consultation with me, or the least attention to me. Dr. F. mentioned the affair of borrowing money. I told him I could not discover that congress had directed us what to do with the money if we borrowed it; that if it was to be expended by us, it was proper we should give an account first of what had already passed through our hands; that I was very uneasy at being responsible for so great a sum of public money, without being able to obtain any account of its expenditure, which I had repeatedly desired might be made out. He answered it was as much my business as his; why did I not make it out? there was no reason to suspect any misapplication. I replied he had certainly misapprehended me. I had suggested no suspicion, but desired that which was just, reasonable, and absolutely necessary. I appealed to him whether I had ever refused to bear my part in doing business; but to make out an account when I was not possessed of a single paper for the purpose, was not possible. A great deal of the money had been expended in my absence, and almost all without consulting me. In consequence I was utterly incapable of giving any account of the expenditure. He said I had as many papers concerning it as he had; that we had sent an account of the principal articles in our last despatches to congress. I said I could not recollect it. He called for the paper, and it appeared to be only the estimate of what we were to expend, with very little account of what we had spent. He then proposed we should altogether collect the account from Mr. Deane's books. But when, he would not determine, and so that went off like every thing else, unsatisfactorily. We went to Mr. [Ferdinand] Grand's, who showed us a note from Count Vergennes desiring to see him, in consequence of which he set out immediately for Fontainbleau.

From "Extracts from the Journal of Mr. Lee," in *Life of Arthur Lee, LL.D.*, ed. Richard Henry Lee, 2 vols. (Boston: Wells and Lilly, 1829), 1: 343–347.

[Franklin at Passy, 1778]

William Greene

The son of Rufus Greene of Boston, William Greene (*fl.* 1777–1778) left New England for the West Indies in 1777 but was captured by the British and taken to New York. In September 1777, he sailed for London, possibly as a prisoner of war. At some point, he obtained his release and left England for France to await the opportunity to return to America. The second week in May 1778 he had the chance to visit Passy and meet both Benjamin Franklin and John Adams. His diary provides a glimpse into Franklin's social life in France. Greene reveals Franklin's gregarious nature, his friendliness, and his enjoyment of both male and female company. Greene's delightful account of a Sunday visit to Bois de Boulogne confirms Franklin's fondess for the ladies of Paris and shows why John Adams grew impatient with Franklin.

FRIDAY, MAY 8, AS SOON AS dresst we sent to the coffee house for breakfast. A man brought coffee, bread, butter, and cost us sixteen sous each. We then discharged our lodging, at the amazing price of eight livres each for two nights, we took coach to Passy to visit Dr. Franklin and Mr. Adams when we reach'd Passy we called on Mr. [Jonathan Loring] Austin and Mr. P. Amiel. Mr. Austin inform'd us that Mr. Adams was then gone to be presented to the King by Dr. Franklin. This was a great disappointment to us, as we shall have to go again tomorrow, we dined with Mr. Austin and Mr. Amiel after tea Mr. Jos. Waldo, who din'd with us, Mr. Austin, etc. walked towards town, we took the Thuilleries in our way the gardens are very pleasant. After two or three turns, we walked to the Garden Royal from thence home to our new lodgings [for] which we are to give forty two livres per month two chambers etc.

Saturday, May 9, morning we took coach for Passy for which [we] gave six livres, we first waited on Mr. Adams, who receiv'd us very genteelly, but he has not wore off the natural restraint which always was in his behaviour, we tarried with him half an hour, from him we went to Doctor Franklin's apartment, he receiv'd us like children, and behaved to us with all the complaisance and tenderness imaginable, we were above half an hour in free discourse with this venerable man on our departure he desired our company to dinner the next day being Sunday; Doctor Franklin is above the common stature seventy-three years of age with his gray locks, quite fat, in good health, a fine constitution, eats very hearty and enjoys company, in general he is very reserved, but in company, and after dinner, he is free and sociable. Mr. Austin who introduced us, told us after we came out we were much honor'd, for he never see the Doctor so free and conversant before. We intended to wait on Mr. [Arthur] Lee, but his being from home, prevented us. We return'd to town in our coach, we dined at a eating house in St. Honoré. The people knowing we were strangers, cheated us intolerably, the afternoon was imploy'd in strolling about.

Sunday, May 10, after we had dresst ourselves, we set out first for Chaillot on foot, I could not help laughing to think, that we were walking three miles to see the Ambassadors from the United States of America, but as prudence was our guide, we could not afford to coach it. We called on Mr. Lee at Chaillot, his situation is very pleasant, he was in his garden in his morning dress reading. I never see the gentleman before, neither did he know us, we sent in our names, the servant came back and desired us to walk in to the garden. Mr. Lee receiv'd us very kindly, and enter'd into close conversation for near an hour, from thence (after walking till two o'clock) to his Excellency's Dr. Franklin. He was alone reading, after seeting a little, we took a turn in the Doctor's garden. I think it is as fine a situation as I ever see, and most delightful gardens, we were soon join'd by more company, here; we walked till dinner time, some went in and play'd at billiards. Our company were, the Doctor, his nephew a young man about twenty-six, his Excellency John Adams Esq'r, a Mr. Milworth and Lady, Mr. Joseph Waldo, formerly of Boston, now belonging to Bristol in England, Mr. Thomas Brattle, Mr. Loring Austin, a French gentleman, and another stranger I knew not [Francis Coffyn], Mr. M. Joy, Mr. F. Johonnot, Mr. Adams' son [John Quincy Adams], and myself; we had a treat, all was jovial, pleasant and appear'd happy, in the afternoon a number of ladies from the neighbourhood came in, and took us all to walk, in the Bois Boulogne the old Doctor still so fond of the fair sex, that one was not enough for him but he must have one on each side, and all the ladies both old and young were ready to eat him up. On the whole I think him an honor to his

country, and it has been much thro' his means that America has so far succeeded in their Independency.

From "Diary of William Greene, 1778," ed. Worthington Chauncey Ford, *Proceedings of the Massachusetts Historical Society* 14 (1920): 103–104.

[Franklin at Passy, 1783]

John Baynes

When his friend Samuel Romilly (1757–1818) began planning a trip to France and Switzerland in 1783, John Baynes (1758–1787) jumped at the chance to accompany him. The two had been good friends ever since reading law together at Gray's Inn. Baynes, an award-winning student, had previously attended Trinity College, Cambridge, where he took his BA in 1777, being elected to a Trinity fellowship in 1779. It was at Cambridge that he met Dr. John Jebb, a fellow of Peterhouse and a prominent political reformer. Since Jebb had become acquainted with Franklin, Baynes asked him for a letter of introduction. Jebb complied. In his letter, he assured Franklin of Baynes's "virtuous attachment to the cause of freedom," calling him "a sincere admirer of your character and virtues" (*Papers* 40: u210). Romilly was pleased with his choice of traveling companion. Baynes's positive attitude and pleasant conversation made the journey a treat. Baynes was especially pleased with the opportunity to meet Franklin. Romilly, who accompanied him on his first visit to Passy on August 27, 1783, was also impressed. Romilly remembered:

> Dr. Franklin was indulgent enough to converse a good deal with us, whom he observed to be young men very desirous of improving by his conversation. Of all the celebrated persons whom, in my life, I have chanced to see, Dr. Franklin, both from his appearance and his conversation, seemed to me the most remarkable. His venerable patriarchal appearance, the simplicity of his manner and language, and the novelty of his observations, at least the novelty of them at that time to me, impressed me with an opinion of him as of one of the most extraordinary men that ever existed. (*Memoirs*, 1: 50)

Romilly continued on to Switzerland, but Baynes lingered in Paris, mainly to spend more time with Franklin. He paid several more visits to Passy in September and October. Baynes's journal contains one of the fullest records of Franklin's personal life in Paris.

WEDNESDAY, AUGUST 27. HIRED A COACH for the day, and went to visit the ambassador ([George Montagu,] the Duke of Manchester), who received me very politely; asked me to dine on Friday. From thence I went to Passy (a pleasant town, two miles from Paris, and on the Seine) to present Dr. Jebb's letter to Dr. Franklin. Mr. Romilly went with me, having inquired most particularly into the propriety of his going, and finding that there would be nothing improper. His house is delightfully situated, and seems very spacious; and he seemed to have a great number of domestics. We sent up the letter, and were then shown up into his bedchamber, where he sat in his nightgown, his feet wrapped up in flannels and resting on a pillow, he having for three or four days been much afflicted with the gout and the gravel. He first inquired particularly after Dr. Jebb, which led us to the subject of parliamentary reformation. I mentioned that Dr. Jebb was for having every man vote: he said he thought Dr. Jebb was right, as the all of one man was as dear to him as the all of another. Afterwards, however, he seemed to qualify this by expressing his approbation of the American system, which excludes minors, servants, and others, who are liable to undue influence. He said that he much doubted whether a parliamentary reform at present would have the desired effect; that we had been much too tender in our economical reform, — that offices ought never to be accompanied with such salaries as will make them the objects of desire. In support of this he read the 36th article of the Pennsylvania Constitution (a most wise and salutary rule). He mentioned the absurd manner in which the *Courrier de l'Europe* had spoken of General Washington's resignation and retirement, as if it were a dissolution of the original compact: he said that the General was an officer appointed by the state, and no integral part of the constitution, and that his retirement could affect the state no more than a constable, or other executive officer, going out of office. I observed how some of our papers had affected to depreciate his motives in retiring, and added that I should always suppose a man to act from good motives till I saw cause to think otherwise. "Yes," said he, "so would every honest man"; and then he took an opportunity of reprobating the maxim that all men were equally corrupt. "And yet," said Mr. Romilly, "that was the favourite maxim of Lord North's Administration." Dr. Franklin observed that such men might hold such opinions with some degree of reason, judging from themselves and the persons they knew: "A man," added he, "who has seen nothing but hospitals, must naturally have a poor opinion of the health of mankind."

Mr. Romilly asked as to the slave-trade in America, whether it was likely to be abolished? He answered that in several states it now did not exist; that in Pennsylvania effective measures were taken for suppressing it; and that, if it had not been for the Board of Trade, he believed it would have been abolished everywhere. To that board he attributed all our misfortunes, the old members corrupting the young ones.

He seemed equally liberal in religious and in political opinions. The excellence of the constitution of Massachusetts in point of religious liberty being mentioned, he observed that they had always shown themselves equally so; that the land was originally granted out to them subject to the payment of a small sum for the support of a presbyterian minister; that, many years ago, on the application of persons of other religions, they agreed that the sum actually paid by any congregation should go to its own minister, whatever was his persuasion. This was certainly a great act of liberality, because they were not bound to do it in point even of justice, the annual payment being in fact the price or rent of the land. He mentioned his having had a conversation with Lord Bristol ([Frederick Augustus Hervey,] the Bishop of Derry [Church of Ireland]) on a similar subject; that the Bishop said he had long had in hand a work for the purpose of freeing Roman Catholics from their present state, and giving them a similar indulgence. "And pray, my Lord, while your hand is in, do extend your plan to dissenters, who are clearly within all the reasons of the rule." His Lordship was astonished—no—he saw some distinction or other, which he could not easily explain. In fact, the revenue of his Lordship would have suffered considerable diminution by suffering dissenters to pay their tithes to their own pastors. He reprobated the statute of Henry VI. for limiting votes to forty-shilling freeholders, and observed that the very next statute in the book was an act full of oppression upon poor artificers.

He conversed with greater freedom and openness than I had any right to expect, which I impute partly to Dr. Jebb's friendly letter, partly to his own disposition. I never enjoyed so much pleasure in my life as in the present conversation with this great and good character. He looked very well, notwithstanding his illness; and, as usual, wore his spectacles, which made him very like a small print I have seen of him in England. He desired us on taking leave to come and visit him again, which we resolved to do. . . .

Monday, September 1. Mr. S. R. left me and set off for Geneva or Lausanne with M. Gautier in a cabriolet or single-horse chair. I never parted with any man more unwillingly; for, besides his excellent disposition, he has such a fund of information on all subjects of importance as must make his company an object of the first consequence. He asked me repeatedly to write to him, which I promised to do.

Monday, September 15. Called on Lieutenant Hernon, and walked with him as far as the *Barrière de la Conference*, on the way to Passy. He left me there, and I proceeded to Dr. Franklin's house. On entering, a confounded Swiss servant told me to go up stairs and I should meet with domestics. I went up, but not a domestic was there; I returned and told him there was nobody. He then walked up with me, and pointing to the room before me told me I might enter and I should find his master alone. I desired him to announce me. "Oh! Monsieur, ce n'est pas nécessaire; entrez, entrez"; on which I proceeded, and, rapping at the door, I perceived that I had disturbed the old man from a sleep he had been taking on a sofa. My confusion was inexpressible. However, he soon relieved me from it, saying that he had risen early that morning, and that the heat of the weather had made a little rest not unacceptable; and desiring me to sit down. He inquired if I had heard from Dr. Jebb. I then showed him an excellent letter which I had just received from him, containing some noble sentiments on the American war, with which he seemed much pleased. The letter contained some sentiments on the American religious constitution, particularly noticing the liberality of that of Massachusetts Bay. Dr. Franklin observed that, notwithstanding its excellence, he thought there was one fault in it: that when the government of that colony had, thirty or forty years ago, upon the application of the dissenters, permitted them to apply their portion of the sum raised for religious purposes to the use of their own minister (as he had mentioned in his former conversation), the Quakers likewise applied for a total exemption from this burden upon this ground, that they did, one among another, *gratis*, the same duties as the other sects paid a duty for performing. "The government," said he, "considered their case and exempted them from the burden, the person claiming an exemption being obliged to produce a certificate from the meeting that he was really *bonâ fide* one of that persuasion. The *present* constitution of Massachusetts Bay does not appear to me to make any provision of this sort in favour of Quakers. Now I own I think this a fault; for if their regulations, one among another, be such that they answer the ends of a minister, I see no good reason why they should be obliged to contribute to a useless expense. We find the Quakers to be as orderly and as good subjects as any other religious sect whatever; and indeed," said he, "in one respect I think their mode of instruction has the advantage; for it is always delivered in language adapted to the audience, and consequently is perfectly intelligible. I remember once in England being at a church near Lord Despencer's with his Lordship, who told me that the clergyman was a very sensible young man, to whom he had just given the living. His sermon was a sensible discourse and in elegant language; but notwithstanding this, I could not perceive that the audience seemed at all struck with it. The Quakers in general attend to some plain sensible man of their sect, whose discourse they all understand. I therefore rather incline to doubt of the necessity of having teachers, or ministers, for the express purpose of instructing the people in their religious duties.

"All this is equally applicable to the law: the Quakers have no lawsuits except such as are determined at their own meetings; there is an appeal from the monthly to the annual meeting. All is done without expense, and nobody grumbles at the trouble of deciding. In fact, the honour of being listened to as a preacher, or of presiding to decide lawsuits, is in itself sufficient. A salary only tends to diminish the honour of the office; and this, if considered, will tend to support the doctrine, held in the Pennsylvania constitutions, which I mentioned to you in our last conversation. Persons will play at chess, by the hour, without being paid for it; this you may see in every coffee-house in Paris. Deciding causes is in fact only a matter of amusement to sensible men."

I mentioned the mode in France of buying seats in the Parliament for the purpose of ennobling themselves. He observed that that very practice would confirm the ideas he had just thrown out. Here a *bourgeois* gives a sum of money for his seat in Parliament as a *conseiller*. The fees of his office do not bring him in 3 per cent., or at least not more. Therefore for the *noblesse* or honour which his seat gives him, he pays two-fifths of the price of the office, and at the same time gives up his labour without any recompense.

In the course of our conversation I asked if they did not still imprison for debt in America? He answered that they did; but he expressed his disapprobation of this usage in very strong terms. He said he could not compare any sum of money with imprisonment—they were not commensurable quantities. Nobody, however, in America who possessed a freehold (and almost everybody had a freehold) could be arrested on mesne process. He inclined to think that all these sorts of methods to compel payment were very impolitic — some people indeed think that credit and consequently commerce would be diminished if such means were not permitted, but he said that he could not think that the diminution of credit was an evil, for that the commerce which arose from credit was in a great measure detrimental to a state. . . .

He mentioned one instance to show how unnecessary such compulsory means were, and he seemed to think that it would be better if there were no legal means of compelling the payment of debts of a certain magnitude. In the interval between the declaration of independence and the formation of the code of laws in America, there was no method of compelling payment of debts, yet, notwithstanding this, the debts were paid as regularly as ever; and if any man had refused to pay a just debt because he was not legally compellable, he durst not have shown his face in the streets. Dr. Jebb having requested me to inquire if there were any good political tracts or pamphlets, I took the liberty to ask if he knew any. He told me that there were a good many upon one particular subject, which had been fully discussed, but which was little known in England as yet. Of these he said one might make a little library. The subject was on the giving information to the public on matters of finance. The books in question had given rise to a set of persons or to a sect called economists, who held that if the people were well informed on matters of finance, it would be unnecessary to use force to compel the raising of money; that the taxes might be too great — so great as in fact to diminish the revenue — for that a farmer should have at the end of the year not only wherewith to pay his rent and to subsist his family, but also enough to defray the expense of the sowing, &c. &c., of next year's crop; otherwise, if the taxes are so high as to prevent this, part of his land must remain unsown, and consequently the crop which is the subject of taxation be diminished, and the taxes of course must suffer the same fate. Some of their principles, he observed, were perhaps not quite tenable. However, the subject was discussed thoroughly. The Marquis de Mirabeau was said to be the author of the system. Dr. Franklin waited on him, but he assured him that he was not the author originally — that the founder was a Dr. Chenelle, or Quenelle [i.e., François Quesnay]. The Marquis introduced Dr. Franklin to him, but he could not make much out of him, having rather an obscure mode of expressing himself.

He said that he was acquainted with an Abbé [Morellet] now abroad, but who would return in a fortnight or so, and who would give him a list of the principal pamphlets on both sides.

I then left him, and he desired me to call from time to time during my stay at Paris. . . .

Tuesday, September 23. Walked to Passy to see Dr. Franklin, but took care to make the servant announce me regularly. Found him with some American gentlemen and ladies, who were conversing upon American commerce, in which the ladies joined. On their departure I was much pleased to see the old man attend them down stairs and hand the ladies to their carriage. On his return I expressed my pleasure in hearing the Americans, and even the ladies, converse entirely upon commerce. He said that it was so throughout the country: not an idle man, and consequently not a poor man, was to be found.

In speaking of American politics, I mentioned Dr. Jebb's sentiments on the famous vote of the House of Commons which put an end to the American war; that he disapproved of the terms of the resolution, which was, on the face of it, founded on our being the better able to combat France, and which therefore could not be very agreeable to America. "Certainly not," said he; "I trust we shall never forget our obligations to France, or prove ungrateful." "You are at so great a distance," said I, "from the European powers, that there does not seem much probability of your quarrelling with any of them unless on account of Canada or the West Indies." He said that he hoped they would keep themselves out of European politics as much as possible, and that they should make a point of adhering to their treaties.

In the course of this conversation, I mentioned the shameful neglect of treaties which so much prevailed at present; the great injustice of several of our own wars, and the triviality of the avowed cause of others. I likewise mentioned Dr. [Richard] Price's plan for a general peace in Europe. He observed that nothing could be more disgraceful than the scandalous inattention to treaties, which appeared in almost every manifesto; and that he thought the world would grow wiser, and wars become less frequent. But he observed that the plans which he had seen for this purpose were in general impracticable in this respect, viz. that they supposed a general agreement among the sovereigns of Europe to send delegates to a particular place. Now though perhaps two or three of them might be willing to come into this measure, it is improbable and next to impossible that all, or even a majority of them, would do it. "But," said he, "if they would have patience, I think they might accomplish it, some way in this manner: — Two or three sovereigns might agree upon an alliance against all aggressors, and agree to refer all disputes between each other to some third person or set of men, or power. Other nations, seeing the advantage of this, would gradually accede; and, perhaps, in 150 or 200 years, all Europe would be included. I will, however," continued he, "mention one plan to you, which came to me in rather an extraordinary manner, and which seems to me to contain some very sensible remarks. In the course of last year, a man very shabbily dressed [Pierre-André Gargaz] — all his dress together was not worth 5s. — came and desired to see me. He was admitted, and, on asking his business, he told me that he had walked from one of the remotest provinces in France, for the purpose of seeing me and showing me a plan which he had formed for a universal and perpetual peace. I took his plan and read it, and found it to contain much good sense. I desired him to print it. He said he had no money: so I printed it for him. He took as many copies as he wished for, and gave several away; but no notice whatever was taken of it." He then went into a closet and brought a copy of this plan, which he gave me. I took the liberty to remind him of his list of books, which he promised not to forget, saying the Abbé was now with Lord Shelburne in Holland.

N.B. — He this day expressed his opinion that in England the executive power might be maintained without all the expense which at present seems to be esteemed so necessary for its establishment. . . .

Thursday, Oct. 2. Walked with M. Hernon to Passy. Called upon Dr. Franklin, who showed me an Irish newspaper he had just received, containing the noble and spirited resolutions of the delegates of the Ulster volunteers at Dungannon, in which they appointed a grand national convention at Dublin. He expressed his sentiments very strongly that they would carry their point; and that, if parliament would not execute their plan of reform, they would drop the parliament and execute it of themselves. On my asking his opinion of our hopes of success in England, he said he feared we were too corrupt a nation to carry the point. "I have not patience," said he, "to read even your newspapers; they are full of nothing but robberies, murders, and executions: and when a nation once comes to that, nothing short of absolute government can keep it in order."

In speaking of the Irish-volunteers I took the liberty of mentioning (what seemed to me an omission in the constitution of America) the want of any sufficient armed force. He said they had a militia who met and exercised five or six days in a year. I objected the smallness of the time, and their serving by substitutes, and in support of personal service mentioned Andrew Fletcher's opinion.

He seemed to think the objections of no great weight, "for," said he, "America is not, like any European power, surrounded by others, every one of which keeps an immense standing army; therefore she is not liable to attacks from her neighbours — at least, if attacked she is on an equal footing with the aggressor; and if attacked by any distant power, she will always have time to form an army. Could she possibly be in a worse situation than at the beginning of this war, and could we have had better success?"

Insensibly we began to converse on standing armies, and he seeming to express an opinion that this system might some time or other be abolished, I took the liberty to ask him in what manner he thought it could be abolished; that at present a compact among the powers of Europe seemed the only way, for one or two powers singly and without the rest would never do it; and that even a compact did not seem likely ever to take place, because a standing army seemed necessary to support an absolute government, of which there were many in Europe. "That is very true," said he; "I admit that if one power singly were to reduce their standing army, it would be instantly overrun by other nations; but yet I think that there is one effect of a standing army, which must in time be felt in such a manner as to bring about the total abolition of the system." On my asking what the effect was to which he alluded, he said he thought they diminished not only the population, but even the breed and the size of the human species. "For," said he, "the army in this and every other country is in fact the flower of the nation — all the most vigorous, stout, and well-made men in a kingdom are to be found in the army. These men in general never marry."

I mentioned to him that in England, our military establishment not being so large, we did not as yet feel these effects, but that the multiplication of the species was dreadfully retarded by other causes, viz.: — 1. Our habits of luxury, which make us fancy that a young man is ruined if he marry early, nobody ever thinking of retrenching their expenses; and 2. Our absurd laws, *e.g.* the Marriage Act and the law of descents, which gives all to the eldest son, whereby younger sons are generally excluded.

"Yes," said he, "I have observed that myself in England. I remember dining at a nobleman's house where they were speaking of a distant relation of his who was prevented from marrying a lady, whom he loved, by the smallness of their fortunes: everybody was lamenting their hard situation, when I took the liberty to ask the amount of their fortunes. 'Why,' said a gentleman near me, 'all they can raise between them will scarce be 40,000*l.*' I was astonished: however, on recollecting myself, I suggested that 40,000*l.* was a pretty handsome fortune; that it would, by being vested in the Three per Cents., bring in 1200*l.* a year. 'And pray, Sir, consider, what is 1200*l.* a year? There is my lord's carriage and my lady's carriage, &c. &c.' So he ran up 1200*l.* in a moment. I did not attempt to confute him; but only added, that notwithstanding all he had said, if he would give me the 40,000*l.*, I would endow 400 American girls with it, every one of whom should be esteemed a fortune in her own country. As to the custom of giving the eldest son more than the others, we have not actually been able to get entirely rid of it in America. The eldest son in Massachusetts has, without either rhyme or reason, a share more than any of the rest. I remember before I was a member of the Assembly, when I was clerk to it, the question was fully agitated. Some were for having the eldest son to have the extraordinary share; others were for giving it to the youngest son, which seemed indeed the most reasonable, as he was the most likely to want his education, which the others might probably have already had from their father. After three days' debate, it was left as it stood before, viz. that the eldest son should have a share more."

I observed that this was the Jewish law of descent. He asked if it was to be found among Moses' laws? I answered that it was. Upon which he said, it was remarkable that he had not seen or heard of it before; "but," said he, "the mention of Moses' laws reminds me of one which always struck me as very extraordinary; and I do not remember an instance where it appears to have been carried into execution — I mean the law prohibiting the alienation of land for a longer time than from Jubilee to Jubilee, *i.e.* for 50 years. This must evidently have been intended to prevent accumulation of landed property, but it seems very difficult to execute; indeed, in one respect, it is perhaps impolitic, for it must necessarily follow that the land will be run out at the end of the term."

"That," said I, "will always be the case even at the end of a fourteen or seven years' lease, and it seems a difficult thing to determine how long a lease in prudence and justice ought to be; these long leases throw too much into the power of the tenant, and in leases from year to year the tenant is too dependent." "That very thing," replied he, "convinces me that no man should cultivate any land but his own. I rather am of opinion that land at present is of too high a value throughout these parts of the world. I was reading the other day some accounts of China, sent over by two young Chinese, who were educated here at the expense of government, and sent into their own country again. They were desired to send over minute accounts of every thing relative to that country, and several volumes have been published already. In the last of these I find that they allow a very high interest on money, (about 30 per cent.,) and it struck me that it was a politic measure, for the consequence would be that no person would be desirous of having a large quantity of land, which therefore must be the more equally divided. All laws for keeping the landed property exactly equal are impracticable on account of the fluctuating state of population; and where at the first the property is equal, if alienation be allowed it will very soon be unequal again. Antigua was at first divided into lots of ten acres; it is not an ancient colony. I remember hearing one who was a very old man when I was a very young one, observe that he recollected there being a great number of ten-acre men in the island, and yet that when he spoke there was hardly a ten-acre man to be met with. At this time I do not believe there is one remaining." I mentioned to him my intention of leaving Paris in ten days: he said he expected his Abbé in less than that time. . . .

Sunday, October 12. Walked to Passy to call on Dr. Franklin. Found him with two French gentlemen, conversing on the subject of the *ballon*. Dr. Franklin said he had subscribed to another *ballon*, and that one of the conditions of the subscription was that a man should be sent up along with it. The gentlemen did not stay long. After they were gone our conversation turned chiefly on the state of the arts here and in other countries, particularly printing and engraving. He admitted that we had one or two artists superior to any French engravers, but he seemed to think the art in much higher perfection here than in England. He showed some engravings (coloured in the engraving) of birds, &c., for Buffon's *Natural History*, which were wonderfully finely executed. I cannot, however, think that they can execute a large print so finely as we do in England. I have never seen a large print engraved here which had not a sort of coarseness not to be found in Bartolozzi. Their small designs, vignettes, &c., are beautiful, both in design and execution.

He showed me, among other specimens of printing, the Spanish Don Quixote, in 5 vols. 4to., which for elegance of typography and engraving equals anything I ever saw except the translation of Sallust by Don Gabriel, the second son of the King of Spain. . . .

I mentioned to him Howard's book on Prisons [John Howard, *The State of the Prisons in England and Wales*], as one of our best printed books. He said he had never seen it; I promised to send it to him.

In the course of conversation he again expressed his doubts of our success in accomplishing a parliamentary reform, and repeated his opinion that we had been too tender of places and pensions: he said that these were in general, either directly or indirectly, the objects of coming into Parliament. This he confirmed by an instance taken from America, where he said that he had sat in the Assembly 12 years and had never solicited a single vote; that this was not peculiar to him — hundreds had done the same; that the office of an Assembly-man was looked upon as an office of trouble, and that you perpetually saw the papers filled with advertisements requesting to decline the honour. And to show that the salary is the thing which makes the office desirable, the Sheriffs place is always sought for by a number of candidates. Anciently when the office of sheriff was instituted in America, the fees were fixed at rather too small a rate to make a sufficient salary, there being then very few writs: the fees were therefore increased; but since that time the number of lawsuits having increased, the salary is increased so much as to make the office an object of desire. He seemed to express a fear that the spirit of the Pennsylvania constitution was not in this instance perfectly kept up; however, he said if he ever went into America, he would endeavour to diminish the sheriff's salary. He therefore strongly recommended us to persist in the present economical reform, as that would at all events save us from ruin, by taking away the object at which most men at present aim who seek a seat in Parliament.

I asked if the Abbé was yet arrived. "Upon my word," said he, "I had actually forgot your list. The Abbé is arrived, and he was one of the gentlemen who were with me when you came in. But I will write him a note to request he will send you the list of books you wish to have." I promised to send him word when I intended to set off, as he wished to send a letter or two by me to England.

Wednesday, Oct. 15. Not being able to get a place for Rouen sooner, engaged one for Friday night. Dr. Franklin having expressed a wish to read *Mason's English Garden*, I sent it to him to-day, with a letter of thanks for his politeness. He returned a most obliging answer.

[97]

Thursday, Oct. 16. Called on M. l'Abbé Morellet, at Dr. Franklin's instance, to get my list, but he was in the country.

Oct. 17. Called again, but he was still in the country; therefore I was at last disappointed of my list.

From "Extracts from Mr. Baynes's Journal," in *Memoirs of the Life of Sir Samuel Romilly*, 3d ed., 2 vols. (London: John Murray, 1841), 1: 447–458.

[This Venerable Nestor of America, 1785]

ANDREW ELLICOTT

Like many ambitious scientific men who established their careers in the 1780s, Andrew Ellicott (1754–1820) was eager to meet Benjamin Franklin. Though nearly a half century younger than the old sage, Ellicott had much in common with him. Ellicott excelled at mathematics and astronomy, talents that helped him edit *The United States Almanack*. An excellent surveyor, Ellicott surveyed the boundary between Virginia and Pennsylvania west of the unfinished Mason and Dixon Line in 1784. In the coming years, he was commissioned to make several other important surveys. He surveyed Pennsylvania's western boundary in 1785, its northern boundary in 1786, and the islands in the Ohio and Allegheny rivers in 1788.

Ellicott's friendship with Philadelphia's most famous astronomer-mathematician, David Rittenhouse, gave him a way to make Franklin's acquaintance. Rittenhouse escorted Ellicott to Franklin Court the evening of Thursday, December 1, 1785. The next night, Ellicott attended a meeting of the American Philosophical Society, where he heard a paper Franklin wrote and a proposal submitted by Jean-Hyacinthe de Magellan. Franklin apparently enjoyed the young man's company well enough to invite him back to Franklin Court on Sunday to spend the day. Ellicott arrived Sunday morning soon after breakfast and stayed until nine that night, obviously thrilled with the opportunity to get to know Benjamin Franklin.

DECEMBER 1ST 1785. . . . SPENT THE EVENING with my Friend David Rittenhouse at the celebrated Dr. Benjamin Franklins the present Governour of this State—the old Gentleman tho infirm in body possesses the former Vigour of his mind—

2. This Evening attended the Meeting of our Philosophical Society we had a proposal of Dr. Magellans laid before us; it was a donation of 200 Guineas with a condition that 10£ yearly should be paid as a prize to the person who should make the best Improvement in Natural Philosophy or Navigation (Natural History excepted) we had likewise a long Paper of Dr. Franklins read proposing some improvements in Navigation—

3. Rainy continued at my Friend D. Rittenhouses —

4. Immediately after brakefast I went by perticular Invitation to spend the Day with Dr. Franklin — I found him in his little Room Among his Papers — he received me very politely and immediately entered into conversation about the Western Country — his Room makes a Singular Appearance, being filled with old philosophical Instruments, Papers, Boxes, Tables, and Stools — About 10 O Clock he sat some water on the fire and not being expert through his great age I desired him to give me the pleasure of assisting him, he thanked me and replied that he ever made it a point to wait upon himself and although he began to find himself infirm he was determined not to encrease his Infirmities by giving way to them — After his water was hot I observed his Object was to shave himself which Operation he performed without a Glass and with great expedition — I Asked him if he never employed a Barber he answered, "no" and continued nearly in the following words "I think happiness does not consist so much in perticular pieces of good fortune that perhaps accidentally fall to a Mans Lot as to be able in his old age to do those little things which was he unable to perform himself would be done by others with a sparing hand — " Several Foreigners of Distinction dined with us — About 9 O Clock in the Evening I took my leave of this Venerable Nestor of America.

From *Andrew Ellicott: His Life and Letters*, ed. Catharine Van Cortlandt Mathews (New York: Grafton Press, 1908), pp. 50–51.

[The Wisdom and Experience of Mellow Old Age, 1785–1789, 1805, 1806]

BENJAMIN RUSH

Born in rural Pennsylvania just outside of Philadelphia, Benjamin Rush (1746–1813) traveled to Edinburgh to study medicine in the 1760s. During his time in Great Britain, he became acquainted with Franklin and even dedicated to him his medical dissertation, *De coctione ciborum in ventriculo* (Wolf and Hayes, no. 2964). In the late 1760s Rush returned to Philadelphia, where he established a thriving medical practice and ultimately became one of the most well-respected American physicians of the eighteenth century. He also became active in Revolutionary politics. In the summer of 1776, he and Franklin briefly served together in the Continental Congress; both were signers of the Declaration of Independence. When Franklin returned from Paris in 1785, Rush tried to spend as much time with him as he could. Regardless of his distinguished medical career, Rush understood that he still had much to learn from Franklin, even when it came to the subject of medicine. Rush frequently dined with him, listening attentively to what he said and recording their conversations in his diary and occasionally his correspondence. Rush appreciated Franklin's humorous anecdotes and general wisdom. In his discussions with Rush and others, Franklin drew on a lifetime of experience. Active in the anti-slavery movement, he was elected president of the Pennsylvania Society for Promoting the Abolition of Slavery. As he and Rush discussed the issue of abolition, Franklin recalled a book he had published in 1737, nearly a half century earlier, Benjamin Lay's *All Slave-Keepers That Keep the Innocent in Bondage* (Miller, no. 134). Always one to shape his anecdotes to suit both audience and situation, Franklin also related many tidbits of medical knowledge he had gleaned from personal experience in his talks with Rush, who wrote some of them down in his notes and his correspondence. Other anecdotes he noted briefly but developed later as part of either *Medical Inquiries and Observations* (1794–1798; second ed., 1805) or *Essays, Literary, Moral and Philosophical* (1798; 2d ed., 1806).

Conversations with Dr. Franklin

1785. — Dined with the Dr. with Dr. [David] Ramsay, Mr. [David] Ritten-house, Mr. Littlepage, 'Littlepage's Salutation,' etc. He [Franklin] said the foundation of the American revolution was laid in 1733, by a clause in a bill to subject the Colonies to being gov'd by Royal instructions which was rejected. He said in 1756, when he went to England, he had a long conversa-tion with Mr. [Charles] Pratt (afterwards Lord Camden) who told him that Britain would drive the colonies to independance. This he said first led him to realise its occurring shortly.

1786 Augt. — I waited on the Dr. with a Dr. [Walter] Minto. He said he believed that Tobacco would in a few years go out of use. That, about 30 years ago, when he went to England, Smoking was universal in taverns, coffe-houses, and private families, but that it was now generally laid aside, that the use of Snuff, from being universal in France, was become unfash-ionable among genteel people, no person of fashion under 30 years of age now snuffed in France. He added that, Sir John Pringle and he had ob-served that tremors of the hands were more frequent in France than else-where, and probably from the excessive use of Snuff. They once saw in a company of 16 but two persons who had not these tremors at a table in France. He said Sir John was cured of a tremor by leaving off Snuff. He concluded that there was no great advantage in using Tobacco in any way, for that he had kept company with persons who used it all his life, and no one had ever advised him to use it. The Dr. in the 81st year of his age de-clared he had never snuffed, chewed, or smoked.

Septem'r 23rd. — Three persons who don't care how little they get for their money, waited upon the Dr. with Mr Bee. He [Franklin] said he believed the Accts. of the plague in Turkey were exaggerated. He once conversed with a Dr. MacKensie who had resided 38 years at Constanti-nople, who told him there were *five* plagues in that town. The plague of the drugger-men or interpreters, who spread false stories of the prevalence of the plague in Order to drive foreign ministers into the country, in order that they might enjoy a little leisure. 2. The plague of debtors, who when dunned, looked out of their windows, and told their creditors, not to come in for the plague is in their houses. 3. The plague of the Doctors, for as they are never paid for their Attendance on such patients as die, Unless it be with the plague, they make most of *fatal* diseases the plague. The Dr.

forgot the other two. He added that Dr. MacKensie upon hearing that 660 dead with the plague, were carried out of one of the gates daily, had the curiosity to stand by that gate for one whole day, and counted only 66.

1786 Sepr. — Waited upon the Dr. with Mr R[ichard]. Stockton, he told us that in 1723, people went to market with cut silver, those who had it not, procured provisions by taking the country people to two Stalls in the market, and giving them goods for them, which goods were charged to their Acct's. and paid for once or twice a year. He added that, it would be an advantage to our country for the Europeans to be the carriers of our produce for many years, for as they could not afford to lye long in our ports, they must always sell 10 percent, lower and buy 10 percent, higher than our own merchants, product of German Industry.

Octbr 1. — Dined with the Dr., with Mr. Bee, Dr. Minto, Dr. [Adam] Kuhn, etc. He [Franklin] said interest was 3 percent per month, for 10 months in China, or 30 percent per anm., which promoted industry, kept down the price of land, and made freeholds more common. Upon another occasion he said that *Credit* produced Idleness and vice, and he wished that all debts should like debts of honor or game Debts be irrecoverable by law. He added this day that in the last 30 years of his life, he had never enjoyed better health, than at present.

Octobr 12. — Waited on him with Dr. [Charles] Nisbet. He observed that by raising the ear with his hand, he heard better than without it, and still better if he formed a concave with his hand round his ear. He spoke in high terms of the game of Chess.

1787 May 3rd. — Drank tea with Dr. F., he spoke in high terms ag'st. negro Slavery, and said he printed a book 40 years ago written by *Ben. Lay* ag'st. it, w'ch. tho' confused, contained just tho'ts and good sense, but in bad order.

April. — Dined with Dr. He spoke of the talkativeness of the French nation, and told a story of the Abbe Raynal, who was a great talker, who came into a company where a French man talked so long and so incessantly that, he could not get in a word. At last he cried out "il e pendu, si il crache." "He is lost, if he spits." His grandson told another story of a Frenchman, who was dining, complaining to his companions that their noise kept him from tasting his Victuals.

1788 April 19th. — Spent half an hour wth Dr. F. in his library. "He observed that a man lost 10 percent on the *value*, by lending his books; that he once knew a man who never returned a borrowed book, because no one ever returned books borrowed from him." He condemned the *foreign* commerce of the United States, and observed that the greatest part of the trade of the World, was carried on for Luxuries most of which were really injurious to health or Society, such as *tea, tobacco, Rum, Sugar,* and *negro Slaves.* He added, "when I read the advertisements in our papers of imported goods for sale, I think of the Speech of a philosopher upon walking thro' a fair, "how happy am I that I want none of these things."

Sepr 22. — Waited upon Dr. Franklin with Doctor Thibou, of Antigua. The Dr. said few but quacks ever made money by physic, and that no bill drawn upon the credulity of the people of London by quacks, was ever protested. He ascribed the success of quacks partly to patients extolling the efficacy of the remedies they took from them, rather than confess their ignorance and credulity, hence it was justly said, "quacks were the greatest lyers in the world, except their patients." He told two stories, the one of a Jew who had peculated in the French army, being told when under confinement that he would be hanged, to wch. the Jew answered, "who ever heard of a man being hanged worth 200,000 livres," and he accordingly escaped. The Judges in Mexico being ordered to prosecute a man for peculation, found him innocent, for wch. they said, "they were sorry both for his own, and their sakes."

British Commissary. Story of ears more faithful than eyes. He added further, that in riding thro' New Eng'd. he overtook a post Rider that was once a shoemaker, and fell into consumption, but upon riding two years as a post in all weathers, between New York, and Connecticut river (140 miles), he recovered perfectly, upon which he returned to his old business, but upon finding a return of his consumption, he rode post again, in which business he continued in good health 30 years. He said that he could have *purchased* the independance of America at 1/10 of the money expended in defending it; such was the venality of the British Court.

Nov. — Spend half an hour with Dr. in company with the Revd. Mr. Bisset and Mr. Goldsborough. He said Sir John Pringle once told him 92 fevers out of 100 cured themselves, 4 were cured by Art, and 4 proved fatal.

About the end of this month, I saw him alone. He talked of Climates; I borrowed some hints from this Conversation for the essay on Climates ["An Account of the Climate of Pennsylvania and Its Influence upon the Human Body"].

1789. June 12th. — Had a long conversation with him on the Latin and Greek languages. He called them the "quackery of literature." He spent only abt. a year at a Latin School, when between 8 and 9 years of Age. At 33, he learned French, after this Italian and Spanish wch. led him to learn Latin wch. he acquired with great ease. He highly approved of learning Geography in early life, and said that he had taught himself it, when a boy, while his father was at prayers, by looking over four large maps which hung in his father's parlour.

From Benjamin Rush to Richard Price, 25 May 1786

Our venerable friend Dr. Franklin continues to enjoy as much health and spirits as are compatible with his time of his life. I dined with him a few days ago in a most agreeable circle where he appeared as chearful and gay as a young man of five and twenty. But his conversation was full of the wisdom and experience of mellow old age. He has destroyed party rage in our State, or to borrow an allusion from one of his discoveries, his presence and advice, like oil upon troubled waters, have composed the contending waves of faction which for so many years agitated the State of Pennsylvania.

From Benjamin Rush to Richard Price, 27 October 1786

Our venerable friend Dr. Franklin has found considerable benefit from the use of the remedy you recommended to him, joined with the blackberry jam. He informed me a few days ago that he had not enjoyed better health for the last 30 years of his life than he does at present. His faculties are still in their full vigor. He amuses himself daily in superintending two or three houses which he is building in the neighbourhood of his dwelling house. One of them is for a printing office for his grandson [Benjamin Franklin Bache], a promising youth who was educated by him in France.

From *Medical Inquiries and Observations* (1805)

Impressions made upon the *ears* of old people, excite sensation and reflection much quicker than when they are made upon their eyes. Mr. Hutton informed me; that he had frequently met his sons in the street without knowing them, until they had spoken to him. Dr. Franklin informed me, that he recognized his friends, after a long absence from them, first by their voices. This fact does not contradict the common opinion, upon the subject of memory, for the recollection, in these instances, is the effect of what is called reminiscence, which differs from memory in being excited only by the renewal of the impression which at first produced the idea which is revived. . . .

The ancient Romans prolonged life by retiring to Naples, as soon as they felt the infirmities of age coming upon them. The aged Portuguese imitate them, by approaching the warm sun of Brazil, in South-America. But heat may be applied to the torpid bodies of old people artificially. 1st. By means of the *warm bath*. Dr. Franklin owed much of the cheerfulness and general vigour of body and mind which characterised his old age, to his regular use of this remedy. It disposed him to sleep, and even produced a respite from the pain of the stone, with which he was afflicted during the last years of his life.

From *Essays, Literary, Moral, and Philosophical* (1806)

In the numerous and frequent disorders of the breast, which occur in all countries, where the body is exposed to a variable temperature of weather, sugar affords the basis of many agreeable remedies. It is useful in weaknesses, and acrid defluxions upon other parts of the body. Many facts might be adduced in favour of this assertion. I shall mention only one, which from the venerable name of the person, Whose case furnished it, cannot fail of commanding attention and credit. Upon my enquiring of Dr. Franklin, at the request of a friend, about a year before he died, whether he had found any relief from the pain of the stone, from the Blackberry-Jam, of which he took large quantities, he told me that he had, but that he believed the medicinal part of the jam, resided wholly in the sugar, and as a reason for thinking so, he added, that he often found the same relief, by taking about half a pint of a syrup, prepared by boiling a little brown sugar in water, just before he Went to bed, that he did from a dose of opium. It has been supposed by some of the early physicians of our country, that the sugar obtained from the maple tree, is more medicinal, than that obtained from the West-India sugar cane, but this opinion I believe is without foundation. It is preferrable in its qualities to the West-India sugar only from its superior cleanliness. . . .

He [Benjamin Lay] wrote a small treatise upon negro-slavery, which he brought to Dr. Franklin to be printed. Upon looking over it, the Doctor told him that it was not paged, and that there appeared to be no order or arrangement in it. "It is no matter said Mr. Lay — print any part thou pleasest first." This book contained many pious sentiments, and strong expressions against negro slavery; but even the address and skill of Dr. Franklin were not sufficient to connect its different parts together, so as to render it an agreeable or useful work.

From "Conversations with Dr. Franklin," *Pennsylvania Magazine of History and Biography* 29 (1905): 23–30.

From *Letters to and from Richard Price, D.D., F.R.S., 1767–1790.* (Cambridge, MA: Harvard University Press, 1903), pp. 85, 95.

From Benjamin Rush, *Medical Inquiries and Observations*, 4 vols., 2d ed. (Philadelphia: J. Conrad, 1805), 1: 437, 449.

From Benjamin Rush, *Essays, Literary, Moral and Philosophical*, 2d ed. (Philadelphia: Thomas and William Bradford, 1806), pp. 284, 299.

[My Dinner with Franklin, 1786]

Winthrop Sargent

After a distinguished military career during the Revolutionary War, Winthrop Sargent (1753–1820) turned his attention to surveying. Congress appointed him surveyor of the Northwest Territory. In 1786, he became a prominent shareholder in the Ohio Company of the United States, which sought to develop land north of the Ohio River in southeastern Ohio. Besides being the Ohio Company's largest shareholder, Sargent was also its secretary. The last week of June 1786 he stopped by Philadelphia on his way to survey land north of the Ohio River.

Through much of his life, Sargent kept a detailed diary, the source of the following passage. He was an excellent observer with a good sense of the material culture. Recording his dinner with Franklin, Sargent even mentioned their simple fare: beer and russet potatoes. Afterward Franklin showed his guest some engraved prints: a commonplace after-dinner activity within well-to-do eighteenth-century families. As their conversation turned to more intellectual topics, Franklin gave Sargent a tour of his library. As he often did, Franklin located a volume ideally suited to his guest's interests, *Connoissance des temps* (Wolf-Hayes, no. 701), a compendium of astronomical and meteorological calculations that the learned astronomer Jérôme de La Lande compiled for the Académie Royale des Sciences.

PASS'D THE WHOLE of the 29th [of June] in Philadelphia and dined with his Excellency President [of Pennsylvania] Franklin. This dignified Character [who] is distinguished in the literary and political world is very much the Object of my Wonder and Admiration. He is now advanced beyond four Score and yet seems perfectly in full Exercise of all his mental Abilities. His Perception is quick and Memory very retentive. From Appearances I should suppose him to enjoy uninterrupted Health and great Vigour of Body for his advanced Life. Our Meal was frugal, but his Excellency indulged as to Quantity, drinking only of Beer and very small Russets. We were alone excepting a Daughter (Mrs Beech [Sarah Franklin Bache]) and two Women from the Country which indulged me with the Opportunity of engrossing him altogether. I found him conversible, communicative *enough*, easy in his Manners and affording all those Attentions which could in Reason be demanded from his Time of Life and Station. He indulged me with the Sight of several Prints executed in Europe, amongst which were General Washington's and that of John Paul Jones — both masterly finished, and [Franklin] was so very obliging as upon my mentioning the Difficulty of procuring a nautical Ephemeris (without knowing him to be possess'd of those Calculations) as to take me to his Library and put into my Hands the *Connoissance des temps* done in Paris.

From *The Winthrop Sargent Papers*, ed. Frederick S. Allis, Roy Bartolomei, and Benjamin Harrison Pershing, 7 reels (Boston: Massachusetts Historical Society, 1965), reel 1, frame 115.

[A Visit to Franklin Court, 1787]

Manasseh Cutler

The Reverend Dr. Manasseh Cutler (1742–1823) was an ardent patriot, having served as chaplain to the American forces in Massachusetts during the late 1770s. After the war he turned his interests toward botany, compiling the first systematic compendium of New England flora. Cutler's "Account of Some of the Vegetable Productions, Naturally Growing in This Part of America" appeared in the first volume of *Memoirs of the American Academy of Arts and Sciences* (1785). Franklin had a copy of this volume in his library (Wolf-Hayes no. 102), which Cutler had the opportunity to see when he visited Franklin Court in 1787. Imagine his excitement upon seeing the volume containing his most important scientific accomplishment in Franklin's personal library. Earlier Cutler had learned from Benjamin Rush that he and Franklin discussed Cutler's article and thought that the *Columbian Magazine* should publish extracts from Cutler's article as a way of disseminating his information further. Cutler's botanical research demonstrates his keen eye for detail, a skill that worked to describe contemporary material culture, as well. Cutler's description of this 1787 meeting in his journal constitutes the fullest contemporary description of Franklin's Philadelphia library. The reference to a friend going to the Ohio country Cutler makes at the beginning of this account indicates where his future interests would lie. A prominent member of the Ohio Company of Associates, a group established to promote the settlement of the Northwest Territory, Cutler strongly encouraged New Englanders to emigrate to Ohio in *An Explanation of the Map . . . of the Federal Lands* (1787). Published the same year he visited Franklin, Cutler's *Explanation* echoes the promotional rhetoric of Franklin's *Information to Those Who Would Remove to America* (1784). Franklin's friends John Vaughan and Elbridge Gerry accompanied Cutler to Franklin Court. Franklin had known Gerry since 1776, when both signed the Declaration of Independence. Gerry was in Philadelphia at this time attending the Constitutional Convention. So was Franklin.

OUR NEXT CALL WAS on Mr. John Vaughan, son of Samuel Vaughan, Esq., and the brother of my friends, Charles and Samuel Vaughan. I had letters to the old gentleman, but, very unfortunately for me, he was gone on a journey into the Ohio country. The young gentleman, however, received me with every expression of warmest friendship, urged me to take lodgings with him, and dismissed all business, to devote himself to me. He mentioned his brothers having often spoken of their acquaintance with me, and was acquainted with the correspondence which his brother Samuel and I had continued from our first acquaintance. He is not married, and, since his mother and sisters went to London in the spring with his brother Samuel, he and his father keep bachelors' hall in a very elegant home in fore street. He is in a very large circle of trade, in partnership with another young gentleman. I informed him of my engagement to go with Mr. Gerry to Dr. Franklin's, and that the hour was then arrived. He could not be denied the pleasure, he said, of going with us, for Dr. Franklin he considered as his father, having lived a number of years with him, and the two families were so strongly connected that they considered themselves as one and the same.

When we came to Mr. Gerry's, he was waiting for us; but, as he supposed we had time enough, and feeling myself much fatigued, we sat about half an hour. There were two young ladies by the name of Hamlinton on a visit to Mr. Gerry. They were dressed very rich indeed, but were entirely sociable and agreeable. Mr. Vaughan took a large share in the conversation, and, with his easy and natural pleasantry, kept us in a burst of laughter. I knew that Mr. Vaughan was not acquainted with Mr. Gerry. I therefore introduced him, which Mr. Gerry likewise did to his lady and the company. But I immediately supposed the young ladies, from his instant and free sociability, were of his most intimate acquaintance. He appeared to me to know every thing about them and every body else that was mentioned in the course of the conversation. But, on our way to Dr. Franklin's, he asked me if those young ladies were of my acquaintance, and what were their names, for they had slipped his memory. This excited my astonishment. I asked him if he had never seen them before. He said no, and he was sure they did not belong to Philadelphia, or he certainly should have had some knowledge of them. Mr. Gerry informed us they were from New York, and of Mrs. Gerry's particular acquaintance. What advantages are derived from a finished education and the best of company! How does it banish that awkward stiffness, so common when strangers meet in company! How does it engage the most perfect strangers in all the freedom of an easy and pleasing sociability, common only to the most intimate friends!

Dr. Franklin lives in Market Street, between Second and Third Streets, but his house stands up a court-yard at some distance from the street. We found him in his Garden, sitting upon a grass plat under a very large Mulberry, with several other gentlemen and two or three ladies. There was no curiosity in Philadelphia which I felt so anxious to see as this great man, who has been the wonder of Europe as well as the glory of America. But a man who stood first in the literary world, and had spent so many years in the Courts of Kings, particularly in the refined Court of France, I conceived would not be of very easy access, and must certainly have much of the air of grandeur and majesty about him. Common folks must expect only to gaze at him at a distance, and answer such questions as he might please to ask. In short, when I entered his house, I felt as if I was going to be introduced to the presence of an European Monarch. But how were my ideas changed, when I saw a short, fat, trunched old man in a plain Quaker dress, bald pate, and short white locks, sitting without his hat under the tree, and, as Mr. Gerry introduced me, rose from his chair, took me by the hand, expressed his joy to see me, welcomed me to the city, and begged me to seat myself close to him. His voice was low, but his countenance open, frank, and pleasing. He instantly reminded me of old Captain Cummings, for he is nearly of his pitch, and no more of the air of superiority about him. I delivered him my letters. After he had read them, he took me again by the hand, and, with the usual compliments, introduced me to the other gentlemen of the company, who were most of them members of the Convention. Here we entered into a free conversation, and spent our time most agreeably until it was dark. The tea-table was spread under the tree, and Mrs. Bache, a very gross and rather homely lady, who is the only daughter of the Doctor and lives with him, served it out to the company. She had three of her children about her, over whom she seemed to have no kind of command, but who appeared to be excessively fond of their Grandpapa. The Doctor showed me a curiosity he had just received, and with which he was much pleased. It was a snake with two heads, preserved in a large vial. It was taken near the confluence of the Schuylkill with the Delaware, about four miles from this city. It was about ten inches long, well proportioned, the heads perfect, and united to the body about one-fourth of an inch below the extremities of the jaws. The snake was of a dark brown, approaching to black, and the back beautifully speckled (if beauty can be applied to a snake) with white; the belly was rather checkered with a reddish color and white. The Doctor supposed it to be full grown, which I think appears probable, and thinks it must be a *sui generis* of that class of animals. He grounds his opinion of its not being an extraordinary production, but a distinct genus, on the perfect form of the snake, the probability of its being of some age, and there having been found a snake entirely similar (of which the Doctor has a drawing, which he showed us) near Lake Champlain, in the time of the late war. The Doctor mentioned the situation of this snake, if it was traveling among bushes, and one head should choose to go on one side of the stem of a bush and the other head should prefer the other side, and that neither of the heads would consent to come back or give way to the other. He was then going to mention a humorous matter that had that day taken place in Convention, in consequence of his comparing the snake to America, for he seemed to forget that every thing in Convention was to be kept a profound secret; but the secrecy of Convention matters was suggested to him, which stopped him, and deprived me of the story he was going to tell. After it was dark, we went into the house, and the Doctor invited me into his library, which is likewise his study. It is a very large chamber, and high studded. The walls were covered with book-shelves filled with books; besides, there are four large alcoves, extending two-thirds of the length of the Chamber, filled in the same manner. I presume this is the largest, and by far the best, private library in America. He showed us a glass machine for exhibiting the circulation of the blood in the arteries and veins of the human body. The circulation is exhibited by the passing of a red fluid from a reservoir into numerous capillary tubes of glass, ramified in every direction, and then returning in similar tubes to the reservoir, which was done with great velocity, without any power to act visibly on the fluid, and had the appearance of perpetual motion. Another great curiosity was a rolling press, for taking the copies of letters or any other writing. A sheet of paper is completely copied in less than two minutes, the copy as fair as the original, and without effacing it in the smallest degree. It is an invention of his own, and extremely useful in many situations in life. He also showed us his long artificial arm and hand, for taking down and putting books up on high shelves which are out of reach; and his great armed chair, with rockers, and a large fan placed over it, with which he fans himself, keeps off flies, etc., while he sits reading, with only a small motion of his foot; and many other curiosities and inventions, all his own, but of lesser note. Over his mantel-tree, he has a prodigious number of medals, busts, and casts in wax or plaster of Paris, which are the effigies of the most noted characters in Europe. But what the Doctor wished principally to show to me was a huge volume on Botany, and which, indeed, afforded me the greatest pleasure of any one thing in his library. It was a single volume, but so large that it was with great difficulty that the Doctor was able to raise it from a low shelf and lift it on to the table; but with that senile ambition common to old people, he insisted on doing it himself, and would permit no person to assist him, merely to show us how much strength he had remaining. It contained the whole of Linnieus Systima Vegetabilia, with large cuts of every plant, and colored from nature. It was a feast to me, and the Doctor seemed to enjoy it as well as myself. We spent a couple of hours in examining this volume, while the other gentlemen amused themselves with other matters. The Doctor is not a Botanist, but lamented that he did not in early life attend to this science. He delights in natural history, and expressed an earnest wish that I would pursue the plan I had begun, and hoped this science, so much neglected in America, would be pursued with as much ardor here as it is now in every part of Europe. I wanted for three months at least to have devoted myself entirely to this one volume. But fearing I should be tedious to the Doctor, I shut up the volume, though he urged me to examine it longer. The Doctor seemed extremely fond, through the course of the visit, of dwelling on Philosophical subjects, and particularly that of natural History, while the other Gentlemen were swallowed up with politics. This was a favorable circumstance to me, for almost the whole of his conversation was addressed to me; and I was highly delighted with the extensive knowledge he appeared to have of every subject, the brightness of his memory, and clearness and vivacity of all his mental faculties. Notwithstanding his age (eighty-four), his manners are perfectly easy, and every thing about him seems to diffuse an unrestrained freedom and happiness. He has an incessant vein of humor, accompanied with an uncommon vivacity, which seems as natural and involuntary as his breathing. He urged me to call on him again, but my short tarry would not admit. We took our leave at ten, and I retired to my lodgings.

From *Life, Journals and Correspondence of Rev. Manasseh Cutler, LL.D.*, ed. William Parker Cutler and Julia Perkins Cutler, 2 vols. (Cincinnati: Robert Clarke, 1888), 1: 265–270.

[Franklin during the Constitutional Convention, 1787]

James Madison

Over the course of his political career, James Madison (1751–1836) gradually rose to prominence through a succession of positions that provided him with a strong basis in parliamentary procedure and a vast knowledge of governance. He was a delegate to the 1776 Virginia Convention, a member of the Virginia Assembly, the Virginia Governor's Council, and delegate to the Continental Congress. Franklin was in France when Madison came on the national political scene in 1780 as a delegate to the Continental Congress, in which capacity he served through 1783 and again in 1787–1788. The two men came together in 1787 when both served in the Constitutional Convention at Philadelphia. Madison's experience with Franklin during the Constitutional Convention resembles Jefferson's experience with him during the Continental Congress. Both were impressed with Franklin's wit, his calm, and his ability to summon an appropriate anecdote to suit the situation. The following record of Madison's interaction with Franklin shows that the old sage and this young whippersnapper shared many important ideas.

Detached Memoranda: Doctor Franklin

I did not become acquainted with Dr. Franklin till after his return from France and election to the Chief Magistracy of Pennsylvania. During the Session of the Grand Convention, of which he was a member and as long after as he lived, I had opportunities of enjoying much of his conversation, which was always a feast to me. I never passed half an hour in his company without hearing some observation or anicdote worth remembering.

Among those which I have often repeated, and can therefore be sure that my memory accurately retains, are the following. Previous to the Convention, and whilst the States were seeking by their respective regulations, to enlarge as much as possible their share of the general commerce, the

Dr. alluding to their jealousies and competitions remarked that it would be best for all of them to let the trade be free, in which case it would level itself, and leave to each its proper share. These contests he said, put him in mind of what had once passed between a little boy and little girl eating milk and bread out of the same bowl, "Brother," cried the little girl, "eat on your side, you get more than your share."

In the Convention, the difference of opinions was often very great, and it occasionally happened that the votes of the States were equally divided, and the questions undecided. On a particular day, when several subjects of great importance were successively discussed, and great diversity of opinions expressed, it happened that on each of them this was the case; so that nothing was done through the whole day and appearances were not a little discouraging, as to a successful issue to the undertaking. After the adjournment, the Doctor observed to several of us who were near him in allusion to the poor sample which had been given, of human reason that there was on board a ship in which he once crossed the Atlantic, a man who had from his birth been without the sense of smelling. On sitting down to dinner one day one of the men, cut off a piece of beef, and putting it to his nose cried out, this beef stinks. The one next to him, cutting and smelling a piece, said not at all, it is as sweet as any meat I ever smelt. A third passing a piece across his nose several times; stinks, says he, no, I believe not: yes, I believe it does, repeating the opposite opinions as often as he made the trial. The same doubts and contrarieties went round as the company, one after the other, expressed their opinions. Now, gentlemen, exclaimed the man, without the sense of smelling, I am satisfied of what I have long suspected, that what you call smelling has no existence, and that it is nothing but mere fancy and prejudice. . . .

In a conversation with him one day whilst he was confined to his bed, the subject of religion with its various dotrines and modes happening to turn up, the Dr. remarked that he should be glad to see an experiment made of a religion that admitted of no pardon for trangressions; the hope of impunity being the great encouragement to them. In illustration of this tendency, he said that when he was a young man he was much subject to fits of indigestion brought on by indulgence at the table. On complaining of it to a friend, he recommended as a remedy a few drops of oil of wormwood, whenever that happened; and that he should carry a little viol of it about him. On trial he said he found the remedy to answer, and then said he, having my absolution in my pocket, I went on sinning more freely than ever.

[117]

On entering his chamber in his extreme age when he had been much exhausted by pain and was particularly sensible of his weakness, Mr. M. said he, these machines of ours however admirably formed will not last always. Mine I find is just worn out. It must have been an uncommonly good one I observed to last so long, especially under the painful malady which had co-operated with age in preying on it; adding that I could not but hope that he was yet to remain some time with us, and that the cause of his suffering might wear out faster than his Constitution. The only alleviation he said to his pain was opium, and that he found as yet to be a pretty sure one. I told him I took for granted he used it as sparingly as possible as frequent doses must otherwise impair his constitutional strength. He was well aware he said that every Dose he took had that effect; but he had no other remedy; and thought the best terms he could make with his complaint was to give up a part of his remaining life, for the greater ease of the rest.

From "Debates in the Federal Convention"

The Constitution being signed by all the members, except Mr. [Edmund] Randolph, Mr. [George] Mason and Mr. [Elbridge] Gerry, who declined giving it the sanction of their names, the Convention dissolved itself by an adjournment sine die.

Whilst the last members were signing, Doctor Franklin, looking towards the President's chair, at the back of which a rising sun happened to be painted, observed to a few members near him, that painters had found it difficult to distinguish in their art, a rising, from a setting, sun. I have, said he, often and often, in the course of the session, and the vicissitudes of my hopes and fears as to its issue, looked at that behind the President, without being able to tell whether it was rising or setting: but now at length, I have the happiness to know, that it is a rising, and not a setting sun.

From "Madison's 'Detached Memoranda,'" ed. Elizabeth Fleet, *William and Mary Quarterly*, 3d ser., 3 (1946): 536–539.

From Henry D. Gilpin, ed., *The Papers of James Madison*, 3 vols. (Washington: Langtree and O'Sullivan, 1840), 3: 1624.

"Closing Scenes of Dr. Franklin's Life: In a Letter from an Eye-Witness" (1790)

Mary Stevenson Hewson

When Franklin came to London in 1757, he found lodgings with a widow named Margaret Stevenson on Craven Street, where he became a mentor to her bright, scientifically inclined daughter Mary Stevenson (1734–1795) or Polly as she was known to friends and family. Franklin helped Polly with her studies and occasionally loaned her books. He liked her well enough to imagine her as his daughter-in-law, but William Franklin's marriage to another dashed his father's hopes. Nonetheless, Mary Stevenson remained a lifelong friend. In 1770, she married William Hewson, a physican and lecturer. When she gave birth to their son William, Benjamin Franklin became the boy's godfather. Sadly, Hewson wounded himself while dissecting a corpse, contracted septicemia, and died in May 1774, four months before the birth of their third child. On Franklin's advice, she and her three children later left England for America. Settling in Philadelphia with them, Mary Hewson stayed near her friend and mentor to comfort him at the end of his life and subsequently wrote this account of the experience in a letter dated May 5, 1790, to "Mr. Viny," an old London friend. Her recipient is usually identified as Thomas Viny, but the address on Blackfriar's Road makes John Viny a likelier possibility: John Viny's renowned wheel manufactory was located on Blackfriar's Road. Regardless, Mary Stevenson's devotion to Benjamin Franklin shows clearly throughout the letter.

THOUGH I AM ALMOST EXHAUSTED with writing letters, I will not let this opportunity pass without one for my friends at Blackfriars.

As bad news flies swift, if it is important, I suppose my letter will not be the first information you will have of Dr. Franklin's death. Yes, we have lost that valued, that venerable, kind friend, whose knowledge enlightened our minds, and whose philanthropy warmed our hearts. But we have the consolation to think, that if a life well spent in acts of universal benevolence to mankind, a grateful acknowledgment of Divine favour, a patient submission under severe chastisement, and an humble trust in Almighty mercy, can insure the happiness of a future state, our present loss is his gain. I was the faithful witness of the closing scene, which he sustained with that calm fortitude which characterized him through life. No repining, no peevish expression ever escaped him, during a confinement of two years, in which, I believe, if every moment of ease could be added together, the sum would not amount to two whole months. When the pain was not too violent to be amused, he employed himself with his books, his pen, or in conversation with his friend; and upon every occasion displayed the clearness of his intellect and the cheerfulness of his temper. Even when the intervals from pain were so short that his words were frequently interrupted, I have known him hold a discourse in a sublime strain of piety. I say this to you because I know it will give you pleasure; for what but piety, which includes charity, can we carry into a future state of happiness? "Whether there be tongues, they shall fail, whether there be knowledge, it shall vanish away"; but love to God and to his creatures, which is certainly what the apostle meant by charity, "never faileth."

I never shall forget one day that I passed with our friend last summer. I found him in bed in great agony, but when that agony abated a little, I asked if I should read to him; he said, Yes; and the first book I met with was [Samuel] Johnson's *Lives of the Poets*. I read the life of Watts, who was a favourite author with Dr. F.; and, instead of lulling him to sleep, it roused him to a display of the powers of his memory and his reason; he repeated several of [Isaac] Watts's Lyric Poems, and descanted upon their sublimity in a strain worthy of them and of their pious author. It is natural for us to wish that an attention to some ceremonies had accompanied that religion of the heart which I am convinced Dr. F. always possessed; but let us who feel the benefit of them continue to practise them, without thinking lightly of that piety which could support pain without a murmur, and meet death without terror.

I will not apologize for filling my paper with this subject, I could not find one more interesting. The public transactions of his life, and the honours paid to his memory, you will hear by other means.

"Closing Scenes of Dr. Franklin's Life: In a Letter from an Eye-Witness," *Monthly Repository* 16 (January 1821): 3–4.

"Short Account of Dr. Franklin's Last Illness by His Attending Physician" (1790)

John Jones

John Jones (1729–1791) studied medicine in colonial America before traveling overseas and continuing his study in Great Britain and France, ultimately
taking his MD at the University of Rheims in 1751. Returning to America, he
established a medical practice in New York in 1752. His private practice, com-
bined with experience as a surgeon during the French and Indian War, established his reputation, which continued to grow throughout his life. In 1767, he
created the department of medicine at Kings College (later, Columbia University) and became its first professor of surgery. He also helped organize
the New York Hospital and published the first American textbook on surgery,
Plain, Concise, Practical Remarks on the Treatment of Wounds and Fractures
(1775). With the outbreak of the Revolutionary War, he helped organize the
medical department of the Continental Army, but the occupation of New York
by British troops forced Jones from the city. He settled in Philadelphia in 1779.
He was elected a physician of the Pennsylvania Hospital, which Benjamin
Franklin had established three decades earlier. During Franklin's final year in
Paris, Jones wrote him to suggest the possibility of establishing sanitary bathing facilities in Philadelphia, which would offer different types of bathing, including "Russian vapour baths," a method of bathing Franklin had alluded to
many years earlier in *An Account of the New Invented Pennsylvanian Fire-Places*
(1744). Franklin appreciated Jones's wide-ranging, public-minded efforts,
and the two became friends upon his return to Philadelphia. Jones attended
Franklin in his final illness and was present at his death on April 17, 1790.

THE STONE, WITH WHICH he had been afflicted for several years, had for
the last twelve months, confined him chiefly to his bed; and during the
extremely-painful paroxysms, he was obliged to take large doses of laudanum to mitigate his tortures. Still, in the intervals of pain, he not only
amused himself with reading and conversing chearfully with his family, and

a few friends, who visited him, but was often employed in doing business of a public as well as private nature, with various persons, who waited on him for that purpose; and in every instance displayed, not only the readiness and disposition to do good, which were the distinguishing characteristic of his life, but the fullest and clearest possession of his uncommon mental abilities: he not unfrequently indulged himself in those *jeux d'esprit* and entertaining anecdotes, which were the delight of all who heard him.

About sixteen days before his death, he was seized with a feverish indisposition, without any particular symptoms attending it, till the third or fourth day, when he complained of a pain in his left breast, which increased till it became extremely acute, attended with a cough and laborious breathing. During this state when the severity of his pains drew forth a groan of complaint, he would observe, that he was afraid he did not bear them as he ought, acknowledged his grateful sense of the many blessings he had received from that Supreme Being, who had raised him, from small and low beginnings to such high rank and consideration among men: and made no doubt, his present afflictions were kindly intended to wean him from a world, in which he was no longer fit to act the part assigned him. In this frame of body and mind he continued till five days before his death, when his pain and difficulty of breathing entirely left him: and his family were flattering themselves with the hopes of his recovery, when an imposthumation, which had formed itself in his lungs, suddenly burst, and discharged a great quantity of matter, which he continued to throw up, while he had sufficient strength to do it, but, as that failed, the organs of respiration became gradually oppressed — a calm lethargic state succeeded — and, on the 17th instant, about eleven o'clock at night, he quietly expired, closing a long and useful life of eighty-four years and three months.

It may not be amiss to add to the above account, that Dr. Franklin, in the year 1735, had had a severe pleurisy, which terminated in an abscess of the left lobe of his lungs: and he was then almost suffocated with the quantity and suddenness of the discharge. A second attack of a similar nature had happened some years after this, from which he soon recovered, and did not appear to suffer any inconvenience in his respiration from these diseases.

"Short Account of Dr. Franklin's Last Illness by His Attending Physician," *American Museum* 7 (May 1790): 266.

On Franklin (1800)

LOUIS LEFEBVRE DE LA ROCHE

Louis Lefebvre de La Roche (1738–1806) is remembered nowadays, if at all, as the editor of Helvétius's and Montesquieu's complete works, published in 1795. Helvétius had left him all his papers, an index of his trust and friendship, but Lefebvre de La Roche did not serve him well, as he shortened some of the works, and even forged some letters of Helvétius to Montesquieu. The son of a farmer, he became a Benedictine monk because that was the best way to cultivate his intellectual inclinations; he was ordained in 1764, becoming a secular priest in 1769, thanks to connections of Helvétius's in Rome. Some verses which he wrote as a young man make it clear he was an unbeliever and bored by all things religious. He was happy to give up the priesthood in 1790, describing religion as "superstition" to the Revolutionary Committee that interviewed him.

He moved into Mme. Helvétius's house in 1775 at the latest, having often stayed with the Helvétiuses since becoming acquainted with M. Helvetius around 1769. M. Helvétius left him a life annuity, to which were added his emoluments as chaplain to the Comte d'Artois at his mansion at Maisons. At Auteuil he undertook to prepare Helvétius's manuscripts for publication. He became mayor of Auteuil in 1791, but withdrew from political life in 1793, after the defeat to the Girondins, who were moderate republicans. He was then arrested and released only after the fall of Robespierre in July 1794. He later became a supporter of Bonaparte.

During Franklin's stay in Passy, Lefebvre de La Roche would often correct what he wrote in French; after Franklin's return to America, they corresponded until Franklin's death. Lefebvre de La Roche wrote the following essay as a letter to the printer Pierre Didot, who was considering a selected edition of Franklin's works, to which he planned to append some of Franklin's characteristic anecdotes. Didot's edition never materialized, and Lefebvre de La Roche's essay remained in manuscript until 1950, when Gilbert Chinard published it in a contribution to the *Proceedings of the American Philosophical Society*. It appears in English for the first time here.

YOU PROPOSE, DEAR FRIEND, TO PRINT a selection of moral pamphlets by Franklin, with the addition of those episodes of his life best able to characterize his personality and his genius. His printed *Memoirs*, and his Eulogy delivered by Condorcet at the Académie des Sciences would provide a great many such episodes. But you believe that my connection with this great man during his stay in France may have enabled me to become privy to certain facts which, though apparently slight, have had, from his own admission, the deepest influence on his personality and on the conduct of his life. The most trivial facts in the history of a famous man become most interesting when they trigger new ideas which, all of a sudden, change the course of his will. Those slight events deserve examination. They often make up the first steps in our education. They would remain ignored if, from the eminence one reaches, one did not look back reflectively on the obscure point from which one started.

I will not say much about what one has already read or may read elsewhere. I will only advert to those facts which may give the thoughtful occasion to reflect on the nature of those inconsiderable causes which, even from childhood, help to shape the personality of an extraordinary man. Those people will enjoy understanding what brought about in Franklin the concatenation of thoughts and actions, the willpower, which enabled him to overcome the obstacles to the growth of his physical and moral faculties.

He was born from needy parents in a new country where the demands of everyday life made manual work a necessity, leaving little time for the cultivation of the mind. Boston, his native town, was then only the meeting-place of a few seamen and adventurers from Europe. Some of the useful arts had barely appeared there. There was no library nor any public seminaries of education. Religious quacks preached absurd dogmas and a fanatical morality, and all the vices of superstitious ignorance were obstacles to the progress of enlightenment. In this eclipse of reason, much resolution is required, when all means are lacking both to enlighten one's mind and to fend off widely accepted errors. The Bible was the only known book and few settlers could do so much as read it.

Young Franklin, a workman in a printing house, could teach himself only from broadsheets and *The Spectator*. And those he had to read stealthily, without his parents' knowledge, and during his hours of rest. After some chance reading of a volume by Plutarch expounding the uses of animal flesh, he decided to give up meat, struck as he had been by the argument of that writer. At table, a family friend who saw him eating fruit and vegetables only asked his mother: "Why does not your child eat meat? It appears, she answered, that he read this in some mad old philosopher."

The slight sarcasm in that remark glanced off him. He only gave up his abstinence after seeing that many large fish fed off smaller ones. He saw in that instinct of living creatures the harsh law which subjects the weaker ones to the sway of the stronger or the defter. He would tell his friends that this observation had early determined him to elude, to the best of his abilities, the amoral force which keeps men under the yoke of despotism; and that he was thenceforth concerned with becoming free, with shaking off false needs and increasing his knowledge and an industry which would make him less dependent. "To be useful to others, he said, and to depend on them as little as possible is to get closer to the perfection of that omnipotent being who is good to everyone and needs no-one." That maxim of an ancient philosopher [Socrates] was to guide him throughout his life.

As a Minister Plenipotentiary of the Republic, in his old age, he only needed one servant. And him he did not use much. He had noticed that with two servants, one really only had half-a-one, and with three, none at all.

Being used to doing everything himself, gifted with a singular cleverness acquired through practice, in a country deprived of all the learned arts of Europe, he needed, in order to make his fine discoveries about electricity, to devise and to make the necessary instruments, which required those tools he called his hands. With much art he simplified those instruments by fitting them for a specific set of effects, and often made them superior to those expensive and complicated machines which do little more than adorn the cabinets of our physicists.

Franklin loved and sought simplicity in everything, and only valued, in his furniture as in his life, actual enjoyment. His benchmark in the appreciation of things was their usefulness or convenience.

"What avails," he would say, "a happiness derived from vanity, what avails all the cumbersome luxury of your finest apartments? I see a plethora of useless marble, china and gilt, elegant chimney pieces which smoke but give off no warmth, tables on which one can write against the light and in freezing cold only, beds and alcoves where a healthy person may sleep in comfort, but a sick person cannot be looked after, read or write commodiously."

When he was in London, a Lord took him to a house he had just had built in a narrow street on an asymmetrical plot which made for the same asymmetry in all the rooms and for a very inconvenient lay-out. Fine columns adorned the frontage and detracted that much more from the depth of the house. "Milord," Franklin told him, "the better to enjoy your house and its superb colonnade, all that you need to do is to rent convenient rooms in the the house across the road."

Thus did this simple man, who achieved so much, appreciate all that did not directly lead to the true enjoyment of a reasonable man. He owed this kind of appreciation to an anecdote from his childhood, from a lesson his sisters taught him when he bought too expensive a whistle. The piquant originality of the letter in which he tells this little story to a female friend of his demonstrates the extent to which the slightest events in our childhood can change our habits. Reading Franklin's *Memoirs*, one willingly believes that nobody was ever as much as he was the sport of chance, but that nobody availed himself of it so well.

At a very early age he left Boston, mainly to escape from his family and the tyrannical ways of an uncle who much mistreated him. He was nearly starved when he reached Philadelphia, and could not afford bare necessaries; he fell in love with a woman whom he only married much later because he was so impecunious. He supported himself through punishing work. Having been duped by his partner, he sailed for England where he became a workman in a printing-house, using his spare time to visit workshops dealing with the useful arts and to seek the conversation of learned men. Once supplied with knowledge he went back to America where he sold books, gathered educated men around him, supervising their work and launching with them subscriptions for the creation of useful establishments.

With the income from little almanacs aimed at spreading enlightenment among his compatriots, he started paper mills. Libraries were set up and each citizen, for a small fee used towards the purchase of new books, would rush there at the end of his working day to improve his mind. Thus did he spread enlightenment, slowly raise his countrymen to the dignity of a free people, and prepare in his country a revolution which will serve as a model to all peoples anxious to recover their rights.

There is no need to recall here all that he did in England and France for the freedom of America. Those particulars are available elsewhere; a few lesser-known anecdotes of his private life will be of more interest, especially if they add to the knowledge of the personality of a man with peculiar traits which set him apart from the greatest personages in the ancient and the modern world.

Franklin lived retired in Passy, entertaining everybody and talking freely with a handful of friends only. The desire to propitiate a nation which he wanted to become friendly to his constrained him to turn down no invitations.

When in a large assembly, he would say little and showed little readiness even to listen to conversations. He told his friends who asked him why that was the case, "If in company four of you French did not speak all together, I could understand what was being said and would not so often leave a large party without knowing what the talk was of."

It was fashionable to ask Franklin to dinner, to give entertainments for him. Women in particular sedulously visited him, talking to him for hours on end without noticing that he understood little because of his limited command of our language. Though they wasted his time he would receive them with a sort of amiable flirtatiousness which they all enjoyed. When each of them, jealous of his preference, asked him if he did not like her more than the others, he would say, "I do, when you are nearest me, as a result of the force of attraction."

His best friend, Helvétius's widow, in whose house he most willingly indulged in free and amusing conversation and spent what time he could away from business, had his portrait taken, in her home. "Keep me entertained, he told his friends, or you will have a very dismal picture of me."

To provide agreeable distraction, his friends would read from collections of witticisms, especially his favorite sort, where the point of the joke always had some philosophical overtones. No witticism would be read out without his answering with one of the same kind which, in somebody his age, involved a prodigious fund of facts and anecdotes which he could choose from and use relevantly, always to bolster some useful moral maxim.

To young people he liked to tell anecdotes likely to give them simple and natural tastes. As he had not forgotten anything of what had most interested his inquisitive mind in the course of a long, very busy life, he could, at no risk of repeating himself, as old people do, enliven a conversation with strokes of ingenuity suited to all ages and all minds. This fertility and versatility, the hallmark of his genius, made it very attractive to consort with him.

He asked a young man about to set off for Italy why he was going there. " — To see the home of arts and talents. — Did you cultivate them yourself? — That is why I am going. — Do you know the masterpieces of your country? — I don't. I shall see them when I am back after learning from my travels. — Don't you know, my dear child, that if you know nothing you will learn very little? In order to learn one needs to hold conversations with others. Conversation is nothing if not a form of exchange. He who does not contribute anything will not benefit from it. If you do not know how to ask the right questions, do you think that enlightened men will bother to impart their knowledge to you, if there is no reciprocation? More is needed to see monuments than eyes; in order to appreciate them, one must have honed one's judgement through comparisons and serious study."

The nephew of friends of Franklin's, on his coming out of school, called on Franklin, and told him he wished that his uncle would give him a piece of furniture he did not need; the philosopher told him that a Quaker friend of his, who had had a house built, offered to show him round it. "I was first struck, he said, by the grandeur of the rooms. The Quaker lived alone and did not entertain much. I asked him what the point was of having such a large antechamber — you have only one servant. No matter, he answered, I can afford it. About each room in the house, about each thing which was foreign to his needs, the same question brought the same answer. When we reached a vast dining-room I saw a large fine mahogany table which could easily sit twenty-five people. Now, said I, why on earth do you need such a large table? He again answered, no matter, I can afford it. Why then, I rejoined, don't you have a hat that large? You can afford it. This is the root of the unreason of men who, preoccupied by artificial needs, neglect actual pleasure. We have but five senses, which are easily gratified. With regard to sight, our only expense is a pair of spectacles, when we get older. What is ruinous are the eyes of others. It is for others that we have expensive attire, sumptuous houses and furniture, that we display jewelry and employ unnecessary footmen, that we travel in a magnificent carriage-and-eight though we have strong legs to walk with."

By eschewing all the factitious needs of vanity Franklin was the better able to spend his time striving towards the true goal of a man — becoming good and happy, becoming useful to his fellow human beings. In charge of important business, he did not neglect lesser matters and had become used to getting behind with none. His health enabled him, if necessary, to work eight days in a row, with no other rest than a little sleep in his armchair.

When, overcome by fatigue he slept for an hour or two, he would wake up to a new morning, he said, with relish for work.

As a young man he had strengthened his body by frequent swimming. He would spend any free day swimming in the sea with his young Boston friends whom he urged to follow him. He would tell how, to test his own stamina and assess how long he would be able to stay afloat if he were shipwrecked, he had often swum three leagues with, on his back, a suitcase weighing thirty pounds, meeting with no accident and not feeling tired. At the age of eighty he would still, early in the morning, go to the bank of the Seine opposite the village of Passy to teach one of his grandsons how to swim, crossing the width of the river with him.

As a minister plenipotentiary who, in the interests of his country, had to correspond with many people across Europe, he only needed one secretary. "I am not surprised, he would say, that French ministries should find it so difficult to complete even simple business with so many departments and clerks. They make it so complicated that it cannot be brought to a conclusion or not wear out the patience of the petitioner. Thus do your leaders use more art to drag out any business than it would take time to complete it."

Aware that Franklin did not like to waste his time on unnecessary words or procedures, Vergennes, the minister, had agreed to discuss America's interests with Franklin only. More transactions were brought to a conclusion in one day thanks to arguments being put frankly on both sides, face to face or in writing, than the different departments expedited in six months. Despite his wish to waste no time, much was stolen from him by those whom mere curiosity brought to his door. He was so obliging as to satisfy the strange and singular requests with which he was importuned.

One day a gentleman from Perche [a province west of Paris] wrote to him that America could not do without a king; and that he, a scion of an ancient family going back to William the Conqueror, had the qualities he deemed necessary to a leader, that he was at his disposal, and that, if Franklin did not succeed in convincing Congress to have him, he would be content with the title of king and a pension of fifteen thousand pounds, while he would stay in his province, allowing Americans to choose for themselves whatever government they wanted. Franklin was much diverted by such letters and never failed to entertain his friends with them.

Adventurers of all stripes begged him to send them to America with letters of recommendation. "What good would a letter do you, as I know you no more than I know the people I would recommend you to?" he would ask. He much liked the letter of a lady from the court recommending a young man roughly in these terms: "Sir, if in your America people have the knack of improving a hateful being who is the bane of his family's life, please dispatch there him who will bring you this introduction. That will be a miracle worthy of you. We will be much obliged, etc." The young man sailed across and died gallantly in battle.

To honor our age and nation, I will say that the enthusiasm of the French for Franklin was extreme. All enlightened men sought his company. Even in public the prettiest women would beg to be allowed to kiss the venerable old man crowned with grand tokens of his services to mankind. The Court, while it favored his cause, did not consider him in the same way. The former queen, who was far from suspecting that there was so much genius behind a modest appearance and such simplicity, marveled that he consorted with the medal-wearing ministers of Europe's great powers.

One day, when she asked a courtier what Franklin did in his country before becoming its ambassador, he said: "He was an overseer in a printing-house." "That is so," a more sensible man said. "In France, he would at most have been a bookseller."

Once peace had been made and American liberty ensured, Franklin proposed to return to his homeland, despite the pangs of a cruel ailment which led his friends to believe that he could not bear the fatigues of a long voyage. Helvétius's widow, whom he was particularly fond of, urged him to stay in France, to be operated on by skillful hands and to end his life at her side, surrounded by friends who held him dear.

On the other hand Jefferson, his friend and successor in France, said: "If I had the misfortune to see this great man stay here and die of the operation offered him, for the good of our country I could not but have him taken back there in his coffin, convinced as I am that the mere presence of his remains would seal the success of our revolution."

Though urged to stay, this man, who had faced so many dangers to serve his country and the cause of liberty, was all the more determined to sacrifice to his country the final moments of his life. "You only make leaving more difficult to me," he would answer his friends. "Do not add to my regrets. Rather bolster the courage I need in order to leave you. My task is not at an end yet. What life I have left I owe to those who have entrusted me with theirs. It is true that I am in pain but nature, who has treated me so well so far, will surely give me the time to grant the wishes of my fellow countrymen. If I recover after completing my duty towards my country, nothing will give me more joy than to end my life in a country where I have tasted so many pleasures amidst the most enlightened men in Europe."

The sincerity of his regrets could be measured by the tears rolling in his eyes. For this matter, his words were always the truthful expression of his feelings. While he sometimes found it prudent not to voice his opinions, he never distorted them. His extreme subtlety did not verge on dissimulation. He would avow that he had always deceived the English ministry by telling the truth and that the American War would not have taken place, if the English had not believed the contrary of what he had said to the King's Council in Parliament.

Age had not deprived his soul of its sensibility. One day when he was having a walk in the Bois de Boulogne and talking of the death of a child of his at the age of seven, forty years before, tears rolled down his cheeks. "Don't be surprised, he told his friend, at the pain such an old wound causes. Alas! I always fancy that this son would have been the best of my children."[1]

Note

1. It is well-known that his only surviving son, during the Revolution, had moved over to the British side and that, having been taken prisoner, he owed his freedom entirely to the extreme regard his father was held in [Lefebvre de La Roche's note].

Appeared in French as "Recollections of Benjamin Franklin," ed. Gilbert Chinard. *Proceedings of the American Philosophical Society* 94 (1950): 218–221. Translation here provided by Isabelle Bour.

[Anecdotes of Doctor Franklin, 1818 and 1821]

THOMAS JEFFERSON

Thomas Jefferson (1743–1826) was aware of Benjamin Franklin's reputation as an important scientist long before the two men ever met. Speaking of Franklin in *Notes on the State of Virginia,* Jefferson observed, "No one of the present age has made more important discoveries, nor has enriched philosophy with more, or more ingenious solutions of the phaenomena of nature." Jefferson knew Franklin's *Experiments and Observations on Electricity* soon after its publication and installed one of Franklin's lightning rods at Monticello. Living on a mountaintop, Jefferson was grateful for it on numerous occasions. Monticello slave Isaac Jefferson recorded a typical remark his master made during electrical storms: "If it hadn't been for that Franklin the whole house would have gone."

Jefferson became good friends with Franklin when the two were delegates to the Continental Congress together. Both served on the committee responsible for drafting the *Declaration of the Causes and Necessity for Taking Up Arms,* the committee to consider Lord North's conciliatory proposal, and, most important, the Committee of Five, that is, the committee assigned the task of writing the Declaration of Independence. Jefferson drafted the document, of course, but Franklin offered several important suggestions. When the Committee of Five completed their work, the Declaration of Independence came before the Continental Congress for debate. Almost every sentence came under discussion. Jefferson found excruciating the process of listening to his finely crafted words being debated, revised, or deleted. Franklin, who sat next to him during these proceedings, recognized the younger man's discomfort and offered an anecdote to make him feel more at ease. Franklin's anecdote had its intended effect. Jefferson remembered it well and repeated it many years later.

Once Congress appointed Jefferson minister plenipotentiary and commissioned him to negotiate treaties of amity and commerce with foreign powers, he went to Paris, where he renewed his friendship with Franklin, who served as minister to the Court of France. Franklin returned to America in 1785, when Jefferson took over as minister to the Court of France. When asked if he was Franklin's replacement, Jefferson famously said, "No one can replace him, I am only his successor." The two would meet once more. When Jefferson returned to the United States, he learned that George Washington had appointed him secretary of state. Traveling from Virginia to New York to assume his new position, Jefferson stopped in Philadelphia to see Franklin. Jefferson found his old friend on his deathbed.

Writing a biography of Franklin in the early nineteenth century for *Delaplaine's Repository of the Lives and Portraits of Distinguished American Characters*, Robert Walsh approached Thomas Jefferson to see if he had any stories about him. Jefferson's 1818 letter to Walsh is an absolute delight. Jefferson included additional episodes featuring Franklin in his own autobiography, as well. Indeed, Jefferson seemed to tell stories about Franklin more readily than he told personal stories about himself. He fleshed out anecdotes into tales, capturing their cultural contexts and Franklin's wonderful sense of humor. Jefferson's stories about Franklin form an important contribution to Franklin's biography—and his own.

From Thomas Jefferson to Robert Walsh, 4 December 1818

Dr. Franklin had many political enemies, as every character must which, with decision enough to have opinions, has energy and talent to give them effect on the feelings of the adversary opinion. These enmities were chiefly in Pennsylvania and Massachusetts: in the former they were merely of the proprietary party; in the latter they did not commence till the revolution, and then sprung chiefly from personal animosities, which spreading by little and little, became at length of some extent. Dr. [Arthur] Lee was his principal calumniator, a man of much malignity, who, besides enlisting his whole family in the same hostility, was enabled, as the agent of Massachusetts with the British government, to infuse it into that State with considerable effect. Mr. [Ralph] Izard, the Doctor's enemy also, but from a pecuniary transaction, never countenanced these charges against him. Mr. [John] Jay, Silas Deane, Mr. [Henry] Laurens, his colleagues also, ever maintained towards him unlimited confidence and respect. That he would have waived the formal recognition of our Independence I never heard on any authority worthy notice. As to the fisheries, England was urgent to retain them exclusively, France neutral; and I believe that had they been ultimately made a *sine quâ non*, our commisioners (Mr. Adams excepted) would have relinquished them rather than have broken off the treaty. To Mr. Adams' perseverance alone on that point, I have always understood we were indebted for their reservation. As to the charge of subservience to France, besides the evidence of his friendly colleagues before named, two years of my own service with him at Paris, daily visits, and the most friendly and confidential conversations, convince me it had not a shadow of foundation. He possessed the confidence of that government in the highest degree, insomuch that it may truly be said that they were more under his influence, than he under theirs. The fact is that his temper was so amiable and conciliatory, his conduct so rational, never urging impossibilities, or even things unreasonably inconvenient to them, in short, so moderate and attentive to their difficulties as well as our own, that what his enemies called subserviency, I saw was only that reasonable disposition, which, sensible that advantages are not all to be on one side, yielding what is just and liberal, is the more certain of obtaining liberality and justice. Mutual confidence produces of course mutual influence, and this was all which subsisted between Dr. Franklin and the government of France.

I state a few anecdotes of Dr. Franklin, within my own knowledge, too much in detail for the scale of Delaplaine's work, but which may find a *cadre* in some of the more particular views you contemplate. . . .

Our revolutionary process, as is well known, commenced by petitions, memorials, remonstrances, etc. from the old Congress. These were followed by a non-importation agreement, as a pacific instrument of coercion. While that was before us, and sundry exceptions, as of arms, ammunition, etc., were moved from different quarters of the house, I was sitting by Dr. Franklin and observed to him that I thought we should except books; that we ought not to exclude science, even coming from an enemy. He thought so too, and I proposed the exception, which was agreed to. Soon after it occurred that medicine should be excepted, and I suggested that also to the Doctor. "As to that," said he "I will tell you a story. When I was in London, in such a year, there was a weekly club of physicians, of which Sir John Pringle was President, and I was invited by my friend Dr. [John] Fothergill to attend when convenient. Their rule was to propose a thesis one week and discuss it the next. I happened there when the question to be considered was whether Physicians had, on the whole, done most good or harm? The young members, particularly, having discussed it very learn-edly and eloquently till the subject was exhausted, one of them observed to Sir John Pringle, that, although it was not usual for the President to take part in a debate, yet they were desirous to know his opinion on the ques-tion. He said they must first tell him whether, under the appellation of Phy-sicians, they meant to include *old women*; if they did he thought they had done more good than harm, otherwise more harm than good."

The confederation of the States, while on the carpet before the old Con-gress, was strenuously opposed by the smaller States, under apprehensions that they would be swallowed up by the larger ones. We were long engaged in the discussion; it produced great heats, much ill humor, and intemper-ate declarations from some members. Dr. Franklin at length brought the debate to a close with one of his little apologues. He observed that "at the time of the Union of England and Scotland, the Duke of Argyle was most violently opposed to that measure, and among other things predicted that, as the whale had swallowed Jonas, so Scotland would be swallowed by England. However," said the Doctor, "when Lord Bute came into the gov-ernment, he soon brought into its administration so many of his country-men that it was found in event that Jonas swallowed the whale." This little story produced a *general* laugh, and restored good humor, and the article of difficulty was passed.

When Dr. Franklin went to France, on his revolutionary mission, his eminence as a philosopher, his venerable appearance, and the cause on which he was sent, rendered him extremely popular. For all ranks and con-ditions of men there, entered warmly into the American interest. He was, therefore, feasted and invited to all the court parties. At these he sometimes met the old Duchess of Bourbon, who, being a chess player of about his force, they very generally played together. Happening once to put her king into prise, the Doctor took it. "Ah," says she, "we do not take kings so." "We do in America," said the Doctor.

At one of these parties the emperor Joseph II. then at Paris, incog., under the title of Count Falkenstein, was overlooking the game, in silence, while the company was engaged in animated conversations on the American question. "How happens it M. le Comte," said the Duchess, "that while we all feel so much interest in the cause of the Americans, you say nothing for them?" "I am a king by trade," said he.

When the Declaration of Independence was under the consideration of

Congress, there were two or three unlucky expressions in it which gave offence to some members. The words "Scotch and other foreign auxiliaries"
excited the ire of a gentleman or two of that country. Severe strictures on
the conduct of the British king, in negotiating our repeated repeals of the
law which permitted the importation of slaves, were disapproved by some
Southern gentlemen, whose reflections were not yet matured to the full ab-
horrence of that traffic. Although the offensive expressions were immediately yielded, these gentlemen continued their depredations on other parts
of the instrument. I was sitting by Dr. Franklin, who perceived that I was
not insensible to these mutilations. "I have made it a rule," said he, "whenever in my power, to avoid becoming the draughtsman of papers to be reviewed by a public body. I took my lesson from an incident which I will
relate to you. When I was a journeyman printer, one of my companions,
an apprentice hatter, having served out his time, was about to open shop
for himself. His first concern was to have a handsome sign-board, with a
proper inscription. He composed it in these words, 'John Thompson, *Hatter, makes* and *sells hats* for ready money,' with a figure of a hat subjoined;
but he thought he would submit it to his friends for their amendments. The
first he showed it to thought the word '*Hatter*' tautologous, because followed by the words 'makes hats,' which show he was a hatter. It was struck
out. The next observed that the word '*makes*' might as well be omitted, because his customers would not care who made the hats. If good and to their
mind, they would buy, by whomsoever made. He struck it out. A third said
he thought the words '*for ready money*' were useless, as it was not the custom of the place to sell on credit. Every one who purchased expected to
pay. They were parted with, and the inscription now stood, 'John Thompson sells hats.' '*Sells hats*' says his next friend! Why nobody will expect you
to give them away, what then is the use of that word? It was stricken out,
and '*hats*' followed it, the rather as there was one painted on the board. So
the inscription was reduced ultimately to 'John Thompson' with the figure
of a hat subjoined."

The Doctor told me at Paris the two following anecdotes of the Abbé
Raynal. He had a party to dine with him one day at Passy, of whom one
half were Americans, the other half French, and among the last was the
Abbé. During the dinner he got on his favorite theory of the degeneracy
of animals, and even of man, in America, and urged it with his usual elo-
quence. The Doctor at length noticing the accidental stature and position

of his guests, at table, "Come," says he, "M. l'Abbé, let us try this question by the fact before us. We are here one half Americans, and one half French, and it happens that the Americans have placed themselves on one side of the table, and our French friends are on the other. Let both parties rise, and we will see on which side nature has degenerated." It happened that his American guests were [William] Carmichael, [Josiah] Harmar, [David] Humphreys, and others of the finest stature and form; while those of the other side were remarkably diminutive, and the Abbé himself particularly was a mere shrimp. He parried the appeal, however, by a complimentary admission of exceptions, among which the Doctor himself was a conspicuous one.

The Doctor and Silas Deane were in conversation one day at Passy, on the numerous errors in the Abbe's *Histoire des deux Indes*, when he happened to step in. After the usual salutations, Silas Deane said to him, "The Doctor and myself, Abbé, were just speaking of the errors of fact into which you have been led in your history." "Oh, no, sir," said the Abbé, "that is impossible. I took the greatest care not to insert a single fact for which I had not the most unquestionable authority." "Why," says Deane, "there is the story of Polly Baker, and the eloquent apology you have put into her mouth, when brought before a court of Massachusetts to suffer punishment under a law which you cite, for having had a bastard. I know there never was such a law in Massachusetts." "Be assured," said the Abbé, "you are mistaken, and that is a true story. I do not immediately recollect indeed the particular information on which I quote it; but I am certain I had for it unquestionable authority." Doctor Franklin, who had been for some time shaking with unrestrained laughter at the Abbé's confidence in his authority for that tale, said, "I will tell you, Abbé, the origin of that story. When I was a printer, and editor of a newspaper, we were sometimes slack of news, and, to amuse our customers, I used to fill up our vacant columns with anecdotes and fables, and fancies of my own, and this of Polly Baker is a story of my making, on one of these occasions." The Abbé, without the least disconcert, exclaimed, with a laugh, "Oh, very well, Doctor, I had rather relate your stories than other men's truths."

From *The Autobiography of Thomas Jefferson* (1821)

The remissness of Congress, and their permanent session began to be a subject of uneasiness; and even some of the legislatures had recommended to them intermissions, and periodical sessions. As the Confederation had made no provision for a visible head of the government, during vacations of Congress, and such a one was necessary to superintend the executive business, to receive and communicate with foreign ministers and nations, and to assemble Congress on sudden and extraordinary emergencies, I proposed, early in April, the appointment of a committee, to be called the "Committee of the States," to consist of a member from each state, who should remain in session during the recess of Congress: that the functions of Congress should be divided into executive and legislative, the latter to be reserved, and the former, by a general resolution, to be delegated to that Committee. This proposition was afterwards agreed to; a Committee appointed, who entered on duty on the subsequent adjournment of Congress, quarrelled very soon, split into two parties, abandoned their post, and left the government without any visible head, until the next meeting of Congress. We have since seen the same thing take place, in the Directory of France: and I believe it will for ever take place in any Executive consisting of a plurality. Our plan, best, I believe, combines wisdom and practicability, by providing a plurality of Counsellors, but a single Arbiter for ultimate decision. I was in France when we heard of this schism, and separation of our Committee, and, speaking with Dr. Franklin of this singular disposition of men to quarrel, and divide into parties, he gave his sentiments, as usual, by way of Apologue. He mentioned the Eddystone light-house, in the British channel, as being built on a rock, in the mid-channel, totally inaccessible in winter, from the boisterous character of that sea, in that season; that, therefore, for the two keepers employed to keep up the lights, all provisions for the winter were necessarily carried to them in autumn, as they could never be visited again till the return of the milder season; that, on the first practicable day in the spring, a boat put off to them with fresh supplies. The boatmen met at the door one of the keepers, and accosted him with a "How goes it, friend?" "Very well." "How is your companion?" "I do not know." "Don't know?" "Is not he here?" "I can't tell." "Have not you seen him to-day?" "No." "When did you see him?" "Not since last fall." "You have killed him?" "Not I, indeed." They were about to lay hold of him, as having certainly murdered his companion; but he desired them to go up stairs and examine for themselves. They went up, and there found the other keeper. They had quarrelled, it seems, soon after being left there, had divided into two parties, assigned the cares below to one, and those above to the other, and had never spoken to, or seen, one another since. . . .

I left Monticello on the 1st of March, 1790, for New York. At Philadelphia I called on the venerable and beloved Franklin. He was then on the bed of sickness from which he never rose. My recent return from a country in which he had left so many friends, and the perilous convulsions to which they had been exposed, revived all his anxieties to know what part they had taken, what had been their course, and what their fate. He went over all in succession, with a rapidity and animation, almost too much for his strength. When all his inquiries were satisfied, and a pause took place, I told him I had learned with much pleasure that, since his return to America, he had been occupied in preparing for the world, the history of his own life. "I cannot say much of that," said he; "but I will give you a sample of what I shall leave": and he directed his little grandson (William Bache) who was standing by the bedside, to hand him a paper from the table, to which he pointed. He did so; and the Doctor putting it into my hands, desired me to take it, and read it at my leisure. It was about a quire of folio paper, written in a large and running hand, very like his own. I looked into it slightly, then shut it, and said I would accept his permission to read it, and would carefully return it. He said, "No, keep it." Not certain of his meaning, I again looked into it, folded it for my pocket, and said again, I would certainly return it. "No," said he, "keep it." I put it into my pocket, and shortly after, took leave of him. He died on the 17th of the ensuing month of April; and as I understood that he had bequeathed all his papers to his grandson, William Temple Franklin, I immediately wrote to Mr. Franklin, to inform him I possessed this paper, which I should consider as his property, and would deliver to his order. He came on immediately to New York, called on me for it, and I delivered it to him. As he put it into his pocket, he said carelessly, he had either the original, or another copy of it, I do not recollect which. This last expression struck my attention forcibly, and for the first time suggested to me the thought, that Dr. Franklin had meant it as a confidential deposite in my hands, and that I had done wrong in parting from it. I have not yet seen the collection he published of Dr. Franklin's works, and therefore, know not if this is among them. I have been told it is not. It contained a narrative of the negotiations between Dr. Franklin and the British Ministry, when he was endeavoring to prevent the contest of

arms which followed. The negotiation was brought about by the interven-
tion of Lord Howe and his sister, who, I believe, was called Lady Howe,
but I may misremember her title. Lord Howe seems to have been friendly
to America, and exceedingly anxious to prevent a rupture. His intimacy
with Dr. Franklin, and his position with the Ministry, induced him to
undertake a mediation between them; in which his sister seemed to have
been associated. They carried from one to the other, backwards and for-
wards, the several propositions and answers which passed, and seconded
with their own intercessions, the importance of mutual sacrifices, to preserve the peace and connection of the two countries. I remember that Lord
North's answers were dry, unyielding, in the spirit of unconditional submission, and betrayed an absolute indifference to the occurrence of a rupture; and he said to the mediators distinctly, at last, that "a rebellion was
not to be deprecated on the part of Great Britain; that the confiscations it
would produce, would provide for many of their friends." This expression
was reported by the mediators to Dr. Franklin, and indicated so cool and
calculated a purpose in the Ministry, as to render compromise hopeless,
and the negotiation was discontinued. If this is not among the papers published, we ask, what has become of it? I delivered it with my own hands,
into those of Temple Franklin. It certainly established views so atrocious
in the British government, that its suppression would, to them, be worth a
great price. But could the grandson of Dr. Franklin be, in such degree, an
accomplice in the parricide of the memory of his immortal grandfather?
The suspension, for more than twenty years, of the general publication,
bequeathed and confided to him, produced for a while, hard suspicions
against him: and if, at last, all are not published, a part of these suspicions
may remain with some.

From "Anecdotes of Doctor Franklin," in *The Writings of Thomas Jefferson*, ed. H. A.
Washington, 9 vols. (New York: Derby & Jackson, 1859), 8: 497–502.

From *Memoir, Correspondence, and Miscellanies*, ed. Thomas Jefferson Randolph, 4 vols.
(Charlottesville: F. Carr, 1829), 1: 44–45, 88–89.

[Anecdotes Relative to Dr. Franklin, 1818]

WILLIAM TEMPLE FRANKLIN

Benjamin Franklin's grandson William Temple Franklin (*c.* 1760–1823) was the illegitimate son of William Franklin and an unknown mother. Temple, as he was called, attended James Elphinston's school in Kensington, visiting his grandfather occasionally on Craven Street in London during the late 1760s and early 1770s. Temple came to Philadelphia with his grandfather when he returned to America in 1775. When Benjamin Franklin went to Europe after the Continental Congress elected him commissioner to negotiate a treaty with France in 1776, Temple accompanied him, as did another grandson, Benjamin Franklin Bache. Temple remained with his grandfather at Passy, becoming his secretary, amanuensis, factotum, protégé, and secretary. In 1785, they returned to Philadelphia, where Benjamin Franklin continued doing what he could for Temple. He even managed to get him elected to the American Philosophical Society, a prestigious, and perhaps unwarranted, honor for a young man in his twenties who had not made any personal contributions to science. Arranging for membership to the Society, Franklin sought to secure his grandson's place in the American intellectual world. As a member, Temple could associate with some of the greatest minds in the nation.

Despite his grandfather's best efforts to secure his grandson's future and make him a leading member of the rising generation of Americans, Temple Franklin turned his back on the United States. Benjamin Franklin bequeathed his personal papers and the bulk of his library to Temple, not only as a token of his affection but also as a reward for past service and a responsibility for the future. The respect Temple Franklin felt for the man did not transfer to the library that man had so lovingly assembled over the course of his life. Few of his grandfather's books held either personal or intellectual value for the grandson. Temple saw the library as capital and sought to convert it into cash after his grandfather's death. Before the end of 1790, he left Philadelphia for England, never to return. He left the library behind to be sold and took his grandfather's personal papers with him, intending to prepare an edition of his writings. Temple's editorial incompetence and other distractions delayed the edition for decades. In 1816, he published his first volume, *The*

Private Correspondence of Benjamin Franklin. The edition is dated 1817, but it was ready as early as December 18, 1816, when he sent James Monroe a copy. In 1818, Temple Franklin published two additional volumes, including *Memoirs of the Life and Writings of Benjamin Franklin.*

Though Temple Franklin had finally delivered his long-promised edition of his grandfather's writings, it still left much to be desired. As part of the manuscript material he inherited, Temple Franklin had possessed the original manuscript of the autobiography in four parts in Benjamin Franklin's hand, but he inexplicably traded it away for a manuscript copy containing only the first three parts of the work. Still, his edition of the autobiography represents the first publication of the second part in English and the first publication of the third part. He tinkered with his grandfather's text in many places, decorously toning down the racy language and graphic imagery. He also included a selection of anecdotes. Perhaps there was no aspect of the edition that was more disappointing. No one had a better chance to be Benjamin Franklin's Boswell than his grandson. He must have heard hundreds of his grandfather's anecdotes, but when it can time to prepare his edition of Franklin's writings, he included only seven anecdotes.

DR. FRANKLIN, WHEN A CHILD, found the long graces used by his father before and after meals very tedious. One day after the winter's provisions had been salted, — "I think, Father," said Benjamin, "if you were to say *Grace* over the whole cask — once for all — it would be a vast *saving of time.*"

In his travels through New England, Franklin had observed, that when he went into an inn, every individual of the family had a question or two to propose to him, relative to his history; and that, till each was satisfied, and they had conferred and compared together their information, there was no possibility of procuring any refreshment. — Therefore the moment he went into any of these places, he enquired for the master, the mistress, the sons, the daughters, the men-servants, and the maid-servants; and having assembled them all together, he began in this manner. "Good people, I am Benjamin Franklin of Philadelphia; by trade a printer; and a bachelor; I have some relations at Boston, to whom I am going to make a visit: my stay will be short, and I shall then return and follow my business, as a prudent man ought to do. This is all I know of myself, and all I can possibly inform you of; I beg, therefore, that you will have pity upon me and my horse, and give us both some refreshment."

When Franklin came to England previous to the breaking out of the American war, he went to Mr. [Richard] Hett's Printing Office in Wild Court, Wild Street, Lincoln's Inn Fields, and entering the Press-room, he went up to a particular press, and thus addressed the two men who were working. "Come, my friends, we will drink together; it is now 40 years since I worked like you at this press as journeyman printer": on this he sent for a gallon of porter, and they drunk "success to printing."

In one of the assemblies in America, wherein there was a majority of Presbyterians, a law was proposed to forbid the praying for the King by the Episcopalians; who, however, could not conveniently omit that prayer, it being prescribed in their Liturgy. Dr. Franklin, one of the members, seeing that such a law would occasion more disturbance than it was worth, said, that he thought it quite *unnecessary*, for, added he, "those people have, to my certain knowledge, been praying constantly these twenty years past, that "*God would give to the King and his counsel wisdom*," and we all know that not the least notice has ever been taken of that prayer; so that it is plain they have no interest in the court of Heaven." The house smiled, and the motion was dropt.

In Philadelphia, where there are no *Noblesse*, but the inhabitants are all either merchants or mechanics, the merchants, many years since, set up an assembly for dancing, and desiring to make a distinction, and to assume a rank above the mechanics, they at first proposed this among the rules for regulating the assembly, "that *no mechanic or mechanic's wife or daughter should be admitted, on any terms*." These rules being shown by a manager to Dr. Franklin for his opinion, he remarked, that one of them excluded GOD ALMIGHTY. *How so*? said the manager. "*Because*," replied the Doctor, "*he is notoriously the greatest mechanic in the universe*; having, as the Scripture testifies, made all things, and that by *weight* and *measure*." The intended *new gentlemen* became ashamed of their rule, and struck it out.

About the year 1752, Dr. Franklin having entered into a correspondence with Samuel Johnson, Doctor in Divinity in the University of Oxford, and afterwards President of King's College, in New York, and having endeavoured to induce the latter to accept the Presidency of the College at Philadelphia, and as an additional motive to his doing so, having offered to procure the erection of a new Episcopal church for him in that city; and Dr. Johnson having expressed some doubts respecting the propriety of such a measure, Dr. Franklin wrote a letter for the purpose of removing his scruples, of which the following extract has been preserved, viz. "Your tenderness of the church's peace is truly laudable; but, methinks, to build a new church in a growing place, is not properly *dividing*, but *multiplying*, and will really be a means of increasing the number of those who worship God in that way. Many who cannot now be accommodated in the church, go to other places, or stay at home; and if we had another church, many who go to other places, or stay at home, would go to church. I had for several years nailed against the wall of my house, a pigeon-box that would hold six pair, and though they bred as fast as my neighbors' pigeons, I never had more than six pair; the old and strong driving out the young and weak, and obliging them to seek new habitations. At length I put up an additional box, with apartments for entertaining twelve pair more, and it was soon filled with inhabitants, by the overflowing of my first box, and of others in the neighborhood. This I take to be a parallel case with the building a *new church* here."

Dr. Franklin was so immoderately fond of chess, that one evening at Passy, he sat at that amusement from six in the afternoon till sun-rise. On the point of losing one of his games, his *king* being attacked, by what is called a check, but an opportunity offering at the same time of giving a fatal blow to his adversary, provided he might neglect the defence of his king, he chose to do so, though contrary to the rules, and made his move. "Sir," said the French gentleman, his antagonist, "you cannot do that, and leave your king *in check*." "I see he is in check," said the Doctor, "but I shall not defend him. If he was a good king like yours, he would deserve the protection of his subjects; but he is a tyrant and has cost them already more than he is worth: — Take him, if you please; I can do without him, and will fight out the rest of the battle, en Républicain — as a Commonwealth's man."

From *Memoirs of the Life and Writings of Benjamin Franklin*, ed. William Temple Franklin (London: Henry Colburn, 1818), pp. 447–449.

[A Conversation with Franklin's
London Friends, 1821]

ROBERT ASPLAND

During his London years, Benjamin Franklin enjoyed the company of several men who met every other Thursday at St. Paul's Coffeehouse and, after 1772, at the London Coffeehouse. He referred to the group as his "Club of Honest Whigs." The men who formed this club shared an interest in scientific experimentation, but, as Franklin's name for the club suggests, they also shared similar political views. Most sympathized with the American cause and dissented from the Church of England. Since their membership and their meetings were informal, details about the club are extremely difficult to locate. Andrew Kippis, one of Franklin's club members, listed several others in his *Biographia Britannica* (3: 222). Besides Joseph Priestley, the group included James Burgh, a political writer; John Canton, a schoolmaster and electrical experimenter; Richard Price; and Abraham Rees, a Presbyterian minister and an encyclopaedist. In a 1966 contribution to the *William and Mary Quarterly*, Verner W. Crane assembled the fullest information about this club, but he was unable to come up with a full list of its members and admitted that he could not independently verify some of the members Kippis listed in *Biographia Britannica*.

Brief as it is, the following excerpt from the diary of Robert Aspland (1782–1845), a Unitarian minister, provides much information to supplement Crane's discussion of Franklin's "Club of Honest Whigs." Aspland recorded some table talk that occured in 1821 at Dr. Williams's Library in Red Cross Street, Cripplegate, an important gathering place for many dissenting ministers in London. Aspland's diary provides independent verification that Abraham Rees was indeed a member of Franklin's club: an exciting discovery. Rees later developed a reputation for his massive *New Cyclopaedia, or, Universal Dictionary of the Arts and Sciences* (1802–1820). Franklin's contact with Rees suggests that he could have influenced his encyclopedic thinking. Aspland's diary also provides the names of three other members of Franklin's club not listed in either Kippis or Crane: Thomas Belsham, another Unitarian minister; Abraham Harris, a Unitarian minister from Swansea; and Dr. William Hebereden, a prominent physician. Aspland's diary demonstrates that Franklin's fellow club members remembered him with great fondness, though they bristled at his religious skepticism. It also indicates Franklin's willingness to welcome strangers to the club and let them speak their minds.

JAN. 11, 1821. — DR. REES RELATED the pleasant meetings of a Club which used to meet at the London Coffee-house, of which Dr. Franklin was a member. Every thing new in the Royal Society was there talked of. Dr. F. was the life of the Club; but when a stranger was introduced was always mute. On the breaking out of the American war, the Club became political: this lessened its usefulness; but the first news of proceedings in America were there to be learned.

Dr. Franklin was exceedingly fond of the air-bath, i.e. of stripping himself and sitting in a strong current of air. Dr. Heberden once told him that he went beyond him in this way; for he not only sat unclothed in a draught, but took a pitcher of water and threw it up to the ceiling, and let it fall on his body.

Mr. Belsham. — Dr. Franklin was sceptical. He told Dr. Priestley that he had never fairly studied the evidences of Christianity, and lamented that, owing to his having in early life been accustomed to hear Christianity ridiculed, he was never able to bring himself to study it seriously. Dr. Kippis and Dr. Harris always looked on Dr. F. with suspicion.

Dr. Rees. — But Dr. Priestley idolized him. Dr. Kippis knew little of the world; Dr. Harris differed from Dr. F. in his politics. The truth lay between the two.

From *Memoir of the Life, Works and Correspondence of . . . Robert Aspland, of Hackney* (London: Edward T. Whitfield, 1850), pp. 400–401.

[Memories of Franklin, 1821]

ANDRÉ MORELLET

Abbé André Morellet (1727–1819) can be described as a polygraph. He published a great many pamphlets on a whole range of subjects, including political economy, a topic on which he shared Franklin's ideas; both could discuss politics and economic reform with Anne Robert Jacques Turgot, baron de l'Aulne, who was finance minister from 1774 to 1776, and whose ideas, had they been implemented, may have made the French Revolution unnecessary. Morellet also wrote several entries, mostly on religious subjects, for Diderot and D'Alembert's *Encyclopédie*. His most famous essay may be *Le Cri des familles* (*The Cry of the Families*, 1795), in which he advocated support for and reparation to the families of the men and women who had fallen victim to revolutionary Terror. To support himself during the Revolution, he translated English fiction; his most important translation, however, is that of Cesare Beccaria's *Dei Delitti et delle pene* (*An Essay on Crimes and Punishments*, 1764). His *Mémoires sur le XVIIIe siècle et sur la Révolution* (*Memoirs on the Eighteenth Century and the Revolution*, 1821), which are really his personal memoirs, remain quite readable and form an excellent source of information on the social aspects of French Enlightenment.

He attended Mme. Helvétius's salon—then in Paris—as early as 1760, and later depended on her generosity (in the form of board and lodging, though he only spent two or three days a week at Mme. Helvétius's) for decades, as his income from his literary work, pensions, or a living he finally obtained in 1788 was only sufficient to support him for a few years before the Revolution. Morellet also attended several other major salons. During Franklin's stay in France, he would visit him once a week with Cabanis and Abbé Lefebvre de La Roche. His friendship with those men and with Mme. Helvétius came to an abrupt end in 1790, when Morellet sided with the more conservative supporters of the Revolution, while the others were in favor of dismantling the *ancien régime*. Soon after learning about Franklin's death, Morellet published a set of anecdotes in *Gazette Nationale, ou Le Moniteur*

Universel, 15 July 1790, which have been frequently reprinted (Zall, nos. 157–166). His memories of Franklin reprinted below betray a certain self-satisfaction, though he was considered a very likeable, very honest man, with a marked satirical bent, which did not prevent him from being, like Franklin, a philanthropist.

· AT MR. TRUDAINE'S I BECAME ACQUAINTED with Lord Shelburne, who has since become marquess of Lansdowne, and who had come to France with Colonel Barré, a Member of the House of Commons; he developed friendly feelings towards me. He urged me to come and see him in England. Mr. Trudaine approved of this plan, thinking that, from that trip, I would bring back useful information concerning trade; I may say that, to the best of my ability, his hope was not disappointed. Out of the coffers of the trade departments he gave me fifty louis for my travel expenses, and Lord Shelburne had had a promise from me that I would stay with him. At the end of April 1772 I crossed the channel.

When I reached London I found that milord was away; but he had left orders regarding my reception.

Moreover, as he had warned his brother Fitzmaurice of my arrival, the latter, while his brother was absent, took me to Wycombe, an estate about seven or eight leagues from London which provided Lord Shelburne with his first aristocratic title, and which today belongs to his son; with him he also took Colonel Barré, Dr. Hawkesworth, the author of Banks's first voyage around the world, as well as [David] Garrick and Franklin, two men who need no introduction.

We spent five or six days at Wycombe, in rather good company, as can be gathered.

It was very difficult for me to understand spoken English; but all had a little French, and were very forbearing with me. They could understand me very well, as my elocution was clear and distinct, as I had a loud voice and a natural and truthful delivery which was instrumental in ascertaining the meaning of words and sentences, all of which Garrick felt, which helped him to understand me, as he told me more than once.

As may be imagined, that time went by very pleasantly for me, in the company of such men as I have since always rejoiced that I knew, and about whom I will say a little here, beginning, as I should, with the most famous of them.

Franklin, who was already for England the politician and the statesman it would soon come to fear, was much better known in Europe then for his great discovery of the identity of electrical fire and of lightning, and for his fine theory about electricity; as I was more concerned with political economy and the question of government than with physics, conversation would naturally turn to those subjects. We discussed at length the general question of the freedom of trade, and two other subsidiary matters of great moment, that of free trade for India and the freedom of the corn trade. I had the satisfaction of seeing him share fully all the principles I had laid down in my *Memoirs* against the Company, and in the Refutation of the Dialogues; it even seemed to me that I removed a few doubts which were left in his mind.

His ideas on population in general, and on that of America in particular, on the relations between colonies and their metropolises, on the progress of America — English America as it was then — and on what other progress could be foreseen, all had their turn in our conversations. We also talked about music, for he loved it, and about physics and morals, but in few words and at long intervals; for nobody was ever a better practitioner of La Fontaine's maxim:

> Le sage est ménager du temps et des paroles.
> [A wise man is sparing of time and of words.]

That was where I saw him stilling waters with oil, an experiment regarded as a fool's tale since Aristotle and Pliny. The waves, it is true, were not those of a sea, but those of a brook which ran in the grounds of Wycombe. It was ruffled by a fresh breeze. He went up river about sixty yards and, pretending to go through a few magical passes, he shook three times over the brook a reed he held in his hand. A moment later, the wavelets gradually grew smaller, and the water surface became as smooth as ice.

When explaining this phenomenon, he told us that the oil in his reed, by fragmenting prodigiously the moment it was thrown, made the water surface smoother, thus preventing the wind from reaching it, especially at the spot in the brook where the first gush fell; underwater, the motion of the waters got less and was not renewed by what lay above, nor passed on further down, so that stillness spread everywhere.

Once back in London, I cultivated the acquaintance of this most interesting man. I often had lunch with him. He had just devised various kinds of fireplace stove, which he then had built by craftsmen; the plans for those may be seen in his works: they combine, as usual, research in physics and grand political views. I thought that it would be useful to have a few models of those in France, and he agreed to sell me the very one which stood in his sitting-room. I paid him twelve guineas for it and sent it to M. Trudaine, who had it installed in Montigny. But only several years later did the French become concerned with the very important art of heating their homes economically.

Since then, and once back in France, I have often discussed fireplace stoves with Franklin. We have tried various new shapes. I improved on those fireplace stoves of his which are fitted with a drawer; I had at least a dozen made, and most of them worked well. But the one I am most pleased about is one in sheet iron, with three cast-iron plates on the outside and a flap operated by a tooth-rack, bell-shaped at the front. They were made by Pérès, the locksmith of the Mint. I ordered one for M. de Vaisnes, exactly similar to mine, which was also very successful. He also made two for the King's sisters in Bellevue.

I will have occasion to say more about Franklin. . . .

In 1786 I published a translation of *Observations on Virginia*, by Mr. Jefferson, the American minister in France, who succeeded Benjamin Franklin in this position, and who has since then been secretary of state in his country and president of the United States.

That book adds to our knowledge of the United States; it is interesting, varied, adorned with philosophical observations which are acute and rational. This considerable piece of work was preyed upon by booksellers, as was the case with nearly all my books: that octavo volume of over 400 pages was of no profit to me.

About that time occurred a great loss to our Auteuil circle, as Franklin left to go back to America; he lived in Passy, and it was easy to travel between Auteuil and Passy. Once a week we would have dinner at his house — Mme. Helvétius, her two house guests, Cabanis and the abbé de la

Roche, as well as myself, who often joined them. He also very often came to dinner in Auteuil, and our gatherings were very merry ones.

For one of those dinners, on some anniversary of his saint's day or of American freedom, I penned the following song:

To the tune of; Camarades, lampons [Let us drink, comrades]

Let history in bronze carve Franklin's name, as for me I will compose a drinking song in his praise; with glass in hand, let us sing our Benjamin.

In politics he is great; at table, merry and frank; while founding an empire, he can be seen drinking and laughing; serious and playful, such is our Benjamin.

Like the bold eagle, he flew up to the heavens and stole the thunder with which they terrified the earth, a felicitous theft by clever Benjamin.

The untamed American recovers his liberty; and this selfless work, another feat of our sage, is completed by Louis and Benjamin.

Never was such a noble cause fought for; they want independence in order to drink French wines, that is the beauty of Benjamin's plan.

Congress declared that they would drink our claret, and for our champagne they started a campaign, having long been prepared by Benjamin.

Beastly Englishmen wanted to confine them to tea; they sold them cloudy wine at a premium, to the grief of their brother Benjamin.

If you see our heroes daring Englishmen, bold at sea, that is in order to have America drink Catholic wine, clear and fine wine, such as Benjamin likes.

I am no advocate of an invasion: what would one do with England? They only drink beer there, an unhappy lot, according to Benjamin.

Those Englishmen are great minds, all their writings are deep ones, they know the weight of air; but if the cellar is poor, in vain are they savants like Benjamin.

Often do they kill themselves while alive; what will moralists do, if the poor people are sad for lack of wine, as Benjamin believes?

May we defeat at sea this jealous and proud people! But after our victory, we will teach them to raise a full glass to toast Benjamin.

Franklin much liked Scottish songs; he remembered, he would say, the strong and sweet feelings they had aroused in him. He told us that while travelling around America, he had found himself, beyond the Allegheny mountains, in the house of a Scotsman who lived in retirement after losing his fortune, with his wife who had once been handsome and a daughter of fifteen or sixteen; on a fine evening, while sitting at her door, the woman had sung a Scottish song, "So Merry as We Have Been," so gently and touchingly that he had burst into tears, and that his recollection of this was still vivid after more than thirty years.

I needed no more encouragement to try and translate or adapt into French the song which had given him so much pleasure. It can be found, with five other similar songs, and the ballad of Mary Stuart, in a collection of music I copied with my own hand.

That was no mean feat; for it is very difficult to fit French words to the original tunes without spoiling them. One of those songs only has masculine rhymes, and three or four two-syllable lines in a row, all musical phrases having stressed, masculine endings. Franklin would sometimes accompany those airs on the glass harmonica, an instrument he invented, as is well-known.

Dealing with him was an exquisite experience, made such by his perfect benevolence, his simple manners, his uprightness which was to be felt in the least matters, extreme indulgence and, above all, a gentle serenity which often paved the way to gaiety; such was sociability with this great man, who made his homeland an independent state, and can boast one of the most important discoveries in the century.

He spoke at length only to tell stories, an art in which he excelled, and which he enjoyed in other people. His tales always had a philosophical aim. Several were apologues which he had made up, and he would apply with infinite relevance those which were not of his own invention.

In my two-volume octavo manuscript *Ana*, written down following Locke's method, I have preserved several of those tales, and many characteristic traits of Franklin. I sent off a few to the journal *Le Moniteur* in the early months of 1790.

From *Mémoires de l'Abbé Morellet de l'Académie Française, sur le Dix-Huitième Siècle et sur la Révolution; Précédés de l'Éloge de l'Abbé Morellet*, 2 vols. (Paris: Ladvocat, 1821), 1: 202–203, 298. Translation here provided by Isabelle Bour.

[A Short Account of Benjamin Franklin, 1825]

Pierre Jean Georges Cabanis

The son of a lawyer and a farmer, Pierre Jean Georges Cabanis (1757–1808) loved reading the classics and John Locke. At sixteen, he became for two years secretary to a Polish gentleman whom he accompanied to his country. Then, as he needed to make a living, he decided to study medicine. Being of delicate health, in 1778, he chose to live in Auteuil, where he met Mme. Helvétius, thanks to Turgot. He became a surrogate son to her who had lost her only boy many years before; he went on living in her house after getting married, and inherited her estate. He died of apoplexy a few years after his benefactor.

As a physician, he was more of a theoretician than a practitioner. In 1789, he published his first book, *Observations sur les hôpitaux (Observations on Hospitals)*. He became a close friend of leading revolutionaries, Mirabeau and Condorcet, attending the former in his final illness, and marrying the latter's sister-in-law. In the 1790s, he was appointed to many important positions in scientific institutions and in politics. His agnosticism and his interests in scientific and philosophical developments made him a welcome addition to the société of Auteuil. Politically, he was a republican who actively supported Napoleon's coup d'état in November 1799, a choice he was to regret. His ideas on biology and medicine, on the nature of man, are a synthesis of the theories of Locke, the materialist La Mettrie, the theorist of sensibility Albrecht von Haller and the sensualist Condillac. He reached a more integrated conception of the human organism, emphasizing the importance of physiology for scientific progress; he rejected a dualistic conception of human nature, though he is not a materialist in the usual sense of the word. His ideas are related to those of Helvétius, though he never met him.

His memoir of Benjamin Franklin glows with kindness and his admiration for the great American diplomat, who clearly enjoyed telling him about his past life. Cabanis also impressed Franklin, who secured his election to the American Philosophical Society (as a foreign member) in 1786, even before he had published any important work.

SUCH WAS BENJAMIN FRANKLIN, certainly more extraordinary in the eyes of his friends, more worthy of being observed in his daily life than he was great in the eyes of America and Europe.

He attended the birth of his own country, so to speak: his name is to be found at the vanguard of all its great achievements. In many ways, the emancipation of the United States was accomplished by him. His memory is hallowed by that revolution, the most useful to human happiness to have occurred on earth at that time, and by one of the most brilliant discoveries of physics.

Eripuit caelo fulmen, sceptrumque tyrannis.
[He snatched lightning from the sky and scepters from tyrants. — Turgot]

But those achievements which epitomize his public life leave aside the most precious in him. His personality was much more valuable than his fame.

Benjamin Franklin depicted himself in *Memoirs* only a fragment of which has been published so far; but that was published by his enemies or incumbents of the Cabinet of Saint James's. They provided dull notes, to which his family should have responded sooner by publishing the rest of the work. In the meantime we will offer here a few insights I have from Franklin's own lips, in the course of an intimate connection which lasted several years.

It is well-known that he was born in Boston in 1705; that he was a printer and bookseller in Philadelphia; that he entered public life only after retiring from trade, about the age of forty; and that his first experiments with electricity happened at about that time. That might seem an unnecessary reminder; but some details from his early life must not be ignored, for they give the key to his personality, or rather because they bring to our knowledge those circumstances which laid the basis of his personality.

His father and mother were prosperous artisans whose daily labor provided all their income. In childhood Franklin wanted nothing; his soul was not injured by need; and the first examples he came across were of hard work, thrift, common sense, virtue and the happiness produced by an industrious life. His mother is said to have been a very sensible woman: she would direct her children's minds towards ideas with applications in daily life, and gave them habits which can make it more pleasant and beneficial. Franklin often told us that on a fun fair day a female relative gave him a little money which he was allowed to spend as he wished; the first thing he noticed on entering the hall where the fair was taking place was a whistle, blown by the vendor who produced sounds Franklin found ravishing: he wanted one, and made it so obvious that all the money in his pocket had to be put down. He went home very happy, blowing away, loud and shrill. His mother asked: "So this whistle is what you liked best?" — Yes, mother. — You did not see anything else which you liked? — Oh, yes, mother; but I had spent all I had on the whistle, and had no more money to purchase anything else. — How do you mean, you spent everything on the whistle! But you could have bought twenty whistles for that amount; and as you only need one, you could have bought a drum, a cart, and many other pretty toys." The little man was left thoughtful and baffled (mark that he was at most five or six years old). His mother went on: "My little friend, before buying a whistle, one should always know how much it is going to cost. Whenever you want something in future, I advise you to ask yourself first: 'How much is the whistle worth?'" Franklin would add that he had never forgotten that lesson, and that since then he had perhaps never hankered after something without repeating to himself this little proverb. When Franklin's son asked the court of Saint James to be given the governorship of one of the thirteen states, a favor which so regrettably connected him with the royalist party, Franklin told him: "Think of what, one day, the whistle may cost you! Why don't you rather become a joiner or a cartwright, as the fortune I leave you seems inadequate to you? At least a man who works for a living remains a free man." But, he added when telling us this story, the young man was infatuated with excellence: he was ashamed of doing as his father had done.

This commonsensical woman had been able to give Benjamin but a mediocre education; but she carefully preserved him from anything which could warp his reason. She would let him play and saunter freely, to make him hardy. All day long he would be roaming about, in winter amidst snow and ice, in summer at the seaside where he bathed. He would sometimes swim for hours on end, several times on the same day. During the bathing season, he often told us, he would feel stronger and heartier: he ate a great deal, but was singularly thin. His mother would often reprimand him for his fondness for pleasure of this sort: but her opinion went the same way as her other sermons; and she was comforted by the thought that he was becoming stronger by the day and was thus acquiring a good without which the most distinguished talents and the most happy circumstances are often to no avail—an excellent health.

Surrounded by the dissipation of his contemporaries, Franklin would read, ponder his reading and try to put it to a good purpose. Before he left his father's home he happened on a few volumes by Plutarch: he read them ravenously. Nothing ever impressed him more than the simple and grand manner, the wise and generous philosophy of that writer, except perhaps for the exquisite good sense and the, as it were, more familiar virtue of Socrates, who is depicted so vividly by Xenophon in his *Memorabilia*. Reading the ancients is a sort of touchstone which may usefully reveal the abilities and the character of young people. There are few truly able men who are not passionate about the ancients, especially Plutarch and Xenophon.

After reading a treatise on the custom of eating flesh, Franklin became convinced that it was a barbarous and pernicious custom; he resolved no longer to eat anything which had been alive.[1]

His mother indulged him, as she was convinced that it was a passing fad. But she soon found that she was wrong; and when her friends asked her who might have put such an idea into his head she would answer, It is some mad philosopher, and would add in a low voice, There is little harm done; it teaches him self-control; he is learning that everything is possible if one really wants it.[2]

Franklin spent his childhood under the eye of such a good mother. But his activity, which wearied of being exercised in a narrow scope, soon made his father's home unbearable. He was barely a teenager when he planned to leave it: the plans of a person of his stamp do not remain in abeyance for long. A cause[3] for discontent arose: he readily availed himself of it and ran away; so here he was, like Adam and Tom Jones, with the world before him, with no other guide than his good fortune, or rather his common sense, which had not yet been honed by experience.

For some time he wandered, as it were at random. He went to Philadelphia, as he hoped it would be easier to find work in that town which the industriousness of its founders had rendered prosperous. He reached it with a mind full of the cheerful prospects of youth, but with no other resources than robust health and the clear determination not to starve. When entering that city, all he had in his pocket was a Dutch six-dollar, that is to say, five pounds of our currency. He immediately expended part of that on three large loaves of bread: he squeezed one under his right arm, one under his left arm, and strode along eating the third; in this manner, which was not improved by his garb, he walked across the town, where a woman noticed him, who was to share his life and make him happy for nearly half a century.

The time Franklin spent in Philadelphia during that first stay, and that he had in London where he tried his luck in a different occupation is remarkable only for the gradual progress of his budding mind and his as yet wavering disposition. All that was new to him, all his successes and his errors were put to good use; everything was nearly equally useful to him. He tells this part of his history in minute detail and is right to do so; no time of life is of more moment for the happiness of the rest. One cannot lay too much emphasis on the dangers one is beset with, even if one's life is habitually governed by common sense and reason; and nothing is more useful than what keeps us from straying off the right path.

All that time Franklin's mind grew: he read a few good English authors. Locke, Collins, Shaftesbury and *The Spectator* kept him interested and busy in turn. Locke taught him how to think; *The Spectator* taught him how to write. He told us that, at that time, he also first read Pascal's *Provincial Letters*, in a rather poor translation; he was delighted by that work and re-read it several times. The *Provincial Letters* are one of the French works which he thought most highly of.

He was so shaken by his reading of Collins that he undertook to discuss all the questions of dogma in short essays. He pondered deeply, in turn, the divine nature of Scripture, Revelation, and the various mysteries: he used up all the subtlety of metaphysics which was still common then. He went so far as to deny the existence of God and, which is no less deplorable, so far as to question the foundations of morals.

But those wanderings of a bold mind who rushes down all the alleys his ratiocination opens up were quite short-lived. Franklin quickly acknowledged that he had been wrong regarding those last two matters. Few philosophers are as certain as he was of the existence of an intelligent being who animates the universe; and nobody has as rigorously demonstrated the principles which, even without that belief, lay down the rules of virtue. He liked to quote two sayings by Bacon; firstly, that it takes more credulity to be an atheist than to believe in God, and secondly, that a superficial study (*levis degustatio*) of physics leads to atheism, but that a deeper knowledge (*pleni haustus*) brings one back to religious ideas and sentiments. As for practical morality, he constantly repeated that it was the only reasonable choice for individual happiness as well as the only guarantee of general happiness. One day, when he had said a lot about that, he concluded with these words, in French nearly always made more forceful or elegant by their unevenness: If scoundrels were aware of all the advantages of virtue, they would become honest out of knavery.

During his first stay in Philadelphia, the interesting woman we mentioned had done him several great services: he became fond of her, and she very fond of him. When in London he completely neglected her. But his mind daily became more thoughtful, and his soul began to feed on the ideas and feelings of moral perfection. He felt he had done wrong, and determined to right that wrong. So, he left London to return to Philadelphia. This was when he designed a master plan for his life which he was never to relinquish; he was no longer a young man groping his way; he could see clearly the road and the goal; and he never ever swerved from it.

When reading the Bible, which he often did, his attention was often particularly drawn to the Book of Proverbs. The so-called Books of Wisdom evince much knowledge of society and of the human heart. That of Proverbs contains excellent lessons applicable to everyday life, expressed in forceful and pithy maxims. There Franklin read: "Length of days is in thy right hand, and in thy left hand riches and honor." This was like a ray of light to him. So, it depends on man if he lives long and acquires enough wealth to be happy! He determined to be a living example of this proverb, on both counts. He was twenty years old then and, at the age of eighty, when recounting this episode he added: "See if I have been wrong. My health has never been better than it is now; I am not affluent, but prosperous beyond my needs; and it is well-known that King George gained nothing from his quarreling with the printer's apprentice."

The *Memorabilia* of Socrates had made the strongest impression on him: the simplicity and moderation, the subtlety and the common sense of that philosopher, particularly suited his way of feeling and of seeing things. There was nobody he wanted to resemble more than Socrates: he took him as his model.

But, when trying to practice the virtues as a whole, he soon found that he could not give each equal attention. It then occurred to him to take them one by one, as analysts do, and to move to the second one only when the first had been secured. He ranked them in the best order he could think of, and immediately started with the major ones. In order to proceed more methodically, he had turned a notebook into a diary, with every day in the week and month. At first, he would devote four or five days to a virtue or a mental ability; sometimes he would give it a week or a whole month; and every evening, when taking stock of the day, he would note his progress and his errors. After dealing separately with the objects of his moral education, he gradually attempted to encompass them within ever more comprehensive wholes, so that eventually this practice became a system of habits which were as natural to him as moving his arms and legs. We were able to peruse this valuable notebook. It provided a sort of chronological story of the soul and the disposition of Franklin: they could be seen developing, getting stronger, shaping up to all the actions which epitomize their perfection as well as the art of living and practicing virtue, learnt in the same way as that of playing an instrument or going on one's first military campaign. The epigraph to this notebook was the proverb mentioned above.

It seems that around that time his relationship with his lifelong partner became an intimate one. They were not quite the same age: this excellent woman was a few years older than he; her poise contributed much to shaping the guidelines for behavior and work followed with so much zeal and constancy by her young friend. He told us several times that what merits he had had he owed in great part to her. To him, a man is whole only when attached to a woman worthy of making him happy: before that his life is imperfect; it is but one half of a whole, which cannot remain thus divided without great disadvantages. "Nature," he would add, "always punishes us, with specific flaws and misfortunes, for a system which flouts her own."

Franklin's wife was nearly as involved as he was in his printing-press, his dealings in newspapers and American almanacs, his bookselling and stationery trade. In shopkeeping of a different kind she had learnt management, neatness and activity, and that helped him, as well as her advice and opinion; she was as quick-witted and tactful as she was commonsensical and experienced. "There was always something which she knew and I did not, Franklin often told us; and if something had escaped me, I could rely on its being what she had noticed." . . .

When still very young, Franklin had felt the need for financial independence. Nearly from the outset of his career he had nurtured the idea and the hope of a decent fortune. But with a soul such as he had he did not seek riches; his very plans for beneficence made it unnecessary. He did not think that it was enough to open one's purse to do good. He had decided in advance what income he wanted to command, and nothing would make him go beyond it. At that time when he was a most prosperous businessman, and when his creditworthiness was at its highest, he suddenly retired to a philosophical life. We often heard him say that he was more sorry to be so well-off than not to be richer. "My heirs," he would say, "will find it much more difficult to be worth something than if they were egged on by the need to shape their own lives; and I would feel guilty towards them, if I tried to gather over their heads assets which can usually be enjoyed in a beneficial fashion only if they were acquired through one's own labor." . . .

When he left France, he gave us the sword which he wore then [during the Revolutionary War], together with the stick he had used for over thirty years in his experiments aimed at stilling choppy waters; its knob contained a small vial of oil. I leave them to you, he told us, as relics and tokens of friendship. It is easy to imagine how we treasure them. . . .

During his last stay in France, which public enthusiasm must have made pleasant to him, Franklin constantly mixed in Paris with people distinguished for their learning, their wit and, above all, for their love of men and of freedom. They met in the houses of Turgot, Helvétius, La Rochefoucault and d'Holbach; he was taken there as soon as he arrived in Paris, and developed several amicable relationships which he sedulously kept up. He liked to quote, and carefully put into practice, the proverb of his friends the savages: Keep the chain of friendship bright. Of the people to whom he became particularly close one may single out the widow of the philosopher Helvétius, whose destiny it was to count among her friends several of the age's great men, and whom, on his departure, he left shedding many tears, honorable to both of them.

That departure had become necessary to his country. It was not easy for Franklin to leave France; he was taking away with him memories which would cause him to miss it; but he was obeying his sense of duty. Mr. Jefferson, who replaced him shortly after in his mission with our government, and who has since then been seen to hold so outstandingly the post of minister for foreign affairs, and to leave it when new guidelines were no longer in agreement with the interests of his country and of mankind — Mr. Jefferson told us then: "This great man must absolutely go back to America; if he died, I would have his remains taken there; his mere coffin would ensure unity among the various parties."

It could be feared that he might be unable to undertake this voyage, or that he would not be given the time. For two or three years he had felt more or less sharp and continuous pain, caused by a stone in his bladder. As the stone kept growing, his pain was sometimes very acute. Franklin would not hear of an operation, though his health, which was otherwise excellent, seemed to ensure success. He felt that he could still be useful to his country; he would not, to spare himself pain, put at risk a life which was bound up with public interest.

He went, with sharp regrets, comforted only by the thought that he would die among men he had served with so much zeal for fifty years, in the arms of his beloved daughter Mrs Beach [i.e., Sarah Franklin Bache] who, during the revolution, had shown the mettle of a patriot, beside the quiet affections and virtues of her sex.

During the crossing, which he bore much better than could be expected, he had the company of his two grandsons, Temple Franklin, who acted as his embassy secretary, and Benjamin Beach [Bache], who has since then become a printer in Philadelphia, and a man worthy of his grandfather, thanks to his common sense and simplicity, his tastes, the way he mapped out his life and his most sincere attachment to republican principles.

But Franklin's regrets on leaving France were not just owing to personal feelings. While deeply touched by individual kindness, he was even more so by services the government and, above all, public opinion, had rendered to the revolution in his country. Of that he spoke with an emotion which age and public business had not abated in him. The men who have since ruled America have not always seemed to wish to follow his lead on that point, as well as on several others. But has not America paid its debt to France by setting such a fine example, which has not gone wasted? With its generous philanthropy, France has calculated better than those cold politicians who believe that any data must be expressed in numbers; for philanthropy, like all the other virtues, creates its own reward; and he who constantly practices it must, in the long run, harvest advantages all the more secure as the superiority they depend on is of a kind which it is in nobody's interest to challenge. . . .

As long as his pain could be borne, or was discontinuous, this rest [afforded by retirement] was filled with peaceful domestic activities, with interesting reading, and the conversation of selected friends. In a letter to his good friend Mme. Helvétius, he told her that he spent most of the day among workmen busy building convenient homes for his grandchildren; that he sometimes renewed his acquaintance with the sages of all ages, and that he tried to gather in his home those of his country; that he also devoted a little time to putting his affairs in order and to completing his *Memoirs*. I reach out to you, he added, despite the vast spread of the seas between us, in the expectation of the celestial kiss I firmly hope to give you one day.

That was his swan song. Soon, as his stone kept growing, with its edges probably becoming more angular, his pain gradually increased: the patient would never consider an operation. Now age was his only reason for opposing the wishes of his friends and rejecting the promises of a celebrated artist. For his life to be bearable, he had to be given opium nearly continually. His constitution, so far sound and robust, slowly deteriorated; and, with unimpaired mental abilities and spiritual serenity, having some time before been dealt a deadly blow, not by his initial illness, but by an abscess in his heart which may have been caused by the migration of the lithic matter in that organ, he died on 17 April, 1790, amidst his family and a grateful people.

Very soon this loss to mankind was known across the ocean; it echoed throughout Europe and, though it had been expected in France for a long time, it caused a great shock here. The Constituent Assembly was sitting; Mirabeau [Honoré-Gabriel Riquetti, comte de Mirabeau] went up to the rostrum: Franklin is dead! He announced with his characteristic lofty tone, science, philosophy, liberty have gathered around his grave, wetting it with their tears. He asked that France, which had, so to speak, adopted Franklin, should honor his memory in a very special way; and the Assembly decreed three days of solemn mourning.

A reading of American newspapers of the time reveals that sorrow was universal in the thirteen states and that even his enemies — for his glory dimmed too many lesser lights for him not to have enemies — had to don the mantle of public grief. But our purpose is not to dwell on those details; it is best to devote a little time to some traits which may contribute to a portrait of Franklin: we will provide them in no particular order, as they occur to our memory.

We saw that in the world he had a prominent place as a scientist, as a politician, as a writer, as a philosopher and as a moralist; from none of these standpoints was he like other men.

The outstanding characteristic of his mind was uprightness, simplicity, sagacity. From an early age he had made it a rule to see things as they were; he would carefully brush aside what might either distort them or obscure them: he did not value extraordinary or dazzling things; he only prized those with immediate application; he would try to bring them to their simplest and most common level; and, while his thought was customarily couched in ingenious and witty terms, that seemed to be only to make it easier to grasp and to put it within the reach of the most ordinary minds. Besides, no man ever saw more promptly and more acutely how to make the most of an idea proffered him or a fact that arose. In something you might chance to say to him, he would find an explanation for, or a link to, a host of discrete observations; in the smallest experiment he could see the general laws of physics; and what we see every day without noticing often provided him with the trigger for the most useful inventions. He had read widely, but was not strictly speaking erudite, and even in physics he had invented more than he had learned. From each book his memory would retain only what he hoped to be able to use; but that was forever. Nor had he forgotten anything of the interesting things he had gathered from human intercourse. The observations or anecdotes relating to that, always vivid in his mind, made up for him a sort of practical science and ethic, which he constantly applied to his daily demeanor or which, forever peppering his conversation, made it equally enjoyable and useful. In a word, nobody had a better claim to say: I carry everything with me.

Besides, it should not be thought that his intellectual acumen made his philosophy dull and austere: there has never been a more sprightly man or one who enjoyed life more. He despised equally the pedantic or meticulous precision which some minds bring to bear on common things and ideas, and the scolding morality which casts a dark veil over life; bad temper he considered a vice, calling it the untidiness of the soul.

In writing, his style was simple and natural, but ingenious and always agreeably colored by the imagination: he had read much poetry, and had himself written verse;[4] like the language of Socrates his style bore the mark of familiarity with the Muses: like that philosopher he was convinced that the Graces should be honored. Even in the most advanced old age his mind had kept its freshness; several of his last pieces bear the true hallmark of youth.

We have said that Franklin's policies consisted in no more than telling the truth. Yet few were more reserved, more guarded than he was: he said that, if faith saves one in the hereafter, it leads to failure in this world. But his acumen he only used to avoid deception, not to deceive others.

With respect to his opinions on social organization, as in the other aspects of his philosophy he had pared everything down. He thought that what was needed were few laws, little government, and he held a deeply rooted belief that, as society moved towards perfection, the number of the former and the direct action of the latter would proportionately decline. According to him, the powers that be had one duty only, to prevent violence: in other areas, all they had to do was *laisser faire*. The idea of limiting the freedom of commerce in general, or in the trade of one merchandise in particular, was one of those absurdities which are reached only with much art and reasoning. He would say, "It took much intellectual application in Europe for you to imagine that the trade in corn must be regulated by laws: nature and common sense on their own would not have taught you that."

He much derided constitutions with a balance of powers: he did not share the admiration of several of our writers, and of a few of his own friends, for the constitution of England which, in his eyes, was but the shapeless outcome of circumstances, supported by corruption; several of whose drawbacks, however, were corrected by public-spiritedness and freedom of the press. As he saw it, anything good in England is the product of public opinion, which, in the constitution, the government has not always the means to corrupt or stifle. We often heard him say that, before the American insurrection, he had often written from London to his fellow countrymen: "You want to shake the yoke; to achieve that, you need a war. Reckon what it must cost you, and send me one quarter of the sum; I promise you that I will buy off Parliament, the ministry and the king himself." He would add: "It would have been easy to keep my word."

But what mainly characterizes Franklin, what would have distinguished him in any century, was the art of faring well with himself and with others, of using in the most advantageous way the tools nature provided man with; in a word, the art of living. To him, the actual merit of any being could be measured by his ability to make the most of his original abilities, and to coordinate them to circumstances: intelligence he thought useful only insofar as it was directed to that grand aim; even virtue he saw only as a necessary condition to the good management and the welfare of life.

Nature had given him a most vigorous constitution: the labors of his youth, as well as the games of his childhood, had made it stronger and stronger. No exertion was needed to keep it up. But he understood early that without good health it was impossible to achieve great things, and very difficult not to spoil many small ones. Thenceforth he set himself a regimen which he adhered to exactly. Not that he felt it necessary to weigh the slightest impressions, like people who are said to be on a diet; but, from time to time, he would give his stomach a feast, as he put it: he left it idle by omitting several meals. From time to time he would swallow either wormwood salt, to melt down the phlegm and the fat which he took often to impair the action of the upper tracts, or quinquina, varying the strength and the frequency of dosing, in order to renew the vigor of solids. The way some people fear fresh air he thought ridiculous. He usually slept with his windows open; he would even often get up to have what he termed an air bath, and sometimes he would spend several hours in one night sitting all but naked at his desk. There is no denying that he thrived on that; but his strong constitution could put up with all the sweating: a few people who were not so sturdy had recourse to the same regimen, and were much the worse for it.

This steady health enabled Franklin to use his time as he deemed suitable; he would eat, sleep, work at any hour, as needed: so that no man was ever less busy, though he undeniably conducted very great business. Whenever one found him, he was available. His house in Passy, where he had fixed his abode because he liked the country and wanted good air, was always open to everybody; he always had an hour to devote to you; and it cannot be said that he relied on the work of his secretaries; for he only had one, his grandson (to whom he left as much time for playing as he himself devoted to conversation), and a copyist who occasionally helped them both. Such were the departmental offices of the minister plenipotentiary of the United States. They were, indeed, enough for him to correspond with his government, with all the American agents spread over Europe, whose operations he was in charge of directing, and with the French government, which it cannot be supposed that he neglected. In truth, he only did what work was strictly necessary. To him, the best way not to see any work through was to demand, as we are used to doing, superabundant, meaningless paperwork from our departments. "You use up much time, work and skill in order not to bring business to completion," he would say. "When one really wants to get business done, there is no need for all that expenditure."

His health probably also accounted in great part for the constant evenness of his temper; but his never-ending self-study, which remained a concern in his old age, had singularly strengthened the predispositions of a most happy nature. He felt that a man who did not enjoy tranquility of soul and presence of mind must always underachieve. There were few points on which he had practiced as carefully. So, it was difficult to display more patience and gentleness than he did, to express less the emotions one might feel or the opinions one had to keep secret; it was difficult to have in readiness more than he did all the faculties of his mind.

Since man is made for society, since mixing with his fellow human beings provides him with his sweetest pleasures, his main object must surely be to improve all aspects of his relationships with them. In order happily to coexist with men it is not enough not to offend against fairness, nor is it enough to make useful deeds; other men must find in you the expression of such amiable benevolence as adorns both him who dispenses it and him who receives it. There lies the principle and the true goal of politeness. Franklin valued it greatly; but by that word he meant neither nods nor bows, nor deferential gestures, nor again that cold respect which is usually but a means to keep people at a distance, and which does not even always rule out contempt. What he held in high esteem was the politeness of the heart, habitual obligingness; that he considered a virtue: he believed that one must be kind, nearly in the same way as one must pay off one's debts, and that only some higher duty can exculpate a good man who distresses another, even about indifferent matters. "The most fraught quarrels, the most violent hatred are often caused," he would say, "by small stings, such as those which unleashed the storms trapped in Ulysses's bags of wind. Much grief, many misfortunes can easily be avoided by a little self-control, and thoughtfulness towards others; even when no actual breach happens, when one has not made the life of the people whose lives one shares as happy as possible, one is wrong. Keep the chain bright."

No philosopher better implemented his own maxims. He was very benevolent towards everybody, he was very thoughtful and attentive towards his friends; and, though because of his natural disposition and the sedate habits he had acquired, he was never zealous in his dealings with other people, there was in his friendship a sort of coquettishness which made its testimonies seem ever more juvenile.

But I am aware that I have been carried away by the pleasure of talking of this great man: my recollection of him, which will ever be dear to me, is paired with such vivid and lasting impressions that I could not have stayed dutifully within the bounds I had set for myself. This memoir was to have run to a few pages only; I would not even have ventured to write it, had Franklin's family published the rest of his *Memoirs*. For indeed, it belonged to him to depict himself, and to his life to provide a proper eulogy.

Publication of those memoirs will not just add to his glory: the public interest also demands it. No document could be of more advantage to the cause of liberty: no reading could be more beneficial to a young man entering into the world. He will see there what diligence, thriftiness and a good timetable can achieve; he will see there that, while living by manual labor one may also cultivate one's mind; that, without being a professional scientist, with analysis and sagacity one may render signal services to the sciences and make one's name thanks to them; that the practice of good behavioral habits and of the virtues may be reduced to an art, the usefulness of which can be demonstrated by calculation, and the practice of which be learned by methodical exercise; in a word, he will behold an exemplary life all of whose actions combine harmoniously, as it were, like the moves of an elaborate game of chess, he will behold the virtually unheard of instance of a spotless political career at the highest level.

Notes

1. In the first part of his memoirs, Franklin said that this idea and determination sprang from his reading a piece by Tryon on the same subject: but his oral account of this episode is such as we give here [Cabanis's note].

2. Later in life he altogether gave up his principles on this point: he explains in his memoirs what led him to resume common habits. He was very fond of fish. During a sea voyage he saw seamen preparing freshly caught cod. In the stomachs of the fish were found several small cod which they had just swallowed. Aha! Franklin said, so you eat one another? Eh! why should man not eat you too? And he added, This comes from being a reasonable being: one always finds plausible rationalizations to excuse all one's passions [Cabanis's note].

3. This cause was ill-treatment on the part of his brother: he said that he was pained to see everybody side against him; and he ascribed to his deeply rooted feeling of rebellion on this occasion his unflinching antagonism to arbitrary power [Cabanis's note].

4. Among the verses by him we are familiar with, there is one which we were particularly struck by; it is a song on the anniversary of his marriage to Mrs. Franklin. They had then been making each other happy for fifty years. One of the stanzas ends with two lines, the gist of which is, I am so used to her faults that they are no more shocking to me now than my own [Cabanis's note].

From *Oeuvres complètes de Cabanis*, 5 vols. (Paris: Bossange Frères, 1823–1825), 5: 225–248, *passim*. Translation here provided by Isabelle Bour.

[The Sawdust Pudding Supper:
Two Versions, 1835 and 1875]

ROBERTS VAUX AND A CANADIAN NUMISMATIST

The story of the sawdust (i.e., bran) pudding, which dates back to when Benjamin Franklin was editor and proprietor of the *Pennsylvania Gazette*, is one of his best-loved anecdotes. It exists in countless versions, though Frankin himself apparently never wrote it down. Isaiah Thomas's *History of Printing in America* (1810) contains the earliest known published version (Zall, no. 216). A much more detailed version appeared in the *Analectic Magazine* 12 (August 1818): 162. This version is specific enough in terms of its detail, especially its references to several of Franklin's early Philadelphia friends, to suggest its authenticity. It was this version that John F. Watson reprinted in 1830 in his *Annals of Philadelphia* (Zall, no. 283). The first version reprinted below, which Roberts Vaux wrote down in a letter to Martin Van Buren in 1835, contains some of the same details as the *Analectic* version, but it includes additional detail, as well. Roberts Vaux (1786–1836) had good reason to possess an insider's knowledge. Though he was much too young to have been friends with Franklin, Roberts Vaux was the grandson and namesake of Hugh Roberts, who was a member of the Junto, the mutual improvement organization that Franklin and his friends formed in 1727. The same year Vaux wrote this letter, he published an article about the members of the Junto from his grandfather's papers. As J. A. Leo Lemay notes in *The Life of Benjamin Franklin*, Vaux's list of Junto members provides much crucial information unavailable elsewhere (1: 336).

Published anonymously over fifty years after its anonymous reporter had first heard this anecdote, the second version of the story of the sawdust supper reprinted below does not even contain a sawdust pudding. It does contain some obvious anachronisms: Franklin was not editing a newspaper when he knew John Hancock, Benjamin Rush, and George Washington. Yet this particular version is worth reprinting for several reasons. For one, it has never been reprinted since it first appeared in 1875 in an obscure Montreal monthly magazine, the *Canadian Antiquarian and Numismatic Journal*. While publishing this anecdote anonymously, this Montreal numismatist attributed it to Franklin's good friend John Vaughan (1756–1841). Wine merchant, librarian, and philanthropist, John Vaughan was the son of Samuel Vaughan, a merchant in the Jamaica trade and one of Franklin's closest friends. In 1778, Samuel sent his son John to Bordeaux, where he studied the wine business. While in France, John became friends with Benjamin Franklin and his grandson William Temple Franklin. John came to Philadelphia in 1782 and began importing Jamaican rum and other spirits, but his social and intellectual activities ultimately took on more importance than his business endeavors. Elected to the American Philosophical Society in 1784, he became its secretary in 1789, its treasurer in 1791, and its librarian in 1803. Vaughan worked tirelessly to make the Society's library one of the finest research collections in the nation. When Franklin's library went on sale, Vaughan acquired for the Society the transactions of numerous scientific societies across Europe and many other books important to history and science. He purchased several books from Franklin's library for his own personal collection, which he later donated to the Society.

Roberts Vaux to Martin Van Buren, 15 August 1835

Soon after Franklin made his first visit to Philadelphia in 1723, he became acquainted with my grandfather. The foundation of a mutual confidence and friendship was then laid, which endured through almost two-thirds of a century when death dissolved this long, and sincere attachment. They were born in the same year 1706, and so were several other members of the *Junto* which they formed in 1727 for the improvement of its associates in moral philosophy and political science. At that time there was but one newspaper in the Province, and Franklin's sagacious mind saw the need of another journal, to rectify public opinion, and disseminate principles, which he deemed essential to the general welfare. It was not however until 1736, that he succeeded in establishing his afterward far famed Pennsylvania *Gazette*, which distributed so much political and economical wisdom, to the People. — A printer himself by profession, but without funds, he was under the necessity of borrowing from two, or three of his friends, money to enable him to commence his labours. — He now rented a room in an obscure alley, where he opened his office and unassisted, composed, struck off, and distributed his paper. — The acute and youthful champion of human rights, soon began to notice with great freedom and force, some of the men and measures of the day, which no one before had the moral courage to arraign. This exhibition, produced a concussion in the primitive community, not less startling, than the shocks which were afterward imparted by his original experiments with the electric fluid. — My Grandfather, and Philip Sing, and Luke Morris and some other members of the Junto, who felt a deep interest in Franklin's success, hearing many complaints of the *tone* of his paragraphs, met one day to consider the propriety of advising him to be more moderate in that respect. — The consultation resulted in the appointment of two of them to administer a caution. — They found the editor with his sleeves rolled up, busy at his press, and on mentioning the purpose of their visit, he excused himself from want of time then, to hear them, but named an early evening when they and their constituents should take supper with him, and talk over the matter at leisure. On the appointed night they assembled at his house, and some time was spent in communicating their opinions and views. — At length Franklin's wife made her appearance — she set out a table — covered it with a coarse tow cloth — placed a trencher and spoon and a penny porringer for each guest, and having deposited on one end of the simple board a large pudding, and on the other a stone pitcher, she retired. — The Philosopher now begged his friends to be seated. — To each he served a slice, and gave some water, and bid them enjoy themselves. — He supplied himself largely, and eat heartily; occasionally saying, "Come gentlemen help yourselves, we have another pudding in the pot." But in vain they endeavored to dispose of their fare. — Finally they looked at one another, and toward their host, and were about to withdraw from the table; at this moment Franklin rose and said. "I am happy to have your company and to listen to your suggestions — some of you have been my benefactors especially — your advice is well meant I know, but I cannot think with you in some respects. You see upon what humble food I can live, and he who can subsist upon Saw Dust Pudding and Water, as can Benjamin Franklin, Printer, needs not the Patronage of any one." Hereupon they parted, cordially shaking hands; the advisers resolving as they walked home, never more to interfere with the intrepid editor.

"Dr. Franklin at Home"

Mr. John Vaughan, Secretary of the American Philosophical Society of Philadelphia, related at a dinner party at Niagara Falls in 1822, the following characteristic anecdote of Dr. Franklin:

Although Mr. Vaughan was much Dr. Franklin's junior, he was intimate with him, because there were points of resemblence in their characters, and because public business threw them often together. At the time spoken of, Franklin was the editor of a young newspaper, advocating uncompromisingly a certain line of American politics.

In those days men were very earnest. One of Franklin's subscribers disapproved of his proceedings, but forbore for some time, hoping for a change; but time only made matters worse.

One day the subscriber met Dr. Franklin in the street, and freely told him that his politics would ruin both him and his country. He finished by desiring him to take his name from the list of his subscribers. Dr. Franklin told him he was sorry to lose him, but that his wishes should be obeyed.

A week or two afterwards, not a little to the old subscriber's surprise, he received from Franklin a little note, inviting him to supper on the coming Friday evening.

He accepted, and went. He found the perverse editor in clean, plain lodgings, at a side-table, leaning on some books in his usual easy humour. Supper was being laid on a round oak table, over which a neat-handed girl had spread a white cloth. She then gradually covered it with a shining, firm cucumber, a pat of butter, a large china jug of water from the spring, a loaf of good bread, three cool lettuces, some leeks, aud a piece of ripe cheese, with a little jug of foaming beer, more brisk than strong.

Just as the last article was placed the table, a tap at the door brought in that friendly man, Dr. Rush, so well known all over the world for his medical skill. Another knock introduced Mr. Vaughan, most probably then full of young projects, and primed for discussion.

To the subscriber's great surprise, after these two Washington himself stepped in, his square, grave face relaxing into good fellowship when he saw his company, and the preparations for making a night of it. Hancock, positive, able, and honest, and one more, made up the company.

They disposed themselves round the table, and fell to. So slender a repast, in such a humble room, for such a party, consisting of the first men in America, puzzled the subscriber severely.

All these guests were in their prime, splendidly and variously endowed. Each had passed the day in labour for the good of others — in the senate, the army, or in private life. They now came together for well-earned relaxation. The hours were only too short for the outpourings of their full minds. Twelve o'clock saw them home.

A few days afterwards the subscriber again met Dr. Franklin in the street. "Ah!" said he, "a thousand thanks for that delightful evening. I saw the lesson you were reading me. You meant to shew that a man who can entertain the first and best of our country upon a cucumber and a glass of cold water, can afford to be politically honest."

"Well, friend," Franklin smilingly replied, "something of that sort."

From William Allen Butler, *A Retrospect of Forty Years, 1825–1865*, ed. Harriet Allen Butler (New York: Charles Scribner's Sons, 1911), pp. 46–48.

"Dr. Franklin at Home," *Canadian Antiquarian and Numismatic Journal* 3 (April 1875): 159–160.

[Memoir of Dr. George Logan of Stenton, 1839]

DEBORAH NORRIS LOGAN

Grandson of Franklin's old friend the great Philadelphia bookman James Logan, George Logan (1753–1821) was born two years after his grandfather's death, but the connection gave him a way of introducing himself to Franklin. George Logan received a good general education in Philadelphia and England before apprenticing in the mercantile trade, but he returned to Great Britain in the late 1770s to study medicine at the University of Edinburgh, where he took his medical degree in 1779. Upon completing school, he took the opportunity to travel through Great Britain and Europe. While in Paris, he visited Passy to meet Franklin, presenting him with a copy of his medical dissertation, *De venenis*, a treatise on poisons (Wolf and Hayes, no. 2087). Happy to help the grandson of his old friend, Franklin welcomed George Logan, who frequently visited Passy during his time in Paris. Logan returned to Philadelphia in 1780, marrying Deborah Norris (1761–1839) the following year. Logan only practiced medicine briefly, devoting most of his attention to his farm. When Franklin returned to Philadelphia in 1785, Logan renewed their friendship. He related their conversations to his wife, which she incorporated in the memoir of her husband she was writing at the time of her death. She, too, met Franklin after he returned to Philadelphia and recorded her impressions of him in a note to this memoir. Her comments are not entirely positive: she critiques Franklin for writing the controversial *Historical Review of the Constitution and Government of Pensylvania* (1759). Her critique is somewhat unfair. Though *Historical Review* was attributed to Franklin in her day, it is now recognized as the work of Franklin's friend Richard Jackson, a British m.p. who sympathized with the American cause.

AFTER HE [GEORGE LOGAN] LEFT SCOTLAND he visited several parts of England and Ireland, and, crossing over to the continent, travelled through Holland, to France, Germany, and Italy. He made the longest stay in France, where he attended the anatomical lectures. Dr. Franklin was then resident at the French Court and was extremely kind and friendly to his young countryman, saying that he was happy to have it in his power to re-

[174]

turn the obligation which he himself had received in his young and inexperienced years from the friendship and wisdom of Dr. Logan's grandfather. At Passy, in the company of the sage, Dr. Logan spent many delightful hours; he was on terms of the greatest intimacy, admitted into his study, and frequently breakfasted and spent the morning with him, and it seemed impossible to be in Franklin's company without feeling yourself to advance in the scale of improvement, his various knowledge, his clear common sense, wit, and intelligence diffusing itself through his easy and unaffected conversation like the corruscations of his own brilliant discoveries from a highly charged object.

An occurrence took place about this time, connected with one of these visits to Passy, which Dr. Logan used in afterlife to mention as what had given him a strong distaste to arbitrary power, and placing in contrast the blessings and benefits of a free constitution where the rights of every individual are placed under the protection of the laws, and the meanest criminal cannot be imprisoned without knowing for what crime it is inflicted and who are his accusers. Dining one day at Passy with other company, a Mr. Adair was introduced by Dr. Franklin as an American gentleman, but from what State I do not recollect. During the entertainment the difficulty of procuring Madeira wine at that time in France was mentioned by Dr. Franklin, when Mr. Adair said he had some very fine and would do himself the pleasure of sending the doctor a few dozen. In the evening, when the company broke up, Dr. Logan asked Mr. Adair to take a seat in his post-chaise, as that gentleman was without a conveyance of his own. He accepted the offer, and it produced an interchange of visits. Shortly after, Dr. Logan, calling at his lodging, was informed by his servant that Mr. Adair had disappeared in an unaccountable manner; his effects were all left behind, his money in his banker's hands, but no intelligence of him had transpired. At length it was known that he had been confined by a *lettre de cachet* in the Bastille upon a suspicion that the wine he had presented to Dr. Franklin was poisoned. The arrest was officially made without the knowledge of our minister, and I believe the liberation was in consequence of his interference.

Dr. Logan continued his attentions to this great man after his return to his native country, and had the pleasure of being ranked among the friends of his declining years. A remarkable trait in his character was that, even in his early youth, he sought the company of his seniors, who were distinguished for their wisdom and virtue.

I have often thought that Dr. Franklin must have sensibly felt the difference between the *éclat* which he enjoyed at the Court of France and the reception which he met with upon his final return to his native country.

The elements of two parties were then fermenting themselves into the form which they afterwards assumed. The mass of the population of Pennsylvania was, as it has been ever since (and may I not say ever was?), decidedly democratic; but there was a contrary spirit then dominant and thinly diffused over the surface of society which rejected the philosopher because they thought he was too much of that popular stamp.

The first constitution of our State after the Revolution, which was his work, though adopted by the great body of the people, was disliked; and I well remember the remark of a fool, though a fashionable party-man at the time, that it was by no means "fashionable" to visit Dr. Franklin. No doubt he was saved from much impertinence by the company of such being withheld; but it may justly be questioned whether those were not greatly the losers who withheld from themselves the entertainment and advantages of his rich and varied conversation. Foreigners of the first distinction thought themselves happy in obtaining such a privilege, and a few of his old and tried friends yet remained to cheer the evening of his eventful life. One of these (the venerable Charles Thomson) was very often with him, and he has told me that, visiting the doctor on his sick-bed a short time before he died, he, in an allusion to a conversation that had formerly passed between them, said, "It is best to believe."[1] . . .

In reading *The Wealth of Nations*, which he [George Logan] justly appreciated without approving of all which the author has advanced, he told me of what Dr. Franklin had related to him of Adam Smith, with whom he was well acquainted. When writing that celebrated work, he was in the habit of taking the chapters as he composed them to his literary friends, and submitting the work to their inspection and criticism. He often availed himself of the benefit of their remarks, so as to rewrite chapters and reverse propositions. Dr. Franklin said he frequently brought it to himself and Dr. [Richard] Price.

Note

1. I have myself had the pleasure of being a few times in Dr. Franklin's society. His conversation was easy, and appeared to grow entirely out of the circumstances that presented themselves to the company, yet I observed that if you did not find you had acquired some-

thing by being with him it must be placed to the account of your own want of attention. His familiar letters give you a good idea of his conversation, — a natural and good-humoured (not sarcastic) wit played cheerfully along and beguiled you into maxims of prudence and wisdom. The man who could make the sayings of "Poor Richard" fashionable in France must have had no ordinary powers of conversation. What a pity there should have been any "errata" in his moral conduct! What a pity that he should have stooped to dishonour his pen by the false statements and glosses of *The Critical Review of the Government of Pennsylvania*! [Deborah Norris Logan's note]

From *Memoir of Dr. George Logan of Stenton*, ed. Frances A. Logan (Philadelphia: Historical Society of Pennsylvania, 1899), pp. 36–47.

"Personal Recollections of Benjamin Franklin" (1864)

ROBERT CARR

Born near Belfast, Ireland, Robert Carr (1778–1866) came to Philadelphia with his parents in 1784. They lived near Franklin Court, and he became friends and playmates with Sarah Franklin Bache's younger children. After Benjamin Franklin returned to Philadelphia in 1785, Carr had the chance to see him regularly. Carr apprenticed in Benjamin Franklin Bache's printshop and later established a distinguished printing career himself, earning in 1804 the first gold medal for general excellence in printing presented by the American Association of Booksellers.

William Bartram Snyder testified to Carr's "remarkably retentive memory" ("Proceedings of Societies," p. 58). Snyder's testimony adds further credence to Carr's reminiscences of Franklin, which are extremely detailed. Throughout his long life, Carr retained fond memories of his adolescent encounters with Franklin. Getting to know Franklin when he was around ten or eleven years old, Carr met him at a time in his life when experiences can take hold of the memory with great tenacity. Carr obviously enjoyed relating his encounters with Franklin. By 1864, when he finally wrote them down, he may have been the oldest living person who had known Franklin personally. The year before he wrote down these memories, Carr visited the New York Historical Society to attend a celebration of the two-hundredth anniversary of the birth of printer William Bradford, which turned out to be a general celebration of printing. Introduced as one of the nation's oldest living printers, Carr regaled those in attendance with firsthand stories of his conversations with Franklin. Perhaps this event compelled Carr to transcribe his memories for posterity. Or perhaps the prominent Philadelphia collector John A. McAllister (1822–1896) goaded him into it. John Van Horne characterizes McAllister as "an avid and pioneering collector of books, pamphlets, autographs, and local history documents dating back to the founding of Pennsylvania." The following account comes from a letter from Carr to McAllister dated May 25, 1864.

IN ANSWER TO YOUR REQUEST that I would give you a few notes of my recollections of Doctor Franklin, in his latter years, I have to state that I can say but very little, and that little only the crude reminiscence of a thoughtless school-boy of eleven or twelve years of age, whose opportunities of seeing the Doctor occurred from the fact of my residing near his house and being intimate with, and the playmates of, his two youngest grandsons.

It is seventy-four years since the Doctor's death, and few persons now remember the location of his house, and none of the present generation could have seen it, as every vestige of the building has been long since entirely obliterated, in the march of improvement.

The Doctor's mansion-house was in the centre of a lot of ground, midway between Third and Fourth-streets, about one hundred feet wide, and extending from Market to Chestnut-streets. A court, or alley, ten feet wide, called "Franklin Court," extended from Market-street to the rear of the house, which was built with the front towards Chestnut-street; but, some time after it was erected, it was discovered that the title to the front of the lot, on Chestnut-street, was defective; and the Doctor, rather than engage in a litigation, or pay an exorbitant price demanded by the claimant of the lot, abandoned it, and used the Market-street avenue. This fact I heard Mr. B. F. Bache, his grandson, relate to Mr. Volney, the traveller, who enquired why the Doctor had built his house fronting the South, to which he had no outlet.

The mansion-house was a plain brick building, three stories high, about forty feet front, and thirty feet deep, with an entry through the centre. There was a large parlor on the East side of the entry, and two rooms on the West side, with a door between them. The kitchen was in the basement, with an ice-house under it. The Doctor's office or study, was the Northwest room, on the first floor; and there was a coal grate, in which he burned Virginia or English coal. Below this grate, on the hearth, there was a small iron plate or trap-door, about five or six inches square, with a hinge and a small ring to raise it by. When this door or valve was raised, a current of air, from the cellar, rushed up through the grate to re-kindle the fire.

The Doctor's bed-chamber was the Southwest room, on the second floor. There were two cords, like bell-pulls, at the head of his bed; one was a bell-pull; and the other, when pulled, raised an iron bolt, about an inch square, and nine or ten inches long, which dropped through staples, at the top of the door, when shut; and until this bolt was raised the door could not be opened.

The house was built before the Revolution; but after the War, he made an addition to the East end, about eighteen feet wide and thirty feet long; the lower room of this addition, was a large reception room, in which the Philosophical Society met, for several years. The second floor was his library; and third floor lodging rooms. His son-in-law, Colonel Richard Bache, and family, resided in the same house with the Doctor.

The doors of the chambers, and nearly all the doors about the house, were lined or edged with green baize, to prevent noise when shutting; and several of them had springs behind them to close them.

On the South side of the house there was a grass lot, about one hundred feet square, containing a few floe plane trees, and surrounded on three sides by a brick wall. From the South wall to Chestnut-street, there were afterwards a tan-yard and currier's-shop. On the North side of the house there was an open lot of the same size, extending to the Printing-office, which was two stories high, built on each side, and over the court or carriage-way opening on Market-street.

This office he had built, after his return to France, for his grandson, Benjamin Franklin Bache, with whom I served my apprenticeship. The Western room, on the lower floor, was a typefoundry: the opposite room, on the East side of the Court, was a book-bindery. The printing-office was on the second floor, and was furnished with every variety of large founte of type, from nonpareil to the largest sizes then used for posting-bills. The Doctor brought them from Paris, when he returned, in 1785.

After the Doctor's death, in April, 1790, there were a great many articles that had belonged to him, stored in the loft, over the office; amongst others, a beautiful and valuable *Orrery* — which I believe was sent to the Philosophical Society — a great variety of electrical apparatus, and a *Sedan-chair*, in which I have often seen him carried by two men, to and from the State House, where he was President of the Supreme Executive Council of Pennsylvania. This Sedan-chair was sent to the Pennsylvania Hospital, where it remained a great many years, in the garret; but on enquiry about it, lately, I ascertained that it had been broken up and burned.

During the latter years of the Doctor's life, he was afflicted with the gout and stone. For the latter, his friends wished him to submit to an operation; but he said that at his age it was not worth while to undergo the pain. Although he suffered much from his afflictions, he was remarkably patient and mild. When able to be out of bed, he passed nearly all his time in his office, reading and writing, and in conversation with his friends; and, when the boys were playing and very noisy, in the lot front of the office, he would open the window and call to them: "Boys, Boys, can't you play without making so much noise. I am reading, and it disturbs me very much." I have heard the servants in his family say that he never used a hasty or angry word to any one.

On one occasion, when his servant was absent, he called me into his office, to carry a letter to the Post-office. Whilst waiting for it, there was a candle burning on the table, with which he had been melting sealing-wax. He told me to put it out and set it away. I took up the candlestick and blew the candle out, when he said: "Stop, my boy, I will show you the right way to put out a candle. Light it again." Accordingly, I lighted the candle; and the Doctor lifted it out of the candlestick, turning the blazing end down, until the tallow had *nearly* extinguished it, when he quickly turned it up, and blew it out. "Now," said he, "it can be lighted again very readily; and the grease will not run down the candle."

The Doctor was remarkable for always having some kind word of advice or encouragement, for those around him. You may recollect the anecdote, which has been published, of his conversation with the man, who was blacking his shoes: "John," said the Doctor, "I was once as poor a man as you; but I was industrious and saved my earnings, until now I have enough to enable me to live in comfort in my old age." "Ah," but Doctor, replied John, "if every one was as saving and as rich as you, who would black your shoes."

"Personal Recollections of Benjamin Franklin," *Historical Magazine* 4 (1868): 59–60.

Permissions

John Adams to Abigail Adams, 23 July 1775, is reprinted by permission of the publisher from *The Adams Papers: Adams Family Correspondence, Volume 1: December 1761–May 1776*, edited by L. H. Butterfield, pp. 252–253, Cambridge, MA: Belknap Press of Harvard University Press, copyright © 1963 by the Massachusetts Historical Society.

[Franklin as a Congressman and a Diplomat, 1775–1776] by John Adams is reprinted by permission of the publisher from *The Adams Papers: Diary and Autobiography of John Adams: Volume 3—Diary 1782–1804, Autobiography through 1776*, edited by L. H. Butterfield, Leonard C. Faber, and Wendell D. Garrett, pp. 41–420, 422, Cambridge, MA: Belknap Press of Harvard University Press, copyright © 1961 by the Massachusetts Historical Society.

[Franklin as a Congressman and a Diplomat, 1777–1778] by John Adams is reprinted by permission of the publisher from *The Adams Papers: Diary and Autobiography of John Adams: Volume 4—Autobiography 1777–1780*, edited by L. H. Butterfield, Leonard C. Faber, and Wendell D. Garrett, pp. 41–44, 46–48, 56–57, 58, 59–62, 63–64, 67–69, 80–81, 92, 104, 105, 117, 143–144, Cambridge, MA: Belknap Press of Harvard University Press, copyright © 1961 by the Massachusetts Historical Society.

Abigail Adams to John Adams, 5 November 1775, is reprinted by permission of the publisher from *The Adams Papers: Adams Family Correspondence, Volume 1: December 1761–May 1776*, edited by L. H. Butterfield, pp. 320–321, Cambridge, MA: Belknap Press of Harvard University Press, copyright © 1963 by the Massachusetts Historical Society.

Abigail Adams to Lucy Cranch, 5 September 1784, and Abigail Adams to Cotton Tufts, 8 September 1784, are reprinted by permission of the publisher from *The Adams Papers: Adams Family Correspondence, Volume 5: October 1782–November 1784*, edited by Richard Alan Ryerson, pp. 436–438, 459, Cambridge, MA: Belknap Press of Harvard University Press, copyright © 1993 by the Massachusetts Historical Society.

[Two Conversations with Benjamin Franklin, 1777–1778] by Philip Gibbes is taken from *The Papers of Benjamin Franklin*, ed. Leonard W. Labaree, et al., 39 vols. to date (New Haven: Yale University Press, 1959–), 23: 281–285; 25: 419–423. Reprinted with permission of The Papers of Benjamin Franklin.

[Franklin during the Constitutional Convention, 1787] by James Madison is taken from Elizabeth Fleet, "Madison's 'Detached Memoranda,'" *William and Mary Quarterly*, 3 (1946): 536–539. Reprinted with permission of the Omohundro Institute of Early American History and Culture.

"On Franklin," by Louis Lefebvre de La Roche is translated from the French in Gilbert Chinard, "Recollections of Benjamin Franklin," *Proceedings of the American Philosophical Society* 94 (1950): 218–221. Reprinted with permission of the American Philosophical Society.

Works Cited

The following bibliography presents a list of works cited in the headnotes to all of the documents included in this collection. Much biographical information for the headnotes comes from the *American National Biography* and the *Oxford Dictionary of National Biography*, which are not cited otherwise.

Adams Family Correspondence. Ed. L. H. Butterfield, et al. 9 vols. to date. Cambridge, MA: Belknap Press of Harvard University Press, 1963–.

American National Biography. Ed. John A. Garraty and Mark C. Carnes. 26 vols. New York: Oxford University Press, 1999.

Crane, Verner W. "The Club of Honest Whigs: Friends of Science and Liberty." *William and Mary Quarterly*, 3d ser. 23 (April 1966): 210–233.

Fisher, Daniel. "Extracts from the Diary of Daniel Fisher." *Pennsylvania Magazine of History and Biography* 17 (1893): 263–278.

———. "To the Printer." *Virginia Gazette*, September 5, 1755. 3.

Franklin, Benjamin. *The Papers of Benjamin Franklin.* Ed. Leonard W. Labaree, et al. 39 vols. to date. New Haven: Yale University Press, 1959–.

———. *The Papers of Benjamin Franklin: The Digital Edition.* Packard Humanities Institute, 2010. <http://franklinpapers.org>.

———. *The Private Correspondence of Benjamin Franklin, LL.D.* Ed. William Temple Franklin. London: H. Colburn, 1817.

Jefferson, Issac. "Memoirs of a Monticello Slave." *Jefferson at Monticello.* Ed. James Adam Bear. Charlottesville: University Press of Virginia, 1967. 1–24.

Kippis, Andrew. *Biographia Britannica: or, The Lives of the Most Eminent Persons Who Have Flourished in Great Britain and Ireland, from the Earliest Ages, to the Present Times.* 5 vols. London: for C. Bathurst, 1778–1793.

Lee, Arthur. "Extracts from the Journal of Mr. Lee." *Life of Arthur Lee, LL.D.* Ed. Richard Henry Lee. 2 vols. Boston: Wells and Lilly, 1829. 1: 333–403.

Lemay, J. A. Leo. *The Life of Benjamin Franklin.* 3 vols. Philadelphia: University of Pennsylvania Press, 2006–2009.

Letters of Delegates to Congress, 1774–1789. Ed. Paul Hubert Smith and Ronald M. Gephart. 26 vols. Washington: Library of Congress, 1976–2000.

"List of Books — With Remarks." *Gentleman's Magazine* 37 (1767): 368–369.

Miller, C. William. *Benjamin Franklin's Philadelphia Printing, 1728–1766: A Descriptive Bibliography*. Philadelphia: American Philosophical Society, 1974.

"Original Anecdote of Franklin." *Analectic Magazine* 12 (August 1818): 162.

Oxford Dictionary of National Biography. Ed. H. C. G. Matthew and Brian Harrison. 60 vols. New York: Oxford University Press, 2004.

Pecquet du Bellet, Louise. *Some Prominent Virginia Families*. 4 vols. Lynchburg: J. P. Bell, 1907.

"Proceedings of Societies." *Historical Magazine* 1 (1867): 50–59.

Romilly, Samuel. *Memoirs of the Life of Sir Samuel Romilly*. 2 vols. London: J. Murray, 1841.

Strahan, William. "Correspondence between William Strahan and David Hall, 1763–1777." *Pennsylvania Magazine of History and Biography* 10 (1886): 86–99, 217–232.

Thomas, Isaiah. *The History of Printing in America: with a Biography of Printers, and an Account of Newspapers*. 2 vols. Worcester, MA: Isaiah Thomas, Jun., 1810.

Tucker, George. *The Life of Thomas Jefferson*. 2 vols. London: Charles Knight, 1837.

Tyler, Moses Coit. *The Literary History of the American Revolution, 1763–1783*. 2 vols. 1897. Reprinted. New York: F. Ungar, 1957.

Van Horne, John C. "Report of the Director." *The Annual Report of the Library Company of Philadelphia for the Year 2004*. Philadelphia: Library Company of Philadelphia, 2005. 8–11.

Vaux, Roberts. "Historical Memoranda Read at the Annual Meeting of the Historical Society of Pennsylvania, Feb. 1835." *Hazards' Register of Pennsylvania* 15 (21 March 1835): 183–184.

Watson, John F. *Annals of Philadelphia: Being a Collection of Memoirs, Anecdotes, and Incidents of the City and Its Inhabitants*. Philadelphia: E. L. Carey & A. Hart, 1830.

Wolf, Edwin, 2d, and Kevin J. Hayes. *The Library of Benjamin Franklin*. Philadelphia: American Philosophical Society and Library Company of Philadelphia, 2006.

Zall, P. M., ed. *Ben Franklin Laughing: Anecdotes from Original Sources by and about Benjamin Franklin*. Berkeley: University of California Press, 1980.

Index